What people say about
MISFITS! Baseball's Worst Ever Team

"It's an anniversary season worth celebrating. Luckily, all the people who might remember it are dead. They've suffered enough."

-Jack DeVries, *1999 Cleveland Indians Yearbook*

"How did they get so bad? And once they got there, how did they manage to make it through an entire season without committing mass suicide? ... Exhaustively detailed."

-Cleveland Plain Dealer

"Hetrick deserves a standing ovation for this meticulous research ... The Spiders' experience does serve as a valuable lesson for self-pitying Cubs and Red Sox fans who only think they know what it means to be cursed."

-Steven Bennett, *The Cooperstown Review*

"It boggles the mind...[a] surrealist exercise in futility."

-Tribe Tract and Testimonial

"MISFITS! tells the sorry tale of the 1899 Cleveland Spiders of the National League. Because of their record (20-134), it is no wonder that they played under more aliases than John Gotti - Misfits, Outcasts, Discards, Leftovers, and those are only the polite ones."

-The News, Southbridge, Massachusetts

"The title would seem to say it all, but if the reader dives into this chronology, there are riches to be savored and discovered."

-The Ohioana Quarterly

A "curious history and esoteric study."

-The People's Almanac Presents the 20ᵗʰ Century

MISFITS!
Baseball's Worst Ever Team
The 1899 Cleveland Spiders

J. Thomas Hetrick

Pocol Press

Cover art by Michael D. Arnold.
Redrawn from *Cleveland Press*, 1899
Titled "April Fool on Cleveland Fans"

POCOL PRESS

Published in the United States of America
by Pocol Press.
6023 Pocol Drive
Clifton, Virginia 20124-1333

Copyright 1999 © by J. Thomas Hetrick.

All rights reserved. No part of this book may be reproduced in any form whatsoever, without the express, written consent of Pocol Press. Exceptions are made for brief quotations for criticism and reviews.

Publisher's Cataloguing-in-Publication

Hetrick, J. Thomas, 1957-
    Misfits! : baseball's worst ever team, the 1899
    Cleveland Spiders / by J. Thomas Hetrick ; cover art by
    Michael D. Arnold. - 2nd ed.
        p. cm.
    Includes bibliographical references (p.) and index.
    ISBN 978-1-929763-00-9

        Cleveland Spiders (Baseball team)-History-19th century.
    I. Arnold, Michael D. II. Title.

    GV875.C76H48 2000   796.357'64'0977132

Formerly *MISFITS! The Cleveland Spiders in 1899*
by McFarland Publishers, Inc., 1991.

Acknowledgments

Special thanks to the Society for American Baseball Research (SABR), the Baseball Hall of Fame's Bill Deane, the Library of Congress' Dave Kelly, biographical researcher Richard Topp, and fellow Spiders aficionado John Phillips.

Even more thanks to Bob Karnes and Gaston Naranjo, my longtime friends, who listened and laughed to exploits of the team.

Finally, recognition is granted to Richard Sedgwick, who put on a glove, pitched some ball games, had a few laughs…and dreamed.

Dedication

Dedicated to the memories of the Cleveland players and Cleveland baseball fans everywhere.

Table of Contents

Illustrations

List of Abbreviations

AA	American Association
AL	American League
BDE	*Brooklyn Daily Eagle*
BG	*Boston Globe*
BTS	*Baltimore: The Sun*
CL	Central League
CP	*Cleveland Press*
CPD	*Cleveland Plain Dealer*
CSL	Connecticut State League
CT	*Chicago Tribune*
EL	Eastern League
GD	*St. Louis Globe-Democrat*
HRL	Hudson River League
LCJ	*Louisville Courier-Journal*
NA	National Association
NL	National League
NYSL	New York State League
NYT	*New York Times*
OI	Ohio Interstate
PE	*Philadelphia Enquirer*
PL	Players League
PP	*Pittsburg Post*
SA	Southern Association
SL	Southern League
SL	*Sporting Life*
TEC	*The Enquirer: Cincinnati*
TL	Texas League
TSN	*The Sporting News*
WCL	Western Canada League
WES	*Washington Evening Star*
WIL	Wisconsin-Illinois League
WL	Western League
WP	*Washington Post*

Preface

Baseball has been a vital part of American sporting culture for a century and a half. Since its beginning, the game has developed a rich literary tradition. This tradition is based largely on the heroic exploits of the stars of the game: from the fiction of Frank Merriwell in the late 1880s to G.H. Fleming's *Murderer's Row* of the 1927 New York Yankees to the inner-city love of the 1950s Brooklyn Dodgers in Roger Kahn's *The Boys of Summer*. In between, stories have been oft-told of baseball's giants, men like Cy Young, Ty Cobb, and Babe Ruth. Photo images of the headfirst slide stay transfixed in the ball fan's mind. The great teams have been analyzed, dissected, and statistics fed into computers. But where has that left the thousands of men who toiled in mediocrity? What of the tales of the unfortunates who were rarely part of the tumultuous cheering or adulation of fans? *Misfits!* is the obscure, true story of major league baseball's worst team ever — the 1899 Cleveland Spiders.

Who? Lafayette Napoleon "Lave" Cross, Joe Quinn, "Foghorn" Tommy Tucker, Crazy Schmit, "Smiling Jim" Hughey, Chief Sockalexis, Sport McAllister, "Buttermilk" Tommy Dowd, Harry Lochhead, Suter Sullivan, Charlie Knepper, Ossee Schreckengost, Joe Sugden, Harry Colliflower — that's who. None of these gentlemen ever set foot near a podium in Cooperstown, New York. For good reason. Incredibly, they rarely set foot in their home city of Cleveland, Ohio. When the Spiders did play in League Park, almost no one came. Bad players? Yes. Bad luck? Definitely.

For rather obvious reasons, there is little mention at all of the 1899 Spiders in baseball's rich histories. It is not exactly the kind of Frank Merriwell sports success story to be proud of. David Q. Voigt gives a fine explanation of the era of syndicate ball and the four teams involved in his book *American Baseball*. Lee Allen wrote that the Spiders "wandered around the league like some sort of lost planet." Bill James offers in his *Historical Baseball Abstract*: "Can you imagine what it was like trying to convince the Cleveland fans to support the 1899 Cleveland Spiders? Well, neither could anybody else. No one went to their home games, and eventually they stopped having them and wound up traveling from road game to road game, serving as virtually an automatic victory for their opponents, and by acclamation, the worst major league team ever." Whitey Lewis barely mentions the Spiders in a history of the Cleveland franchise. The body of the text written about the 1899 Misfits resides in the *Cleveland Plain Dealer*. Few kind words were written about them.

This book examines the "Misfits" strange and funny season of pathos. The story is a daily narrative that mixes colorful jargon, reportage of the day, quotes from players and owners, player profiles, statistics, and quaint tales of 1890s ball. There were pranks on umpires, lawsuits against the teams, betting on teams, detectives hired to "shadow" players — all against a backdrop of baseball's most violent time, the "rowdy ball" era. Casey Stengel, manager of the worst team this side of 1900 (1962 New York Mets) would have been proud.

Why do a book on the Misfits? Glance at the team section in the Macmillan *Baseball Encyclopedia* for the 1899 National League. Note Cleveland. The standings proclaim them to be 35 games behind the 11th place Washington Senators. Surely, a computer misprint. It's no typo, however, nor hoax, nor joke, especially to the players who endured.

What's the old standard mountain climber's line? Because it's there. This book was written for the same reason. The result is the following. Enjoy.

-J. Thomas Hetrick
Stafford, Virginia
December 1990

Cleveland Baseball and the Brothers Robison

Baseball in Cleveland before the turn of the century was colorful, exciting, and controversial. In 1865 the first amateur team organized and the Forest City club lost to a college nine from Oberlin, 67-28. Four years later, a group of gentlemanly $75-a-month Cleveland professionals, wearing white pantaloons and bright blue stockings, were defeated by the legendary Cincinnati Red Stockings, 25-6. The Red Stockings sported "racy knickerbocker-type pants." Later in the season, the barnstorming Red Stockings returned to Cleveland and swamped the locals 43-20 (Condon, 266).

The next year, the Cleveland home towners had improved so much that they squeezed by the Atlantic Club of Brooklyn, New York. With a 52-run first inning rally and 54 in the third inning, the Clevelands won 132-1 (Condon, 267).

By 1871, Cleveland had a charter team in the National Association of Professional Baseball Players. Season ticket prices to Cleveland games were $6 with a $10 special for lady and carriage (Reidenbaugh, *Take Me Out to the Ball Park*, 98). The early league entry lasted but two years.

With baseball gaining popularity as a college and amateur sport, the city was awarded a National League franchise in 1879. The new National League Cleveland club was purchased by J. Ford Evans, among others (Shannon and Kalinsky, 84). That debut season, the Clevelands weren't very successful, finishing 27-55. For five more seasons, Cleveland hovered near the bottom of the league. In 1882, Evans even tried managing the team, but his president replacement, C.H. Bulkley, fired him for a fifth place finish. In those infant NL days, Cleveland's only distinction was a plethora of odd player names. One Arm Dailey and The Only Nolan pitched. Alderman Fatty Briody and Father Kick Kelly squatted at catcher. Pebbly Jack Glasscock and Germany Smith worked the infield dirt. Orator Shaffer patrolled the outfield garden. But, financial troubles plagued the franchise and they stayed out of the National League until 1889.

Cleveland also played two more seasons in the short-lived American Association. The club was owned by the traction magnate brothers, the self-assured Frank DeHaas Robison and genial Matthew Stanley Robison (pronounced Roe-bi-son). They built a new playground for their team at East 66th and Lexington Avenues, right on their trolley lines. The wooden, single-deck structure with a pavilion near first base was called League Park. The ballpark was constructed around two residences and a saloon because the owners refused to sell their properties. As a result, some unusual dimensions formed the field. It was 375 to left field, 420 to center and only 290 feet to right field. The teams featured a toy first baseman (Jim), a one-armed pitcher (Dailey) and a deacon (McGuire).

By 1889, Cleveland was ready for big time National League ball again; the city itself gaining industrial momentum as a top oil, coal, and iron-ore producer. The Robisons jumped at the chance and brought Cleveland back into the league. They were called the Cleveland Babes. Those first two teams offered first basemen Jake Virtue and Peek-A-Boo Veach. Chief Zimmer was the catcher. Pitchers with prominent American names like Jack Wadsworth and Ezra Lincoln tossed the ball. A rookie from Ohio's Tuscawaras County was signed. His name was Denton True Young. But, like most Cleveland clubs, the team wallowed. A nickname was added, however. At a spring practice, someone commented on the spindly physiques of the players, and said that the white and dark blue attired athletes looked like a lot of underfed Spiders. Newspapers quickly discovered the term and the nickname stuck (*TSN*, Feb. 18, 1899).

The National League season of 1890 was marked by a player revolt against club ownerships. It resulted in the short-lived Players League. Several of the Cleveland players jumped ship but returned to the Forest City for the next campaign. Then, mean Patsy Tebeau was hired by Frank DeHaas Robison to manage in 1891 and the club discovered winning. Coincidentally, Frank Robison discovered bragging and throughout the 1890s would boast that his team would knock the stuffing out of all comers. Some of the time, Robison was right. The 1892 version of the Spiders shared the league title in a split season with Boston. The Frank Selee-managed Beantowners relied on outfielder Hugh Duffy, first baseman Tommy Tucker, shortstop Herman Long and pitchers Kid Nichols and Jack Stivetts. Cleveland heroes included second baseman Cupid Childs, catcher Chief Zimmer, and pitchers Cy Young and Nig Cuppy. A best of nine championship series resulted in a Beantown victory.

Tebeau's style preached rowdyism. Baseball, with one umpire simply unable to watch all the action, became brutal. Players resorted to any means to win, literally fighting for the pennant. On-the-field brawls were common. Umpires were shoved around. Even fans were involved in the fisticuffs. But it all may been symptomatic of the owners cheating players out of salaries and falsely reporting gate receipts in order to profit. It was an age of robber barons so corrupted that money, and the making of tons of it, seemed their only purpose. Baseball ownership was no different. Not only was baseball a dirty sport, but it was played with a dirty ball. An historian describes the sphere as "scuffed, dirtied, grass-stained, and just about battered out of shape. Such balls were harder to see, soggier to hit, and more likely behaved eccentrically in flight" (Suchsdorf, 32).

Boston's Frank Selee and Baltimore's Ned Hanlon helped roughhouse play evolve. Throughout the rest of the nineties, Boston, Baltimore, and Cleveland

2

battled tooth and nail. Tebeau's Spiders never finished first but were involved in two Temple Cup championship series. The Cup series matched the league's first and second place clubs.

In 1895, the Orioles edged out the Spiders in the championship race but Cleveland defeated the Baltimore "Oysters" four games to one in one of baseball's wildest showdowns. It was wild, not because of the players on the field, but because of the fans and the irresponsible newspaper reporting of the contests. The Spiders swept the first three games in Cleveland with crowds shouting epithets at the Baltimore players and hurling various vegetables. Cleveland's *Plain Dealer* newspaper barely mentioned the incidents and chose to devote its ink to revel in the size of the gathering and the maddening din of "cow bells, rattles and all the devices of the modern fan" (*CPD*, Oct. 2, 1895). The *Baltimore Sun* exploded in criticism of Cleveland club management to note that police protection was almost nonexistent. The *Sun* also complained of Spiders' fan behavior and warned of a vengeful Baltimore faithful. Besides ducking vegetables in Cleveland, Baltimore outfielder Joe Kelley was interfered with by spectators while attempting to catch a fly in game one. The series concluded in Baltimore with Cleveland players under police protection. After the fourth game, the Spiders had to hit the floor of their horse-drawn bus as projectiles hurtled their way by no less than a mob of Baltimore crazies. One missle that was tossed in the bus was described by the *Plain Dealer* as a rock "slag" and illustrated in a full size drawing. A Baltimore paper said that Tebeau was angry that a crowd of boys could cause such trouble. Tebeau responded: "Boys! Guess you didn't see what kind of stuff was fired at that bus. Why things came in here that no boy could lift" (*CPD*, Oct. 10, 1895). But, when it was over, the Spiders could thank pitching heroes Cy Young and Nig Cuppy and batting stars Jesse Burkett and Chief Zimmer. The *Plain Dealer* proclaimed that on the Spiders' return train trip, "on every town this side of Pittsburg there were shouts for the victorious Spiders" and that Chief Zimmer was in danger of being torn apart by happy fans as much as he was mean ones in Baltimore (Oct. 10, 1895). For their winning efforts, the Spiders received $528.33 per man.

There were some interesting historical touches to the series. A crowd showed up at Cleveland's Music Hall to hear a mimic re-creation of the game, presumably by telegraph reports. An announcer would relay the batter's result and the audience would applaud appropriately. One Cleveland fan tooted a giant horn that the *Plain Dealer* described as eight feet long, while the *Sun* reported it to be 15 feet long! Other Cleveland ball "cranks" contributed poems to the local Cleveland papers to describe the wondrous Cleveland victory. One poem referred to Baltimore as a dish for the Spiders to devour. "Oysters Done Up Brown" was the title. Another poem trumpeted Patsy Tebeau and his brilliant leadership.

3

In 1896, the Orioles gained sweet revenge with a four to zero sweep of Cleveland in the Temple Cup.

Throughout the 1890s, the Spiders boasted a galaxy of baseball luminaries like catcher Chief Zimmer and Jack O'Connor; infielders Patsy Tebeau, Cupid Childs, Ed McKean, Chippy McGarr, and Bobby Wallace; outfielders Jimmy McAleer, Jesse Burkett, Harry Blake and Louis Sockalexis; and pitchers Cy Young, Nig Cuppy, John Clarkson, and Jack Powell.

But not only were the Spiders a star contingent, but principal owner Frank DeHaas Robison gained quite a reputation of the oppressed "base hitter and fly gobbler," reportedly assisting them whenever possible and helping them invest their money for careers after baseball (*TSN*, Feb. 18, 1899). In 1896, the garish Robison stood up for Tebeau after his manager was fined $200 for his violent behavior in Pittsburg. Robison refused to allow Tebeau to pay, went to court and won his case, and defrayed all of Tebeau's expenses for the trouble (*TSN*, Feb. 18, 1899). On another occasion, Robison himself boasted of his relationship with Tebeau:

"Never once in my life," said Mr. Robison the other night, "Did I ask Tebeau who was going to pitch of fill any other position. Once I took a trainload of Ohio legislators from Columbus to Cincinnati to see the opening game of the season in which my team opposed Cincinnati. The lawmakers were dead game sportsmen and every one of them put a little bet on the game; that is the men from the territory tributary to Cincinnati and those from Northern Ohio bet on Cleveland. The sums were small, but I wanted the team to win for my friends, and I asked Mr. Tebeau as a special favor to pitch Cy Young, who we then regarded as our best pitcher. Mr. Tebeau obliged me and we won a hard game by a score of 2 to 1. This is the only time I have asked a manager to do me a favor as far as playing the men went. If he had said, 'I deem it imprudent to pitch Young and I will not do it,' I should not have said a word. I have never gone to him after losing a game and said even in the kindest way that he or any of his players had made the slightest mistake. I knew that the best of players - which mine are - cannot avoid losing a game or making a mistake once in a while" (*TSN*, Feb. 18, 1899).

Unlike his brother, M. Stanley Robison was content to be far less outgoing. He was a practical man with a pleasant disposition; much quieter than his brother, yet fond of a good joke every once in a while (*SL*, Apr. 1, 1911).

By the late 1890s, America's entertainment industry was booming. Theatres had joined forces in a syndicate. Baseball was becoming such a big business than Baltimore and Brooklyn aligned themselves to pool the best players in the best location for the biggest profits. Ex-Baltimore star Ned Hanlon became manager of the Brooklyn Bridegrooms along with Harry Von der Horst who was part owner of the Baltimore club at the same time. Several of the crackerjack Baltimore players like Hughie Jennings, Wee Willie Keeler, and

Joe Kelley went to Flatbush, where in the lights and glamour of New York, money was believed to be found. It seemed to be a conflict of interest and it was.

In 1898, American became involved in a war with Spain in the Philippines. Baseball attendance dropped off. Some owners blamed the weather, others blamed the expanded 154 game schedule. Many fans blamed "Brushism," an effort to suppress obscene language on the field of play. The author of the plan was John T. Brush, owner of the Cincinnati team and Frank Robison's friend. However, the idea was ludicrous because it singled out only players with the supposition they would police themselves. No mention was made of club officials, fans, umpires, or fighting on the field. Brushism, or the Brush Vermiform Index, as it was sometimes called, was a complete flop.

Most National League owners understood their losses to be a direct result of America's preoccupation with the war and a new phenomenon called yellow journalism. But proud Cleveland magnate Frank Robison forced his club to play out its late season games on the road. It was an effort to "punish" fans (Voigt, 265). Robison's excuse was that baseball was a business and not a public service (Voigt, 265).

In late March, just before the 1899 season was about to begin, Frank Robison and his brother bought out the pathetic St. Louis Browns from the wacky and bankrupt German mogul Chris Von der Ahe. The sale was consummated at a sheriff's auction after months of legal bickering and secret negotiations. Before the deal, local Cleveland and St. Louis papers used all their sport ink speculating about "the fate of Mr. Tebeau." Just prior to the announcement, the *Cleveland Press* printed a front-page cartoon depicting an Indian being pulled by a hearty cowboy with "St. Louis" on his hat (Von der Ahe) and a puritan-looking gentleman with "Cleveland" stitched into his coat (Mar. 18). This was a caricature of Frank Robison. But the real Frank Robison had been keeping silent on the details and informed his on-the-field boss, Patsy Tebeau, not to talk either. Then came the announcement that the Robisons would switch the Cleveland and St. Louis franchises with each other. Frank Robison telegrammed Tebeau: "I will transfer the Cleveland players to our company in St. Louis, and you will have the same control that you have always had, since you have been manager of the Cleveland club. If we don't win the pennant, it won't be our fault" (*CP*, Mar. 25).

The Brothers Robison cited dissatisfaction with Cleveland as a city, poor attendance, a small park, and the ban on Sunday ball (*TSN*, Jan. 28, 1899). St. Louis would be the strong team, changing its team colors from brown to flaming red. Frank Robison haughtily announced that his brother M. Stanley would be placed in charge of Cleveland as a "side show" while serving as treasurer of the St. Louis team (Voigt, 267).

Immediately, the St. Louis arm of the syndicate went to work revitalizing Sportsman's Park. Frank Robison rode his St. Louis trolley lines to personally inspect the ball yard and ordered the present grandstands improved, old bleachers torn down and replaced, and a sun cover constructed over the new right field stands. Another image change was the banning of beer from the ball park and concession sales in the grandstand (*GD*, Mar. 28). Ticket prices would range from a quarter to 75 cents. Robison believed that with these changes, crowds would be better behaved and classier in St. Louis.

Because of the Robison's transfer actions, sporting papers of the day were livid. The *Cleveland Plain Dealer* wasn't too excited about the prospect of acquiring the St. Louis Browns - dead last in '97-'98. *The Sporting News* blasted the Robisons, the fans (or lack therof) in Cleveland, and the *Sporting Life* for sympathizing with the Robison's transfers because the park was supposedly too small. Cleveland attendance in 1898 was sparse at best, but *TSN* sarcastically commented that Cleveland was "just bulging over with baseball enthusiasm, with streets filled with men, women, and children engaged in animated discussions about the latest happenings in the field of fan" (Jan. 28, 1899). Meanwhile, *Sporting Life* added, "Cleveland writers have taken to roasting Mr. Frank Robison now that the removal of the Indians to St. Louis is assured. Some of the statements made about him are almost libelous" (Apr. 15, 1899).

While Frank Robison was remaining hush about the affair, M. Stanley Robison was being given advice from the *Plain Dealer* on how to properly conduct an interview. This fanciful account, complete with parenthetical commentary, ate at the heart of syndicate ball:

Yes, we will have the best team in the league. (With the possible exception of 11.) We are prepared to spend any amount of money (up to a dollar fifty) to strengthen the team, but I hardly think that it will need much strengthening (to land at the bottom). The men are a fine lot of ball players (nit) and they are all delighted to come to Cleveland, where they are sure to be appreciated. (Nit some more.)

The players think that under a popular management (that's me) and in the city where they command a little respect (goodness knows where that is) they can put up winning baseball (against any 14-year-old team).

The team will be a little late in reporting, it is true, but we are going to try an experiment. I have a theory that there is nothing in southern training (it costs money), and that the players will do just as well if they begin their work in the climate in which they are to play. If my theory works out well there will soon be an end to all southern practice and I will have been the means of saving the league thousands of dollars every year.

I do not know just how the team will be arranged, the players are all so good that they are able to fill one position almost as well as one another. (And that's no kid.)

6

I have my eyes open for new players all the time and if I find any man who will help us out I will get him (if he don't cost anything). I believe that the coming season will be a great one for the national game (somewhere else) and that the Cleveland club (the old one) will be well up in the race (Mar. 30).

Thus, amid swirling controversy, the 1899 Cleveland Spiders, "weighted down with all manner of non-descript talent," were born (Reidenbaugh, *100 years*, 45). Their story begins, fittingly, on April Fool's Day.

Saturday, April 1. It was two weeks from the beginning of the season and the National League was in turmoil. The sale of St. Louis and subsequent switch of the Cleveland and St. Louis franchises and the new Brooklyn-Baltimore syndicate made ball fans scream of dishonesty in the sport. Chris Von der Ahe was suing the National League for a conspiracy among owners to dump him. The 1899 schedule was released which, in effect, shut off the Louisville team from playing Sunday dates so critical to its revenue. The Louisville owner, Barney Dreyfuss, protested.

The league had long since become an unwieldy 12-headed monster. Many thought that a ten- or eight-team league was the answer. Louisville and Washington were probably to be bought out by the league shortly into the season. Baltimore and Cleveland also entered the year in a state of limbo. Cleveland was rumored to be switched to the minors - the Western League.

National League President Nicholas Young was heavily criticized for his suspect two-man-to-a-game umpiring crews.

The *Cleveland Press*, meanwhile, printed a front-page cartoon depicting a group of old, decrepit men. One was dumpy and had a broken arm. Another had spectacles and a goatee. A third was as skinny as a rail. These were the new Cleveland baseball players, recently removed from St. Louis. The caption read, "April Fool on Cleveland Fans" (Apr. 1). As per the owners Robison, the "team of leftovers" from the 1898 St. Louis club was to round up in Terre Haute, Indiana, by April 7. The nucleus of the team were catchers Jack Clements and Joe Sugden; pitchers Jim Hughey, Still Bill Hill, Lewis "Sport" McAllister, and Kid Carsey; infielders Tommy Tucker, Joe Quinn, Lave Cross and shortstop Morehead; and outfielders Dick Harley, Louis Sockalexis, Tommy Dowd and Jake Stenzel. Pat Tebeau of the new St. Louis squad had the option of retaining Dowd and Stenzel and transferring Harry Blake and "Snags" Heidrick to Cleveland (*CPD*, Mar. 27). The manager of the team was to be "Scrappy Bill" Joyce, currently under contract with the New York Giants. Joyce had recently purchased a saloon in his hometown St. Louis in case managing Cleveland didn't work out (*CP*, Apr. 1).

Curiously, the *Cleveland Press* had printed this advertisement the day before in its sporting pages: "WEAK MEN - Instant Relief. Cure in 15 days.

7

Never returns. I will gladly send to any sufferer in a plain sealed envelope FREE a prescription with full directions for a quick, private cure for Lost Manhood, Night Losses, Nervous Disability, Small Weak Parts, Varicosis, etc. G.B. WRIGHT" (Mar. 31). What exactly "small weak parts" were is unclear. But, the Cleveland baseball team would begin its season in exactly 15 days.

Conversely, the new St. Louis team had been training in Hot Springs, Arkansas. Its veteran club was to include catchers Jack O'Connor, Lou Criger, Chief Zimmer, and Ossee Schreckengost; pitchers Cy Young, Jack Powell, Nig Cuppy, Frank Bates, Cowboy Jones, Pete McBride and Willie Sudhoff; infielders Pat Tebeau, Cupid Childs, Ed McKean, and Bobby Wallace; and outfielders Jesse Burkett, Mike Griffin, and Harry Blake with Stenzel and possibly Tommy Dowd as substitutes. Said St. Louis' native Patsy Tebeau: "This is a pennant winning combination, and with a permanent location I feel more confident of winning the championship than ever" (*CPD*, Mar. 27). Slugger Jesse Burkett had said a few days earlier, "All balls look like balloons to me" (*CP*, Mar. 26).

St. Louis was to challenge Boston and Brooklyn for league honors. Indeed, the new St. Louis squad was off to a good start. Practice was brisk. The pitchers were sharp. Players were running 7-8 miles a day to and from the ball park and every man at Hot Springs was "working like a Trojan" (*CPD*, Mar. 27).

Sunday, April 2. Terre Haute was bitter cold. The new Cleveland baseball team, with a total of eight men on hand, stayed inside to practice in a gymnasium. The squad was composed of first baseman Tommy Tucker, second baseman Joe Quinn, short stop-pitcher Harry Maupin, Lave Cross at third, outfielder Tommy Dowd, utilitymen Sport McAllister and Suter Sullivan, and catcher Joe Sugden. Outfielder Dick Harley was on his way after coaching at Villanova University for the past two months.

The *Cleveland Press* called it a "shameful travesty" that "Tebeau's seasoned warriors" were to go against a "handful of half-frozen has-beens from an alleged training camp at Terre Haute" (Apr. 2). Cleveland was to play St. Louis April 15 in the opener in St. Louis. Brother Stanley kidded Frank Robison about the game: "We are going to beat you, and beat you sure on opening day and the series will be about our size. I think I am going to have a pretty warm team myself. The old Browns may prove a surprise party, and if we get a good start, look out for us" (*GD*, Mar. 30). As much as 20,000 fans were expected for the game. With Cleveland's tenuous situation, their share of the receipts could pay their salaries, rail fares, and hotel bills for a month (*CPD*, Apr. 3).

Lefthander Still Bill Hill telegraphed M. Stanley Robison from Cincinnati to say that he wasn't in shape to pitch. The *Cleveland Press* reported that Hill could become the best southpaw since Toad Ramsey. Hill had all the best qualities except the "ability to care for himself" (Mar. 31).

Monday, April 3. Tom Loftus, manager of the Columbus team of the Western League, was in Cleveland "to visit friends." However, Loftus had just ordered new jerseys for his team with the giant letter "C" across the front. He explained, "We can't tell what might happen before the season is over. 'C' would stand as well for Cleveland as it does for Columbus" (*CP*, Apr. 3). Loftus had managed Cleveland in the American Association in 1888-89.

Sport McAllister, pitcher and jack-of-all-trades fielder, was disappointed on his transfer to Cleveland. Just a few days before, McAllister had been in Hot Springs training with the new St. Louis Perfectos. He was reported to be in good physical shape (*CP*, Apr. 3). Willie Sudhoff was now a member of Cleveland also, having held out for more money from Tebeau's club. Four Cleveland players were holding out for more money. They were outfielder Dick Harley, catcher Jack Clements, and pitchers Kid Carsey and Jim Hughey. As the *Cleveland Press* explained, it was "not known on what they base such demands" Apr. 3).

Wednesday, April 5. After a few days of practice in the chill of Terre Haute, the Clevelands played their first game against Indianapolis of the Western League. By this time, they could put nine men on the field - barely. Still Bill Hill had shown up to pitch just like he said, out of shape. He gave up seven runs, two hit batsman and one wild pitch in one inning. The *Cleveland Press* remarked of Hill, "He hopes to make Cy Young look like 20 cents in the great contests at St. Louis" (Apr. 6).

As Bill Joyce's salary demands were far too high for the Robisons, Lave Cross was named captain and manager. Cross was voted into the job due to the requests of other team members. As Cross was the only bright spot on the team, John Brush of Cincinnati made overtures for the Cleveland third baseman. The *Cleveland Press* deadpanned: "Lave Playing Too Well for Leftovers" (Apr. 6).

Three more players were acquired by Cleveland. Utility man Jimmy Donely tentatively was signed to play third base if Cross departed to the Reds. Infielders Suter Sullivan and George Bristow became Clevelands. Bristow, however, was to remain in Hot Springs with Tebeau and report to Brother Stan's team in time for the opener (*CP*, Apr. 7).

Thursday, April 6. With the season just over a week away, Willie Sudhoff was picked to start the opener for Cleveland. McAllister was originally the frontrunner for the assignment, but Sport balked at pitching and was interested in catching. Hill then became the number one, but his performance versus Indianapolis was horrid.

The *Cleveland Press* sarcastically remarked about the new Clevelands in the opener: "The report that preliminary betting is 100 to 0 in favor of St. Louis is probably erroneous. It is only 90 to 0" (Apr. 7).

"Cross says his men are off to a 'Fast gait,'" trumpeted the *St. Louis Globe-Democrat* on April 6. Snow began to fall in Terre Haute.

Friday, April 7. Controversy concerning the new Cleveland club continued to surface. Staunch Cleveland fan Dan Kellacky refused to re-lease a portion of his property to League Park unless assurances from the management were made not to transfer games. Kellacky had complained to the city authorities. To counteract, the Robison syndicate simply built a house-high fence near Kellacky's property. The fence shut out sunlight on one side of Kellacky's building.

Said the victim:

Of course, it is nothing but spite work, and there is nothing for me to do but suffer. The ballclub owners have had the use of my property for eight years and they have never paid a cent for it. Not that I have asked them that they either pay a reasonable price for it or assure me they will play their games here, they come back at me with this spite work. It will be impossible for me to rent my house, and I will be greatly annoyed by the fence near the house that I live in, but there is nothing for me to do but make the best of it. I am sorry for anyone who is unfortunate enough to be so located that the owners of the Cleveland Baseball club can get a chance to make it unpleasant for him (*CPD*, Apr. 8).

Saturday, April 8. On Saturday, the new Clevelands defeated Indianapolis 6-4 in a five-inning contest. The game was played before 1200 spectators in the rain. Righthander Amos Rusie, "The Hoosier Thunderbolt," one of the most dominant pitchers of the 1890s for the Giants, worked out with the Western League squad. He surrendered three first inning runs. Willie Sudhoff and Harry Maupin pitched for Cleveland. The new Clevelands evened their exhibition record at 1-1.

Catcher Jack Clements and pitcher Jack Stivetts had yet to report to the new Cleveland camp at Terre Haute because of the snowy weather and the lack of funds. The Robisons had refused to advance them rail fare. Both Clements and Stivetts were out of shape and certainly not eager to walk cross-country (*CPD*, Apr. 19). Said Stivetts: "You can't expect a fellow to have any money left six months after his last ghost walk" (*CP*, Apr. 10). The *Cleveland Press* reported that the combined salaries of the Cleveland Left Overs was $21,500 (Apr. 10).

Monday, April 10. It was a remarkable victory. Coming back from a 7-0 first inning deficit, the new Clevelands beat Indianapolis 12 to 10. Still Bill Hill spent most of the afternoon throwing balls out of the strike zone. Harry Maupin relieved. Cleveland scored most of their runs in the seventh inning and then were helped by a marvelous Joe Quinn fielding stop at second base. Quinn's lunge saved at least two runs and the game.

First baseman Tommy Tucker took his foghorn voice to the coaching box and "gingered up the Misfits" (*CPD*, Apr. 11). With a 2-1 practice record, Lave Cross' gang was beginning to jell.

April

"The Players are in a Wretched Condition"

Wednesday, April 12. Fresh from their recent victory, the new Cleveland ball team continued to practice in Terre Haute. The weather, though, remained uncomfortably chilly and not at all conducive to baseball warm-ups. Nonetheless, the players went doggedly on with their manager Cross stressing that he wanted to get in as much work as possible. The players now in camp were Jack Clements and Joe Sugden at catcher; Wee Willie Sudhoff, Still Bill Hill, Jim Hughey, Kid Carsey, Sport McAllister and Harry Maupin the pitchers; Tommy Tucker, Joe Quinn, Lave Cross, George Bristow, Tommy Dowd, Suter Sullivan, and Dick Harley as the infielders and outfielders. Unfortunately for the Spiders, virtually all of the newspapers predicting the order of finish for the National League season of 1899, picked Cleveland for last place, including the eminent baseball weeklies *Sporting Life* and *The Sporting News*. A quick look at the roster shows why.

Blond **Joe Sugden** began his ball playing for a semi-pro outfit called the Ox Athletic Club of Philadelphia. He was paid $5 per game in the early 1890s. That paycheck was enough for Sunday shoes, a dozen eggs, and a couple of trolley rides.

In 1893, while Sugden was playing for a Charleston, South Carolina team, Pittsburg Pirate catcher Connie Mack broke his leg. Sugden was signed immediately and appeared in 19 straight games for the Buccaneers. The enthusiastic youngster held his own and gained fans along the way. When Mack returned, Sugden spelled him occasionally and under old rules, Sugden was a pinch runner every time Connie came to bat. After the first time, Joe was prompted to say, "He nearly ran my legs off that afternoon" (*TSN*, Jun. 28, 1899).

For the next several seasons, backup catcher Sugden's batting eye improved significantly. He was a switch-hitter, a rarity for a catcher. His catching skills also sharpened. With the up-and-down Pirates, Sugden handled the likes of Lefty Frank Killen and Emerson P. "Pink"Hawley. In 1898, he was traded to the St. Louis Browns, an abysmal group, and Sugden shared the catching duties with tough Jack Clements. Here, Joe learned catching humility, handling nondescript hurlers like Jack Taylor (15-29), Wee Willie Sudhoff (11-27), Jim Hughey (7-24), and Kid Carsey (2-12).

Over the years, due to the rough-and-tumble profession of catching baseballs for a living, Sugden developed badly gnarled hands. Once someone suggested that shaking Joe's hands was like "grabbing a bags of peanuts" (*Philadelphia Bulletin*, June 28, 1959).

Considered one of the finest backstops of his era, **Jack Clements** spent most of his career with the Philadelphia Phillies. Described by contemporaries as a "wide shouldered, grim-lipped man with a stature of growing oak," Clements' catching skills were effective for their finesse. As a hitter, he also shone. With the hard-hitting Philadelphia team of the mid-1890s, lefthander Jack kept his average above .340. By 1897 though, he was on the down side of his playing days. He performed for St. Louis in 1898, but by then his batting and fielding skills had eroded.

Hailing from Chattanooga, Tennessee, lefthander pitcher **William C. Hill** began his big league career in 1896. He was a 22-year-old with a tail-end Louisville team and proceeded to help them along. He won only 9 of 37 decisions. The next year the team improved to 11th place and so did Mr. Hill. He was 7-17. Still Bill went to Cincinnati and fashioned a 13-14 record in 1898. The Reds finished 3rd. Hill was known as a gentlemanly ballplayer and polo player.

Righthanded pitcher **John William Sudhoff** graduated from the baseball lots of St. Louis. In the 1890s such luminaries as Scrappy Bill Joyce, Patsy Tebeau, Jack O'Connor, and Ted Breitenstein all came from that area.

Called Wee Willie for his smallish frame, Sudhoff also earned the unusual nickname of "Cottontop" (Phillips, *The Cleveland Spiders Who Was Who*). He played shortstop with Padukah of the Central League in 1897. Converted into a pitcher, Sudhoff showed "curves, speed, and remarkable mental ability" (*TSN*, May 17, 1917). He broke into the National League with his hometown team, the St. Louis Browns. In 1897 and 1898, the Browns were the laughingstock of baseball, synonymous with losing. Willie played his part, going 2-7 as a rookie and 11-27 in his sophomore year. Even though Sudhoff's arm was less than spectacular, many observers said he had promising pitching skills.

Born near Coldwater, Michigan, **James Ulysses Hughey** was so named during President Ulysses S. Grant's tenure in the White House. It was a name that promised greatness, whatever endeavor young James would care to choose. It didn't quite tun out that way.

For the strapping six-foot Hughey, mediocrity and catcher Joe Sugden followed him around wherever he went in baseball. Known for his Cheshire cat grin, Hughey got his first real big league chance with a fair Pittsburg outfit in 1896. Connie Mack was the manager. Joe Sugden was the catcher. Hughey went 6-8. In 1897, Mack was out at manager, Patsy Donovan was in. Joe Sugden caught and Hughey worked to a 6-10 mark. St. Louis beckoned Hughey and Sugden in 1898. Off they went. Inspired by Jack Taylor's 15-29 showing and Willie Sudhoff's 11-27, Hughey won 7 of 31 decisions.

13

By the 1890s, America's wild west was becoming pretty tame. But out of New York City rode **Wilfred "Kid" Carsey**, a righthanded junkball pitcher whose tosses were slow or slower, though not often straight. Carsey pitched briefly with Washington of the American Association in '91, briefly because he was 14-27 and gave up 513 hits and 161 walks. Carsey then went to the hard-hitting Phillies. He did have some success…sort of. Though he continued to give up a frightful total of hits and walks, Carsey compiled winning records for four consecutive years. His best year was 1895 when he was 24-16. By 1897, Carsey's pitching skills had ridden off into the sunset. He was signed by St. Louis, where he fired blanks for two years.

Lewis McAllister learned his ball playing on the sandlots of Forth Worth, Texas. Soon thereafter, he was making a name as a utility player in the Texas League.

Begun in 1896 in Cleveland, Sport McAllister has a curious league career. Possessing little talent to excel in any one position, McAllister played them all. His 68 big league games included some time behind the plate, on the mound, all around the infield, and all over the outfield. McAllister did a lot of running around - perhaps. Manager Patsy Tebeau kept trying to find a position for the stock, switch-hitting utilitarian. More likely, though, McAllister was a full-time fill-in, performing only when players were hurt or hung over. One thing is certain: he wasn't a particularly adept pitcher, hitter, or fielder.

In baseball, "a cup of coffee" is when a player appears briefly in the league. Pitcher **Harry Maupin**'s coffee was cold. Wellesville, Missouri native Henry Carr Maupin twirled all of two games for the 1898 St. Louis Browns. Those credentials being enough, Maupin was transferred to Cleveland.

As a coal miner in Ashland, Pennsylvania, **John Elmer "Happy Jack" Stivetts** made $1 a day. But his strong and tall physique helped him to a successful career. Staring with a York, Pennsylvania minor league outfit, 21-year-old Stivetts pitched three years with St. Louis of the American Association. From 1889-1891, Stivetts won 69 games against 50 defeats. His strikeout records were remarkable and, he was soon hailed as "the Peer of Any Pitcher Living." But, Stivetts was also a fearsome hitter, with seven home runs in both 1890 and 1891.

In 1892 Stivetts went to the Boston Beaneaters of the National League. On that squad were pitchers Kid Nichols and John Clarkson, first baseman Tommy Tucker, second baseman Joe Quinn, shortstop Herman Long, and outfielders Hugh Duffy and Bobby Lowe. The manager was Frank Selee. Stivetts helped Boston to a first place finish, easily outdistancing Pat Tebeau's improving Spiders. Stivetts had a banner 35-victory season, hurling a perfect game August 6 versus Brooklyn. Nine weeks later, Stivetts tossed a five-inning no-hitter against Washington. Players would say of his pitches, "You can't hit 'em if you can't see 'em." Stivetts was said to be as "full of confidence as an egg is of meat" (*SL*, July 12, 1890).

The next season, 1893, Boston took first again, but Jack's pitching effectiveness suffered. Perhaps it was due to arm strain. Stivetts had just concluded three straight seasons of 400+ innings. Boston relinquished the standings' top rung for the next three season but Stivetts plugged away, hurling in a ton of games and even appearing as a novel curiosity: a relief pitcher who went in with the bases loaded and struck out the side. Stivetts continued to hit as well as many league regulars. Happy Jack bopped eight homers in 1894. Occasionally, Stivetts filled holes in the outfield and first base. By 1897-98, Frank Selee's bunch had built another two-year champion team, but Stivett's arm had weakened. His pitching career was upstaged by Kid Nichols, Fred Klobedanz, Ted Lewis, and Vic Willis. Stivetts was relegated to more outfield duties in the next two seasons. By 1899, the 11-year veteran Stivetts went to Cleveland. Most followers described him, at that point, as finished.

Joe Quinn was born on Christmas Day in 1864 in a city not very well acquainted with baseball, Sydney, Australia. At an early age, his family migrated from the land down under to Dubuque, Iowa. As a boy, young Joe Quinn learned to play and love baseball. By the time he was 19, Quinn was playing infield on a highly regarded Dubuque amateur team with Charlie Comiskey.

One year later, Quinn was playing first base on a crack outfit for the Union Association's St. Louis team. Because of St. Louis' outstanding record, they were awarded a National League franchise in 1885. But for two years, the St. Louis Maroons foundered. Quinn didn't hit much and was moved to outfield on a club populated by such names as shortstop Pebbly Jack Glasscock and pitchers One Arm Daily and Egyptian Healy.

By 1887, Quinn was in the minor leagues at Duluth and Des Moines. In 1888, he moved to Boston, where the Beaneaters were beginning to assemble the nucleus of a strong team. Quinn was shifted to second base, a much more natural position. He stayed for two years with the Beaneaters, but it was enough to be selected for the quirky studio-posed Old Judge Cigarette baseball cards. Joe is shown on two of the cards; standing near what appear to be tombstones! The other pose shows Quinn sliding into base head first, arms outstretched, and one eye staring right at the camera.

In 1890, Quinn jumped to the champion Boston club of the Players League. This short-lived league, born out of player grievances with ownership, lasted one season. Quinn returned to the Beaneaters for two more years to be part of their championship clubs. On those clubs were the likes of Tommy Tucker, Herman Long, Harry Stovey, Bobby Lowe, King Kelly, Hugh Duffy, and pitchers Jack Stivetts, John Clarkson, and Kid Nichols. Quinn wasn't hitting much in those years, but he survived on his sportsmanship, guile, and his outstanding defensive play. One contemporary account describes Quinn's fielding as "a knickerbockered child out for a day of sand digging on the beach" (*TSN*, May 13, 1899). So fine a gentleman was Joseph J. Quinn that he was given a watch with a diamond setting as the most popular player in the United States. The award came from the St. Louis-based sporting weekly, *The Sporting News*.

In the mid-1890s, Quinn returned to St. Louis. There, he manned second base gallantly, performing on clubs redefining National League mediocrity. Knowing that baseball wouldn't last forever, he learned his father-in-law's trade - undertaker. With his hitting improving, he became involved in a whirlwind group of baseball cutthroats, the rough-and-tumble champion Baltimore Orioles. With the Birds, Quinn played one full season and parts of two others. But the mild-mannered Quinn seemed out of place on the Orioles and soon he went back to the St. Louis Browns for 1898. If the Orioles of the era were baseball's thugs, the Browns were clowns, and played accordingly. In 1899, after 14 seasons in the big leagues, Quinn was shifted to Cleveland.

They didn't make them any tougher than **Thomas Joseph Tucker** of Holyoke, Massachusetts. The 5-foot-11-inch Tucker began his baseball odyssey at 18 years of age. He was a switch-hitting right fielder/first baseman with his town semipro team. In 1884, he played minor league ball for Springfield of the Eastern New England League and then was with Newark for two seasons. Tucker was signed to play with Baltimore in the old American Association. There he excelled as an adept fielding first baseman and aggressive hitter. Two years later, in 1889, Tucker was the champion batsman of the American Association, creaming pitching at a .372 clip and gaining a "stormy petrol" reputation (*TSN*, Nov. 31, 1935). Tucker even appeared on an 1888 Old Judge Cigarette card, standing straight up and cupping a baseball in a strange fashion.

After the season of 1889, the newly formed Players Brotherhood League team in Brooklyn demanded his services, as did Baltimore of the AA and Boston of the National League. To please them, Tucker "managed, without compunction" to sign a contract with each team between November and January of 1890 (*SL*, Jan. 15, 1890). Tucker probably did so because two of the contracts promised up-front cash. Finally, though, the confusion was ironed out with Tucker going to work in Boston.

Throughout the nineties, the Beaneaters were managed by Frank Selee, who had an eye for talent so keen that he could spot a ballplayer in street clothes (Porter, 325). The rambunctious Tucker would have played in street clothes. For seven years, Tucker manned the first sack for Selee's changes, helping them to three straight league championships between 1891-1893. Meanwhile, Tucker's nifty first base play was being rivaled by his own unique coaching style on the basepath. For his constant screeching, Tucker earned the sobriquets "Foghorn

Tom" and "Noisy Tom." Boston fans loved Tucker but fans of other cities didn't think too highly of his theatrics.

The Beaneaters went into a three-year-long slump in 1894. In July of that year, Tucker was used as a scapegoat by rival Philadelphia fans. In a game in the City of Brotherly Love, Philadelphia cranks assaulted Tucker. "Rain starting, the Boston players stalled to delay the game, being ahead in the eighth inning. Umpire Campbell ordered them to resume, but Captain Nash refused and the Boston players entered their bus outside of the grounds. Tucker got out of the bus and re-entered the grounds to go to the clubhouse for his sweater, when the crowd rushed in and trampled him, breaking his jaw" (*TSN*, Oct. 31, 1935). For the next three seasons, Baltimore's rowdy bunch assumed the top rung of the league. Tucker though, pushed onward, using a miniscule glove and wowing admirers with his one-handed stops of errant throws. The Beaneaters eventually gave up on Tommy and traded him to Washington in 1897.

Tucker hit well with the Senators. Once against the White Stockings pitcher Clark Griffith, Tucker was struck out looking, "confounded" by an arching underhanded pitch. With Griffith laughing, Tucker charged the mound with his bat, and yelling and screaming, he chased the hurler all over the ball yard. When Tucker was finally exhausted, play continued. In his next at bat, Tucker blasted a home run off the startled Griffith (*TSN*, Oct. 31, 1935).

On another occasion, Tucker challenged Baltimore's John McGraw to a gentlemanly duel - not with rapiers or guns - but with baseballs thrown at each other (Phillips, *The Cleveland Spiders Who Was Who*). In 1898, Tucker divided his time equally between two horrid ball clubs, tenth place Brooklyn and 12th place St. Louis.

George Bristow was a rookie outfielder with the Cleveland Spiders in 1899.

Shortly after the Civil War, **Lafayette Napoleon Cross** was born in Milwaukee, Wisconsin. Lave was the son of Czech immigrants. Like teammate Jim Hughey, Cross had to live up to a famous name, two in fact. Had his two famous French general namesakes known him or the uniquely American sport of baseball, they would have been proud.

In a career that bridged barehanded days to finger gloves, the bowlegged Cross had a sterling diamond life. He performed his best in Louisville and Philadelphia in the American Association, Philadelphia in the Players League, and Philadelphia in the National League. He began in 1885 with a Findlay, Ohio team and the next year worked in Altoona, Pennsylvania. A major league contract was drawn up for Lave in Louisville in 1887. Cross started out as a slow-footed catcher, but soon he took his catcher's glove (for what it was) to third base. At the hot corner, Cross became known for his fielding exploits. He was a master at foul pop flies. Cross would backpedal, spit in and pound his glove, and scream, "Get out of the way, I've got it!" (*SL*, Apr., 1906). Cross was also one of the top run producers of his time and learned to be quite a student of the intricacies of the game. From 1892 to 1897, Lave captained the Phillies. On the 1894 squad he hit .386, finishing seventh in the league and fifth on his team. The slugging Phils were paced by a .400 hitting outfield of Sam Thompson (.407), Ed Delahanty (.407), and Sliding Billy Hamilton (.404). For good measure, sub outfielder Tuck Turner batted .416. Cross was gaining quite a reputation for his exemplary ballplaying attitude in Philadelphia.

In 1898, Cross' hitting had so slackened that he found himself in St. Louis. There, playing on the miserable Browns, Cross was easily the star of the team.

Philadelphia-born **Richard Joseph Harley** graduated from Washington, D.C.'s Georgetown University in 1896. He had captained that university's baseball nine.

The next season, Harley signed with the St. Louis Browns. The speedy lefthanded hitter did well. The Browns did not. Managed in part by outfielder Tommy Dowd, Scotsman Hugh Nicol, second baseman Bill Hallman, and owner Chris Von der Ahe, the Browns finished with a record of 29-102 and dead last. The next year, 1898, the Browns regrouped. Every regular player left except Harley and pitcher Kid Carsey. Both should have received medals for heroism. The Browns did improve by ten whole games, but they won only 39 of 150 contests. With his career off to a flying start, Harley was transferred to the Spiders the next season.

Called "Buttermilk," **Thomas Jefferson Dowd** hailed from Holyoke, Massachusetts just like future teammate Tommy Tucker. For four years, the swift-footed, ex-footballer Dowd caught center field flies for Brown University. That was from 1888 to 1891.

Upon graduation, Tommy Dowd began an astonishing big league run. It was astonishing because losing followed Dowd like the plague does a rat. In eight seasons beginning with Washington of the American Association, and the perennially poor St. Louis Browns, Dowd played on eight consecutive losing ball clubs. But, not only were they losers, they were aggregations buried deep in the bowels of the standings. They were ball clubs that finished last three times, 11th twice, tenth twice and ninth once. The best team that Tommy played on was the 1893 St. Louis club (57-75). And yet, Dowd went right on tracking down pitchers' mistakes and possibly believing that this was his karma. He also lost his hair in the process. Buttermilk was perhaps a special appellation that Dowd gained because of all the sour teams he was part of. For all his efforts, Dowd was a decent batsman and an excellent flychaser.

Suter Sullivan began his big league career by signing with the 1898 St. Louis Browns. That was his first mistake. He was transferred to Cleveland in the St. Louis-Cleveland franchise shift of 1899. That was his second mistake. In many ways, Baltimore-born Sullivan was like Sport McAllister. When McAllister and Sullivan weren't playing, they would spend their time warming up by bouncing balls against the grandstand and chasing them down like kids dreaming of the pro league. Sullivan was a versatile, substitute performer, who could play many positions on the diamond. But, unlike McAllister, Sullivan did not catch or pitch.

Judging by this group, it was easy to make a prediction. Talent was a bit lacking. Yet, they were all big leaguers, which meant that someone thought highly enough of their skills. Said Mr. Robison (it is not sure which one), "The Cleveland team will be in the front rank all the time as it always has been" (*SL*, Mar. 25). Strangely enough, it was not even certain which Cleveland club he was speaking of - the old or the new.

Thursday, April 13. As the new Clevelands practiced in the frost of Terre Haute, the "old Clevelands" were just finishing up their spring training at Hot Springs, Arkansas and arriving in their new home of St. Louis, Missouri. They had been at Hot Springs since early March in the charge of Manager Patsy Tebeau. Originally, the plans of owner Robison called for the boys to take the day off, but since the weather in St. Louis was so cheery, practice commenced in the afternoon. At the beginning of this new St. Louis baseball gathering, the usual formalities of photographs and appearances before the fans were in order. However, once the warm-ups began, the team was all business. In a two hour "fast" practice, they showed off their baseball skills catching nearly every grounder that came their way and whipping the ball around the infield. Outfielders covered their positions and caught the soaring spheroids while the pitchers conducted a light workout with the catchers.

The crisp, clean practice was a far cry from what was going on in Terre Haute. The Spiders had just six or seven days of work in Terre Haute but they were trying desperately to get in shape. Manager Lave Cross said he was not expecting much from his men in April but "they are playing winning ball and are bound to finish well up in the second division." (*SL*, Apr 22). Unlike the Perfectos, there was no team photo taken of the Cleveland team and scant few fans were interested in watching the players limber up.

Fri April 14 On the eve of the season opening game between Cleveland and St. Louis in St. Louis, the moods of the ball fans and their cities newspaper coverage was in complete contrast. The *Cleveland Plain Dealer*'s name, which came from an old English term for an "honest, straight-forward type of person," blasted the management of the "alleged Cleveland Baseball Co." saying that it had nothing to create local enthusiasm for the team (Condon 99). The headline of the sports page screamed "Not One Word of Encouragement Has Yet Been

Heard" and also prophesied, "The Dark Outlook in this City." It also went on to say that in 1898, management tried to drive fans to support good men, but management's abrasive tactics did not suit well with the fans and attendance plummeted. The 1899 strategy was just the opposite, showing an indifference towards the fans while providing a proven, lousy baseball aggregation. The opening of the baseball season in Cleveland was not to be noticed, according to the *Plain Dealer*. Conversely, the *St. Louis Globe-Democrat* trumpeted the new ball season, proclaiming fan interest at an all-time high for baseball in the city. Pat Tebeau's team was compared favorably with the other top front-runners, Boston and Brooklyn. An early morning Saturday parade around the city of St. Louis was planned, to be headed by owners Frank Robison and Mr. Stanley Robison of the Cleveland team. Fully one thousand invitations to the game were sent to business and sporting men, all part of a finely orchestrated buildup. The hoopla was to continue at the stadium with a band concert, speeches by the Mayor and Police Commissioner and a first-ball pitch by the Mayor. Even the weather man got into the act, indicating a partly cloudy, but pleasant day.

Two last minute player arrivals surfaced for Cleveland. One was the reportedly overweight Jack Stivetts, a long-time National League pitcher, and shortstop Harry Lochhead from his home in San Francisco. Lochhead had spent previous seasons in the California League known for his fine hitting and fielding. Earlier, the *Cleveland Press* had misnamed him "Morehead."

"Al. Hathaway wired Lave Cross an offer of a new suit, a spring overcoat, a new hat and dinner at the club, if he will throw down Tebeau's gang in the opening game." (*CP*, Apr 14).

Sat Apr 15 A full slate of National League games were played as the season opened in full swing. In St. Louis, the parade and pre-game hoopla went as expected with a crowd of fifteen thousand. The VIP's stared from their boxes, the sale of score cards was up, and the hoi-polloi came not necessarily to watch a game, whose result seemed a foregone conclusion, but to praise the sport of baseball itself. So said the *St. Louis Globe-Democrat*, who chose to describe the action of the ball game in intimate detail, outlining each player's at bat and result (Apr 16). *Sporting Life* related, "Cow bells, tin horns and tally-ho bugles helped out in the noise-producing. The early spring rooters were careless with their vocal chords, but there was slashing batting and sensational fielding to tempt the most bronchial throat to do itself mischief." The Cardinals, led by the pitching of Cy Young, defeated the Spiders and the slants of Willie Sudhoff, 10-1.

Besides the on-field action, the *Globe-Democrat* reported on the unveiling of a baby gray fox mascot from a cage before the fifth inning. The animal was a present from a fan in Lebanon, Missouri. In that same inning, "the wind blew up and the skies darkened. Somebody cried cyclone and a stampede was narrowly averted." (*CPD*, Apr 16). The conclusion of the contest featured a nearly nasty spectacle of seat cushion throwing by an unruly fan. Several of the cushions hit other spectators, including the fair sex, and groundskeeper Murphy. No one was seriously hurt.

The mood of the contest was decidedly upbeat, the fans even applauding loudly for the Cleveland players (*GD*, Apr 16). Perhaps, that was due to the fact that the city was rid of them, after the '98 debacle. After the game President Stanley Robison of the Cleveland club talked with a reporter of the *Plain Dealer* regarding the intentions of management in the Forest City and said emphatically:

It is our honest intention to build up in Cleveland a club that will rank with the one that has been transferred to St. Louis. Cleveland will not, contrary to the impression that some persons have been trying to get abroad, be a farm for the St. Louis team. Not a single man who is now with Cleveland will be transferred to St. Louis this season. If there is any transferring at all, it will come from St. Louis to Cleveland, and then only in the case the St. Louis club has more than it wants, and they are of the caliber that will strengthen our team. We won't put any 'cast-offs' in Cleveland, but men who are at the top of their profession, but who may not be needed in St. Louis for the reason that others just as good are there to fill their places. You can say positively, too, that Cleveland will play every game that is scheduled for the season know that there has been some talk about disbanding after the season is well under way, and thereby forcing, as it were, a reduction of the league circuit, but so far as the Cleveland club is concerned there is absolutely nothing to that rumor. We are in the game and propose to remain in it to the finish. (Apr. 16).

"How about arrangements to strengthen the team?" he was asked.

"Well," he replied, "we can't say yet what will be done. Cross is manager now. I don't know whether a change will be made. We will strengthen the team gradually, but our plan in that regard are definitely not formed just yet."

Sun April 16 An overflow Sunday audience of an estimated sixteen thousand baseball souls turned out at the ballpark to witness the second game of the series. Ropes were strung around the outfield to accommodate at least six thousand, the grandstand and bleachers were packed, and many of the spectators stood at the player's clubhouses. Due to the large audience, special ground rules about balls hit deep to the outfield had to be observed. Normal Sunday crowds were generally brawl-oriented, often mimicking the behavior of the players on the field. This crowd tended to behave itself quite well (*GD*, Apr 17).

An exciting contest followed. The St. Louis team sent their second ace Jack Powell against Cleveland's Kid Carsey. St. Louis took at 6-0 lead into the seventh with their scoring highlighted by catcher Lou Criger's home run. However, Cleveland rallied to the delight of the unsure crowd with three tallies in the eighth and one in the ninth, a key blow being Harry Lochhead's double. But, St. Louis second baseman "Cupid" Childs' sensational stop of Tommy Dowd's smash in the final frame proved to be the difference. The Perfectos barely escaped with a 6-5 victory.

The *Cleveland Plain Dealer* again exhibited negativity in its reportage of the Spiders team, commenting that a "timely error and wildness saved them from the catastrophe" (Apr 17). The catastrophe was winning.

After the game, Criger received a hat and a pair of shoes for his home run effort. The owner of the St. Louis team, Frank Robison, brazenly boasted of his new team to Cincinnati magnate John Brush (*GD*, Apr 17).

Wed April 18 Elmer E. Bates, covering the new Cleveland team for *Sporting Life*, wrote that little preparation was taking place for the Cleveland home games. Some in the city doubted that games would be played. There were no official schedules issued. Indeed, League Park in Cleveland was being described as "rough and uninviting." But, the brothers Robison insisted that all games would be played even if the attendance was a groundskeeper, an official scorer, a peanut and a lemonade boy (Apr 22).

Thur April 20 After three days off, the Spiders hopped a steam locomotive to Louisville, Kentucky to play Fred Clarke's Colonels. Already there were signs that the team was not quite ready for the season. Several players were reported to be overweight. In the words of the *Plain Dealer*, the players were in "wretched condition." (Apr 21). Burly first baseman Tommy Tucker, catcher Jack Clements, and late arriving pitcher Jack Stivetts were all reported to have excessive stomach girth.

Manager Lave Cross' face was beginning to show signs of worry (*LCJ*, Apr 21). Of course, it might. The Spiders lost their third consecutive game 11-2 to Louisville. Pete Dowling, who "didn't half try to pitch" threw for the Colonels while Willie Sudhoff was "anything but a puzzle" for the Louisville hitters (*CPD*, Apr 21). The home team battered Willie for fifteen hits and handed him his second straight loss. Leftfielder Clarke banged out four safeties. Honus Wagner had a double and a triple and pitcher Dowling smacked a pair of two-baggers. The Colonels stole bases at will on Sudhoff and catcher Clements.

Joe Quinn was he only bright spot for the losers with his fine hitting and fielding. Portly Stivetts started in place of Dick Harley in left field and went hitless. Harley had injured his hand after being inadvertently spiked by Childs in St. Louis.

Fri April 21   Once again the Colonels easily handled the Spiders, this time 11-4. The game featured "slight, slender, delicate" twirler Harry Maupin, who was "offered as sacrifice" for the Cleveland team. After a four run first inning for the Colonels, helped by Spider shortstop Harry Lochhead's "rheumatic throw", Magee turned "senile", giving up a spate of walks and hits for three Cleveland tallies (*CPD*, Apr 22). He was replaced by Deacon Phillippe, who was pitching in his first major league game. Phillippe shut the door on the Clevelands and even managed a single and a double at bat. George Bristow started the game in left field for the Spiders, but when he sprained an ankle in the fifth inning, Stivetts came on. The *Plain Dealer* continued its relentless criticism, headlining the game as the "Same Hopeless Proposition" (Apr 22).

Sat April 22   For the first time in the young season, their Spiders managed to win a game. They defeated the homestanding Louisville Colonels in game one of a doubleheader. The final score was 6 to 5. Still, the *Plain Dealer* berated the team, even in victory. They said the win was "due more to an accident than good playing" and that the Spiders "won a game but it was no fault of their own." (Apr 23). However, the second game didn't go as well for the upstarts. Louisville pasted them 15-2. After the beating, the *Plain Dealer* called for censure of the Cleveland team (Apr 23).

For their trouble on this day, the team acquired a new nickname; "Misfits." Ironically, the *Cleveland Press* had exhibited an advertisement in its March 11 editions entitled "What are Misfits?" The ad applied to "suits, overcoats, pants, and vests -- made up by merchant tailors -- which are either misfitted or uncalled for garments." Cleveland baseball fans certainly hadn't called for this team.

In the first game, two thousand Louisville fans watched Bert Cunningham go up against Jim Hughey. The Clevelands took and early 2-0 lead and then relinquished the advantage. Sloppy pitching by Hughey led to his being relieved by Kid Carsey, and Louisville held a late-inning edge. In the sixth, with the score close, Louisville player-manager Fred Clarke was caught in a rundown between first and second base. Cleveland shortstop Harry Lochhead chased him down and made the tag. However, Clarke thought Lochhead was a bit too rough and proceeded to kick the infielder in the shins. Lochhead then punched Clarke but before the scene got too ugly, Joe Quinn and Tommy Tucker pulled Clarke away. Both players were ejected and fined five dollars. Somehow though, luck, fate, or whatever, intervened. The Spiders rallied on errors, Dick Harley's 8th inning double, and Lave Cross' single for the winning run. Even the *Louisville*

Courier-Journal couldn't help but criticize the Cleveland team after their victory. The newspaper reported that "before yesterday's game it was even money that Cleveland would not win a game the entire season."

After fifteen minutes, play resumed for game two. Still Bill Hill started for Cleveland against Walt Woods for Louisville. Hill was pitching against his former teammates. A few days before he had boasted that he'd win the game "with any kind of team behind him." But, the Spiders were not "any kind of team." Despite being given warm applause before the game, Hill was "as wild as the proverbial March hare." (*CPD*, Apr 23). He managed five bases on balls and was dismissed early on. Jack Stivetts came on to retire one batter, but not before he had let in six runs with three wild pitches, three bases on balls, and numerous hits. Manager Cross then called on infield volunteers. By this time, several players were laughing at the spectacle. Finally, erstwhile pugilist/shortstop Harry Lochhead tried his pitching hand with no experience in this area of endeavor. The *Louisville Courier-Journal* described Lochhead as knowing "as much about pitching as he does about the science of electricity, and he has never seen a dynamo, a duplex sounder, or a quad." (Apr 23). Yet, Lochhead tossed three scoreless innings.

Sun April 23   Rain postponed a doubleheader that was to be played between the Spiders and St. Louis and the Spiders and the Spiders and Louisville in Kentucky. Instead, the players and manager Lave Cross spent the day wondering how they were to get healthy. Due to the late training start and lack of conditioning, several players were on the mend. Outfielder Sport McAllister was suffering from a broken finger. Former pitcher/converted outfielder George Bristow sprained an ankle. Pitcher/infielder Harry Maupin, Kid Carsey, and "Coldwater" Jim Hughey all complained of stiffness. But, despite the rash of injuries and bad luck, the Spiders remained in good spirits. To a man they vowed to make a better showing.

Unfortunately for the Spiders, many factors were conspiring against them. First and foremost was the disastrous syndicate ball plan. Poor conditioning also played a major part. Thirdly, because of a goofy schedule concocted by the National League, conflicts existed. These snafus placed some teams in different cities playing different teams on the same day! Due to a ban on Sunday ball in Cleveland, the "what-do-you-call-'ems" would have to interrupt a series and travel to another city to accommodate the schedule (*CP*, Mar 30).

Almost all sportswriters and fans were in agreement that the league was being shoddily run. Several games scheduled in Cleveland were already postponed and the season was only a week old. Finally, Cleveland newspapers, most notably the *Plain Dealer*, blasted syndicate owner and players alike. A telephone interview with Frank Robison is typical.

Q. "Is there anything new in baseball, Mr. Robison? This is the *Plain Dealer*."

A. "Nothing for the *Plain Dealer* until it stops its vilifying attacks on me."

Click. End of interview.

Mon April 24 No game was played on this day, due to yet another scheduling conflict. The Spiders spent another day in limbo. Their only consolation was that they were not in last place. The Washington Senators were busy losing eight of their first nine games.

Meanwhile, the *Plain Dealer* focused its frustrations on the St. Louis franchise and its fans. Editorializing mightily, the *Plain Dealer* commented on the Perfecto's undefeated 6-0 start. Their remarks came a day after a hotly contested game between the "old Clevelands" and Chicago in St. Louis. Only 1500 people were in attendance for the 11-inning affair. The *Plain Dealer* criticized owner Frank Robison and the city attitude towards a team which had a good chance at the pennant. A "warning" was even issued by the newspaper that unless the city supported the team, it would be moved.

First baseman Tommy Tucker said, "The trouble is that nobody takes us seriously. We 'Misfits', so called, are doing our best, but the patrons of the game tend to look upon our presence on the diamond as a joke." (*CPD*, Apr 25).

Full-blooded Penobscot Indian Louis Sockalexis, the once great Cleveland outfielder, dismissed in 1898 for his predilection to alcohol, was seen practicing at League Park. Sockalexis swore his sobriety, hoping for another baseball chance. He boasted, "I will be in right field when the bell tinkles Friday, and if I feel as I do today, I'll knock the ball over to Lexington av." (*CPD*, Apr 25).

In October of 1898, this article appeared in the *Pittsburg Leader* about Sockalexis, an extreme example of anti-Indian prejudice (Oct 21).

A Fallen Hero

Poor Lo Sockalexis, of the tribe of Penobscot and Tebeau, will probably be placed under the hammer of the fire, smoke and water sale of damaged baseball goods which is to be one of the features of the annual league meeting. Sock swears by his feathers of his ancestors that he hasn't removed the scalp from even one glass of the foamy beer since early last spring, when he whooped up a dance on Superior Street, in Cleveland, and was discovered the next morning by Tebeau in the act of fastening a half-Nelson to a lamppost in front of the Hollenden house. Sock might draw his own salary as a freak feature in the minor league or a wild west show, but the wiles and temptations of the big cities stimulate poor Lo's thirst and set him forth in search of the red paint.

Sporting Life magazine reported on the Cleveland team, commenting that one local paper was "roasting" the sore, still unfit players. The reporter also related the criticism wasn't helping matters. It was not known what newspaper *Sporting Life* was referring to, but it probably was the *Cleveland Plain Dealer*. *Sporting Life* told of a feeling akin to anger from the patrons of the city towards the management of the Spiders. The magazine also reported three players from St. Louis were to be sent to Cleveland. They were Frank Bates, a 2-1 pitcher with the '98 Clevelands, pitcher Zeke Wilson, and colorful catcher Ossee Schreckengost. The key player was Bates, whom Tebeau called the "next Cuppy." (Apr 29). Nig Cuppy was the diminutive St. Louis righthander. Early in the decade, Cuppy was the hero in the Spiders 1895 Temple Cup victory over Baltimore.

Tue April 25 The home season opener for the Spiders was two days off, yet preparations were strangely silent. Unlike Saturday in St. Louis, there was to be no parade, nor band to greet the players, nor governor to throw out the first ball. The League Park stadium sign that said "Standing Room Only" was not repainted. Even the flannel Cleveland team uniforms still showed the stitching where the words "St. Louis" used to be. The city's baseball offices in the Cuyahoga building were deserted save for club stenographer Miss Lizzie Doyle. There were no pictures on the wall and no official schedules issued (*SL*, Apr 22). The syndicate owners had done nothing to stir up fan enthusiasm, probably thinking it a lost cause.

The *Plain Dealer* spent the day doing what the ownership had not done. Trying to drum up fan interest, they described the players on the Spiders as a gallant lot of men, doing their best, and worthy of sympathy but not getting any (Apr 26). It was quite a change of tact for the newspaper.

Wed April 26 For 65 cents, Cincinnati ball fans could watch the Spiders play their home town boys from the grandstand. For 75 cents, they could sit in a reserved box seat (*TEC*, Apr 27). So, after several days of postponements, the Spiders once again took to the field to do battle with the Reds. In a sloppy contest before just over 1000 people, the Reds defeated the Spiders 10-5. Eleven of the runs in the game were scored in the sixth inning, six by the Reds and five by Cleveland. Willie Sudhoff answered the call for the Spiders and showed that his curves didn't and his fastballs weren't. But, since manager Cross had only two other pitchers healthy, Stivetts and Hill, Sudhoff was again the choice. The Reds countered with Ted Breitenstein, who allowed the Spiders some good hitting, especially by Tommy Tucker and Cross. According to the *Plain Dealer*, the "Exiles drove him to tall timber", a euphemism for being knocked out of the game. Said Breitenstein afterward to the *Cincinnati*

Enquirer, "I am willing to bet a little money that they will not be tail-enders." It was a moral victory of sorts but Cleveland still lost, looked woefully out of shape, and seemingly devoid of teamwork. Syndicate owner Frank Robison insisted that the Spiders would play much better once they were in condition.

As the season home opener neared, some of the players said they intended to wear rubber suits as uniforms, fearing flying vegetable projectiles from the Cleveland "Fans." The *Plain Dealer* reported that the players were in fear of a so-called "hen-fruit reception." (Apr 27). The Spiders certainly had done nothing on the field to endear Cleveland baseball patrons to them, losing six of their first seven games.

Nonetheless, the *Plain Dealer* announced that the Cleveland Spiders practice at League Park on the 27th was to be open to all baseball cranks. The paper went on to say that those unfortunates who could not make it to the ballpark, could watch through the knotholes of the fence. The *Plain Dealer* also issued a tongue-in-cheek warning to the thousands of fans expected to make the trek to Cleveland to see their beloved Spiders. Erroneously, the newspaper had reported an earlier start date for the season opener.

Thur April 27 On Wednesday, the young daughter of Mr. and Mrs. Frank Robison, a Miss Marie Allison Robison, died unexpectedly. Upon hearing the tragic news, the Secretary of the Cleveland team, Mr. Muir, telegraphed President Barney Dreyfuss of Louisville to request a delay in their scheduled game. Mr. Dreyfuss agreed and the teams worked out plans for doubleheaders on Monday and Tuesday of the following week.

After arriving by train from Cincinnati, many of the players remained nervous about the season opener and their morale was hurt further still by Miss Robison's untimely death. However, the late signing of Charles Louis (Chief) Zimmer buoyed their spirits a bit. The stocky-built, hard-hitting Zimmer had been the regular Cleveland catcher for the better part of ten years. He had become somewhat of a Cleveland institution, proud to play for the fans of the city. *Sporting Life* wrote that Zimmer would be valuable to pitchers on the Cleveland team (*SL*, May 6).

Fri Apr 28 With another day off from playing, the Spiders got in a hard practice at League Park, conducting themselves in a "tired but cheerful" manner (*CPD*, Apr 29). The *Plain Dealer* headlined "They Expect the Worst" though it was not known who "they" was. Suffice to say, "They" were probably the players, but equal time here could be given to the ownership, manager Lave Cross, the opposing team, National League umpires, stadium vendors, and groundskeepers. From their previous commentary, the *Plain Dealer* certainly didn't expect a great deal from the club.

As manager Cross put his team through their paces, several of the players found time to speak on the home opener. It was not altogether known if their comments were serious. Utility man Sport McAllister was hoping his broken finger would be healed in time to play. Speaking to McAllister, catcher Jack Clements replied, "You will be pretty lucky to be out of the game. How do you know how heavy the things will be that they though at us?"

Pitcher Bill Hill chirped, "I am glad that I am not a catcher. I will have the satisfaction of not being shot in the back when I play first game. It will be a good thing to have Zimmer in the first game; they might spare him for old times sake."

Willie Sudhoff said, "I am mighty glad that they have finished paving the street out by the grounds. I am told that the work was completed only recently, and just imagine what we might have got if the streets were full of paving stones." (*CPD*, Apr 28) Rocks were considerably harder than fruits and vegetables. But, perhaps, Willie wasn't just speaking for the team. He was, at this point of the season, an extremely discouraged man. His pitching record was no wins and three losses. So far in the young season he was busy dodging baseballs flying past his head while he pitched. Sudhoff had just completed a contract squabble with St. Louis manager Patsy Tebeau. Tebeau had wanted Sudhoff for St. Louis and was willing to offer him a substantial increase after the transfer of teams. Sudhoff reportedly wanted $300 more. When Tebeau nixed the deal, he was Spiders property and sent packing to Cleveland.

Sat April 29 The recent warm weather and hard practices in Cleveland had Spider players optimistic and confident of winning. Despite Frank Robison's daughter's death and the initial decision to postpone games, M. Stanley Robison related that Cincinnati wanted to play on April 30. The Spiders management agreed and twelve members of the team traveled back to the Queen City. The Spiders were to play a single game before Monday's home opener.

Sun April 30 The Reds shut out the Spiders 9-0 in front of five thousand in Cincinnati. Despite the score, the game was well played by both teams, with several key plays affecting the outcome. The much-maligned Cincinnati pitcher Jack Taylor, 15-29 for St. Louis in 1898, went up against the Spiders' Kid Carsey. Slow Carsey pitched well until a five run eighth for the Reds. Twice the Spiders mounted threats against Taylor and both times Cross was the victim. Two solid line drives by the Cleveland manager were turned into nice double plays by the Cincinnati infield. On another occasion in the game, the daring baserunning of Reds' outfielder Dusty Miller had the Cleveland team shaking their collective heads. Miller managed to score from third after tagging on a short fly just behind second base. Overall, the Clevelands fielded well, highlighted by two Tommy Dowd running catches in center field.

Strangely enough, the game was played without the presence of National League umpires. Since National League President Nick Young neglected to send any, each team appointed one man as game arbiters. The move harkened back to bygone days when umpires were selected from spectators and worked for free (Gerlach 80-81). The Reds selected pitcher Frank Dwyer and the Spiders chose McAllister. Fortunately, there were no close plays in the game to put the replacements in an awkward position.

After the game, the Cleveland team boarded a train back to Cleveland for their home opener with the Louisville Colonels. The confidant Colonels also traveled on the same train, having arrived in Cincinnati to facilitate travel arrangements. Some good-natured kidding took place on the short journey, according to the *Cincinnati Enquirer*. Colonels outfielder Charlie Dexter chided Lave Cross, "I'll bet a new hat that we don't have a thousand people for the opening."

Proud Lave replied, "I've got you. You forget that I am a Cleveland man and that there are at least a dozen amateur teams there that I used to play on. The members of all these teams are sure to be on hand." (*TEC*, May 1).

It was not known who in Cleveland may have heard these quotes, but they may have been wondering why those amateur teams weren't representing the city. *Sporting Life* reported that wagers were taking place around Cleveland with odds 4-1 against attendance exceeding 2000 in the opener (Apr 29).

While rumors abounded over the reduction of the National League, due to pathetic attendance in Washington and financial troubles in Cleveland, manager Cross defended his team. He said that his charges would finish in seventh place (*SL*, May 6). Cross also related that he was negotiating with several players to bolster the club (*SL*, May 6).

Second baseman Quinn defended Cross: "I anticipate very clever treatment in Cleveland. I know the Cleveland people are angry at losing their old team, but I do not think that they blame the players for it. We had nothing to do with it. Our team is not a bad one. Two or three changes will make us strong. The few days of practice we had at Cleveland did us a good deal of good." (*SL*, May 6).

Despite the Cleveland team's financial woes, *Sporting Life* reported that center fielder Tommy Dowd was the possessor of $30,000 in cold cash. "In the language of a New York paper as applied to a politician, 'Where did he get it?'" (May 6). That figure represented considerably more than the salaries of the entire Cleveland team.

The *Cincinnati Enquirer* reported a rumor of Jack Clements release by the Cleveland club and the Cincinnati team's desire to sign him.

Arrival of the Misfits
Cleveland Press

Artist: Michael D. Arnold

Opening Game at League Park
Cleveland Press

Artist: Michael D. Arnold

"And Still They Lose."

Mon May 1   A sparse crowd of only one hundred rooters braved threatening weather conditions in Cleveland for the Spiders home opening doubleheader with Louisville.   The only preparation by team ownership was to paint the League Park outfield fences green.   The playing field remained rutty (*SL*, Apr 29).   After the sun came out and the conditions cleared, five hundred spectators were on hand.   They witnessed two closely played, thrilling contests.   The *Plain Dealer* reported that the Spiders "won one game and were entitled to another." (May 2).   The paper also lamented that the Spiders didn't always play Louisville.

The day started with a small gathering of baseball cranks watching newly acquired Louis Sockalexis warm up.   In years past, "Soc" had excited fans with his hard hitting and sensational outfield maneuvers.   But, Sockalexis did not play on this day.   Instead, the *Plain Dealer* resorted to make comparisons to the old Cleveland players, combining the names of their old heroes with the new ones.   Cupid Childs Quinn, Jimmy McAleer Dowd, Jesse Burkett Harley, P. Tebeau Tucker, and B. Wallace Cross were mentioned in jest.   The Cupid Childs Quinn moniker was especially amusing since an afternoon Cleveland paper had printed a photograph of a healthy appearing boy about fourteen years of age.   The caption underneath read "Old Joe Quinn." (*SL*, Apr 29).

As the first contest began the fans were considerate to the Clevelands, applauding each man as he strode to the plate.   Soon, the applause turned to enthusiasm and then hard rooting.   The Spiders kept the game close because of Jim Hughey and Willie Sudhoff's twirling.   They won out in their half of the 14th on Chief Zimmer's scratch single that scored Lave Cross.   It ended 5-4. Oddly, the *Plain Dealer* reported Louisville shortstop Clingman as both shortstop and pitcher in the box score, a difficult feat indeed.   The Spiders had been maligned before, but when the opposition players were that fast, it was mighty difficult to win.   The typist had erred in confusing Clingman with Colonels pitcher Cunningham.

In game two the Spiders sent Still Bill Hill to the rubber against the Colonels' Pete Dowling.   Both moundsmen were superb and a tie of 1-1 existed into the ninth.   Then, confusion over the finish enraged Cleveland fans.   As was their choice, the home team batted first in the top of the inning and were out. Louisville came to bat.   Clingman grounded to Lochhead at shortstop.   Harry bobbled the ball and threw wildly to first.   The throw enabled Clingman to take second base.   Catcher Kittredge then lined a single to center and Clingman raced home. Tommy Dowd made a sensational throw to the plate apparently nailing Clingman. The Louisville runner was called out by umpire Brennan. A scuffle ensued around the plate amidst the flying dirt. Meanwhile, Kittredge, possibly the slowest runner in the league, gathered steam and "sneaked home from second base, ignoring third entirely." (*LCJ*, May 2). Brennan, unaware of everything that was happening, declared Kittredge safe and Louisville a 2-1 winner. Naturally, the Spiders protested with howling home team fans in a frenzy that threatened to lynch Brennan. The umpire had to be escorted from the field. In a post-game explanation, Brennan said that Clingman was really safe, nullifying the illegal baserunning activity of Kittredge (*CPD*, May 2). Now, to add to their troubles, bad umpiring was going against the Spiders.

During the games, first baseman Tommy Tucker was noticed pushing runners off first base. When he tried the stunt against Honus Wagner, a shoving match developed. Umpire Day intervened and play resumed.

With their victory, the Spiders moved ahead of the slumping Pirates to 11th place. The *Louisville Courier-Journal* praised the efforts of the Spiders, saying, "they played us to a dead-fret, copper-riveted finish." (May 2).

Tue May 2　　Another doubleheader split occurred on this day; Louisville winning the first by 3-2 and Cleveland the finale by 9-5. Unlike Monday's games, these two affairs were not as exciting. Far more interesting was Buffalo Bill's Wild West Show currently touring Louisville replete with "rough riders, cavalry, Indians, and Filipinos." (*LCJ*, May 3). However, the fans were treated to some good playing by the Spiders and there was reason to be hopeful. The *Plain Dealer*, ever mindful, gave the locals a new nickname to go with "Misfits" and "Exiles." The new name was "Forsakens."

In game one, the Colonels sent Deacon Phillippe took the mound against Kid Carsey. With attendance running about the same as the day before, the game began rather promisingly for the Spiders. Tommy Dowd led off, walked, stole second and third, and scored on Joe Quinn's sacrifice. But, Phillippe bore down and allowed the Spiders only one more tally. Carsey's flutterballs kept Louisville off balance but Harry Lochhead's throwing error in the fifth led to the Colonels' decisive run. Indian Louis Sockalexis, making his 1899 debut, struck out batting for Carsey in the late innings.

In game two the Clevelands sent workhorse Willie Sudhoff to face Louisville's Bill Magee. The spotty Magee, who was poor in a previous outing against the Spiders, was no better this time. Poor fielding and a late eighth inning outburst of four runs did in the Colonels. The key blow came from the bat of Sudhoff. Willie popped a fly ball to shallow center field. Dummy Hoy, a deaf-mute major leaguer who would make a little squeaky sound to call for a ball, camped under it. With runners on first and second base, the *Plain Dealer* described. "Sudhoff sent a high fly to Hoy. The only way the silent man could lose it was drop dead or fall down. As he is averse to dying he fell down and the hit went for three bases and scored Tucker and Sullivan." (*CPD*, May 3). Sudhoff had his second win a row.

At the end of the eighth inning, both sides thought the game was over, prompted by the chalkboard score boy who got one inning ahead of himself. The Cleveland players ran to their dressing room while the Colonels made their way to their horse-drawn bus. The official scorers finally noticed the silliness and informed the umpires. The players were summoned back to the field to complete the game (*LCJ*, May 3).

With the first home series a success on the field but a failure for revenues, the *Plain Dealer* made a few comments about the team. The paper raved over Joe Quinn's fine fielding at second base. Quinn handled twelve chances perfectly in game one. Fans were turning on to Tommy Tucker's antics at first base. Tucker would do anything to get an edge on the opposition and his spirited yelling kept team morale high. Lave Cross' "crowd of uncertainties" were playing good ball and were to be admired (*SL*, May 6). The *Plain Dealer* praised the aggressive, yet somewhat erratic shortstop Harry Lochhead. It was Lochhead's light hitting that prompted some mild criticism. With a series coming up against the Chicago Cubs, the Spiders would need a new nickname, should their improved play continue (May 3).

Cleveland club secretary, George W. Muir, commented on syndicate ball:

It is unfortunate that even for a few weeks there must be a joint ownership of National League clubs. The imputation that this will affect the reputation of the game for sterling honesty is, however, too silly to require denials or even attention. I would stake all that is near and dear to me in life on the absolute honesty of every game of ball that will be played in the National League this season. (*SL*, May 6).

Meanwhile, in Pittsburg, the St. Louis team was beaten 4-3 in an ugly contest marred by unpopular umpire decisions. After six close calls went against the visitors, the Pittsburg fans stormed the field at game's end. The mob heaped abusive language on arbiters Smith and Burns and had to be held back by ushers and police using mace. A coach was summoned to hustle the umpires off the grounds (*CPD*, May 3).

Wed May 3 In front of only 350 faithful in Cleveland, Tom Burns' Chicago Cubs defeated the Spiders 7-4 in 10 innings. (Burns was no relation to the league umpire of the same name.) The Spiders played a strong game, holding a 4-2 lead in the seventh inning. But, according to the *Plain Dealer*, umpire Jack Brennan's highly questionable safe call on a Chicago bunt helped lead to the tying runs. Earlier, Brennan had missed several other plays, including Chicago third baseman Harry Wolverton, who "was so impolite as to sit on the head of the venerable Joe Quinn, thus preventing him from reaching the plate, with what otherwise would have been the winning run." (*CT*, May 4). It was the second time in three days that controversial umpiring had gone against the Spiders.

Paunchy Jack Stivetts pitched for Cleveland, insisting to manager Cross that he be given the assignment over Jim Hughey. Stivetts pitched and even hit well, but his bulk prevented him from advancing farther than second base on a long hit to center field. For the Cubs, Jack Taylor was the twirler of record, becoming the second Jack Taylor to pitch against the Spiders. The other Jack Taylor was a member of the Cincinnati team. The *Chicago Tribune* wrote that "Taylor pitched through all the game unruffled. Easy flies fell safe in the sun, but he minded it not. DeMont erred behind him, but Taylor smiled serenely and pitched on. Umpires declared against him, but the youngster only turned on more speed, and pitched his team on to victory." (May 4). In the 10th inning, Stivetts tired as Chicago outfielders Danny Green and Jimmy Ryan doubled for the game winning runs. Ryan was atoning for his earlier poor fielding in left, the sun field.

Despite the creditable game against a good opponent, the Spiders were hampered by a lack of teamwork on the field. On one occasion, no one covered second base on a throw from Lave Cross. Another time Chief Zimmer threw Chicago's Barry McCormick out stealing while the tying run trotted home.

A prominent Pittsburg newspaper reported that in Pittsburgh, Pirates President Kerr sent a protest telegram to the National League boss Nick Young. The irate Kerr complained about the May 2nd debacle and asked for the withdrawal of the umpiring duo of Burns and Smith from his city. Young's reply was not known. However, after the umpires were hustled off the field, they turned on each other. Burns called Smith, "the rottenest thing that has ever happened." Smith's gentlemanly reply was, "You are so rotten that the stench reaches the sky." Fortunately, the abusive language did not lead to fisticuffs. Meanwhile, the *Plain Dealer* reported that umpires Brennan and O'Day, who were working in Cleveland, had packed up their belongings. Although the movements of the umpires were secret, there was speculation that the crews were about to switch cities. This was obviously an attempt to cool tempers.

Thur May 4   The detective work done by the *Plain Dealer* about the Pittsburg and Cleveland umpire situation was proven 100% correct on this day. Nick Young had apparently caved in to President Kerr's demands and attempted to diffuse both situations by switching umpires and cities. But, Young's decision only cooled matters in Pittsburg. In Cleveland, the *Plain Dealer* ranted and raved about the switch like a crying child in a sandbox.

It didn't really matter that Chicago destroyed the Spiders 10-2 behind Clark Griffith's fine pitching and batting. Nor did it matter that Jim Hughey was ineffective for the Spiders. What did matter was the mere presence of Messrs. Smith and Burns, whom the newspaper, players, and fans focused much of their frustration on. Umpire Smith made several calls against the home team, the worst of which was an out call in the 8th inning after Lochhead had beat out an infield throw by a "block." The fans screamed. The *Plain Dealer* headline: "Chicago and an umpire too much for Clevelands" and "Smith Made Good on His Pittsburg Reputation." They even wrote that "everything bad in baseball is dumped on Cleveland." (May 5). The *Plain Dealer* also related that a riot would have ensued had there been enough people for one. This jab was not only directed at Smith, but at the Cleveland ownership who had done nothing to make the city proud of their team. The Spiders were 3-11.

The only real feature in the lifeless game was this incident: "Two queer accidents befell Wolverton while at bat in the sixth. First he ducked a wild pitch. The ball hit his bat and Burns called it a strike. While Wolverton was protesting, Hughey pitched. Again the ball struck the bat, but this time went fair and Wolverton was thrown out." (*CT*, May 5).

Fri May 5   For the third straight day, the Spiders lost to a far superior Chicago squad. "The Cowboys, being in a hurry to catch a train, simply walloped Cross' comedians in waltz time, and packing up their new percentage, started for Chicago." (*CT*, May 6). This time the score was 11-2. Once again the *Plain Dealer* ridiculed the work of Smith, going so far as accusing him of taking bribes, though the newspaper did not know the source. Smith's bad decisions were so impartial as to be "amusing" and a "curiosity." The Spiders played very poorly, especially in the field, making four miscues. The usually steady Joe Quinn was a puzzle, fumbling two ground balls.

Nixey Callahan started for Chicago. Kid Carsey pitched for the Spiders and had about as much chance to win "as the proverbial snowflake to reach the inner precincts of the infernal region." (*CPD*, May 6). The sportswriter also described the contest as "tame, tiresome and ladylike." After a promising series with the Colonels, the Spiders had been outscored by Chicago 28-8.

Sat May 6   The Chicago and Cleveland ball clubs traveled west to resume their one-sided series at the West Side Grounds. Cleveland must have felt like they were playing in the Chicago stockyards.

Windy City fans seemed rather content that their team was fattening up at the expense of the Misfits. As a result, the Cubs moved into second place, just behind front-running St. Louis. The *Chicago Tribune* said that the fans were "howling with delight" over the victory (May 7). Lefthander Bill Hill was the sacrificial pitcher sent up by manager Cross while Tom Burns called on Jack Taylor. Just three days before, Taylor had outlasted Jack Stivetts. This time, neither pitcher fooled many batters, the difference being that the Cubs bunched their hits. The final score was 10-5. The highlight was a remarkable shoestring catch and double play by Jimmy Ryan of Chicago. In the seventh inning, Ryan reached down for a sinking liner off the bat of Lave Cross. Catching the ball just off the grass, Ryan flipped the ball in one motion to first base, doubling up a scrambling Joe Quinn. The *Chicago Tribune* reported astonishment, then silence in the crowd. Then, after realizing what they had just witnessed, they rose in a five-minute ovation to Ryan and the Cubs (*CT*, May 7). The *Plain Dealer* descried the Cross men as lacking "ginger." (May 7).

Sun May 7   There were a few baseball stories concerning the city of Cleveland today. The ball game scheduled between the Spiders and Cubs was rained out.

According to the *Plain Dealer*, the Cleveland team had secured righthanded pitcher Charles Knepper from the Indianapolis team. Knepper was a man long sought after in Cleveland. In 1898, manager Patsy Tebeau of Cleveland wanted both Knepper and his battery mate Ossee Schreckengost from Youngstown. Tebeau succeeded in landing "Schreck", but as the Indianapolis team had a claim on Knepper, the dispute went to arbitration. The ruling favored the Indianapolis team. The St. Louis/Cleveland syndicate remained interested in Knepper. But, the Spiders' management finally settled the matter with Indianapolis. Since the Robison brothers decided that there were enough pitchers on St. Louis, Charlie Knepper went to the Spiders.

President M. Stanley Robison praised his men saying they had the "right spirit" and that the Knepper acquisition would "help us out greatly." (*CPD*, May 8).

The Cleveland Outing club was completing arrangements for "one day of old-time baseball" to welcome the Old Clevelands/St. Louis team back to Cleveland. St. Louis was scheduled to begin a series of games with the Spiders on Tuesday. James Jefferson Buckley, the President of the organization, prepared a musical program based on the favorite selections of the players. The tunes were to be played by a 15-piece brass band as the players came to bat during the game. Club members were to have a special trolley car and were to arrive early on the grounds to greet their heroes. One hundred seats in the grand stand were reserved for the club.

Since heroes were evidently lacking on the new Cleveland club, the *Plain Dealer* devoted a vivid narrative to a childhood incident in the great Jesse Burkett's life. Burkett was the star outfielder for the St. Louis team, and an old-time favorite of the fans in Cleveland. As a lad of sixteen, Burkett dove into a flood river to try to save the lives of two youngsters (May 8).

Mon May 8 For the finale of the Chicago-Cleveland series, a rousing contest was the order of the day. The game had everything a baseball crank could possibly want. There was good pitching and hitting, sensational and forgettable play afield, arguments, ejections, a near fatal injury, and high drama. Manager Tom Burns sent Clark Griffith to the mound for Chicago against Wee Willie Sudhoff. It was a seesaw-scoring affair.

In inning six, Cub second baseman Barry McCormick was knocked senseless on the temple by an errant Sudhoff toss. McCormick barely escaped serious injury. Lave Cross' argument over Harry Wolverton taking a base on a hit batsman led to his being denied to bat in the seventh by Umpire Burns. Lave's foul language put a "crimp in the Brush rule," wrote the *Plain Dealer* (May 9). Lave's replacement, George Bristow, smacked a double. Cleveland straightened Griffith's curves "to the four winds", and with the help of six Cub errors, the Spiders held a 7-5 lead into the ninth (*CPD*, May 9). Three outs away from victory, the bizarre happened. Griffith flied out to Harley in left field but Jimmy Ryan singled off Sudhoff's glove. Outfielder Green was given first on balls, after enduring three straight strikeouts. The batter was now Wolverton, who had managed two errors in the field. At this point, the *Chicago Tribune* reported some fans "jeering sarcastically" while leaving the ball yard (May 9). Wolverton then proceeded to blast the ball far into right field, hitting "The Tribune" newspaper ad sign. It was a game winning home run. As "volumes of gladsome noise" cheered Wolverton's heroics, the Chicago players rounded up the third baseman and did a "war dance of joy. The saddened Clevelands mournfully packed their bat bags and quietly slunk away." (*CPD*, May 9). It was another bitter pill for the "Discards," a new name given them by the *Chicago Tribune* (May 9). Eight to seven.

Despite their losses, Elmer E. Bates of *Sporting Life* continued to support the Clevelands. He singled out several players for their good work. Second baseman Joe Quinn was having another reliable year. Lave Cross was aggressive at third base. Tommy Tucker was playing a fancy game at first. Harry Lochhead was hard working and conscientious at shortstop and right fielder Suter Sullivan was "doing most timely hitting" and covering his position in "good style." It would only be a matter of time before the pitching was squared away. The whole team was playing in earnest but to small crowds. Unlike St. Louis on opening day, there was no need in Cleveland to stretch ropes around the outfield for fan control (May 13).

With the St. Louis team prepared to invade their old stomping grounds, plenty of support still existed in the Forest City. The *Plain Dealer* devoted their lead sports article to a team that was no longer representing Cleveland. Patsy Tebeau gave an extensive interview about the reception, the confidence of his first place club, and syndicate ball.

Tues May 9   With Cleveland fan enthusiasm at a season high, a crowd of about fifteen hundred showed up at League Park to cheer on their old heroes. The Cleveland Outing Club organized much of the merriment and yelled like collegians. A wondrous brass band serenaded the players. The *Cleveland Plain Dealer* newspaper described the gathering as showing no partiality in the rooting.

The result of the game was no surprise. The Spiders fell by 8-1, being stopped again by Cy Young. Jack Stivetts attempted to regain some of his old glory for Cleveland, but couldn't. But, despite a lopsided score, the contest was close. Only in the 8th inning did the Spiders weaken. With Joe Quinn's miscue at second base and decidedly "rank umpiring" by Spider nemesis Brennan, St. Louis tallied five times to put the game out of reach (*CPD*, May 10). The highlight for the Spiders was the lineup presence of Cleveland old timers Chief Zimmer, Louis Sockalexis, and Sport McAllister. The latter, who played shortstop in the contest, insisted that he had pitched his last game.

The real story of the day was not the game itself, but the bittersweetness of the St. Louis team playing in Cleveland. The visitors received the warmest of welcomes with the band providing appropriate music; the National Anthem was not yet a baseball tradition (Einstein 11). But, "Home Sweet Home" was played for the St. Louis team and the *Plain Dealer* related that there was "far more pathos than humor in the situation." (May 10). The great batsman, Jesse Burkett, who was threatening retirement, was greeted with "Say, Au Revoir, but Not Goodbye" and the tune "Twere better far had we never met, we loved you then, we love you yet." To this strain, the newspaper reported that the normally stoic Burkett was quite moved. Other players were welcomed with songs chosen especially for them. Cupid Childs heard Mendelssohn's "Wedding March" to signify his soon-to-be status. Manager Tebeau was serenaded with "He's the Warmest Baby in the Bunch." The band even greeted a few of the new Clevelands. Lave Cross was treated to the rousing "For He's a Jolly, Good Fellow", though it was not known if this actually described his mood after having to manage the Spiders. Off-season undertaker Joe Quinn was reminded of his profession with the "Death March." Louis Sockalexis was serenaded with an Indian war dance. Chief Zimmer heard a tune of his German ancestry (*CPD*, May 10).

National League President Nick Young denied rumors of a proposed reorganization of the league, saying that all the clubs were financially stable.

Wed May 10   It was a case of first place playing last and last was outclassed. The locals were demolished by the ex-locals 12-2. The *Plain Dealer* said the "element of sport in the second game between Cleveland and St. Louis was about equal to that afforded a contest between a hungry fox terrier and a sick rat." (May 11). With a mediocre lefthander named Cowboy Jones twirling for St. Louis versus Still Bill Hill, the Spiders must have figured they would have a chance. But, once again, bad bounces, lack of team work, spotty pitching, poor fielding, inconsistent hitting (all early season Spiders' hallmarks), led to a 7th straight loss. St. Louis made the base paths their personal racecourse, tallying a dozen runs. The Spiders' base running was pathetic; the once swift-footed Penobscot Louis Sockalexis was thrown out at home on a single. It would not have been so bad had Sockalexis not started from third base. Related the *Plain Dealer* on the subject of Cleveland's fielding, "A wooden Indian might get through the season without an error, and so might some of the Cleveland players if they continued to keep away from the ball as they did yesterday(May 11).

Thursday May 11 It was almost a "serious accident" said the *Plain Dealer* (May 12). The Spiders almost won a game from St. Louis in League Park. However, bad luck continued to plague Lave Cross' bunch. Perhaps, though, the Cleveland players just forgot to put good luck token red bandanna handkerchiefs in their uniforms (Schlossberg 68).

This contest involved brutal hitting with St. Louis hammering 16 hits off Sudhoff and the Spiders nailing 18 off Jack Powell. Rightfielder Louis Sockalexis was back in form with a brilliant 5 for 5 day at bat. In baseball comeback parlance, Soc was "still on earth." (*SL*, May 20). Leftfielder Dick Harley rapped out four safeties. But, with all the hitting, the game turned on fielding plays. On the negative side, Sockalexis committed two outfield muffs while Harley added one. The errors contributed much to the St. Louis offense. Sockalexis' poor fielding nullified his hitting and his great outfield assist to double Cupid Childs at third base.

The ninth inning was as exciting as any at League Park on the season. Trailing 8-6, the Spiders loaded the bases on Powell with one out. Singles by Joe Quinn, Sockalexis, and McAllister did the damage. Then, up stepped Tommy Tucker, the talkative first baseman. Tucker smacked a high one over third base that looked, for a second, like it would equate to three runs and a stunning victory. But Rhody Wallace leaped high to snare the ball and stepped on the bag to get Quinn, who had strayed off base. It was an unassisted double play and the game was over. Like the instantaneous act of a Spider catching a fly, this fly had caught the Spiders, handing the locals another defeat.

Friday May 12 Off the heels of the previous day's disappointing loss, the Spiders regrouped. In the finale of the four game series, they played a tight ten-inning game against the front runners. Kid Carsey started for the Cross Men against little-used Zeke Wilson for Tebeau's charges. Both hurlers threw well. According to the *Plain Dealer*, "the way hits were killed by sharp fielding was

40

simply slaughter." (May 13). Shortstop Harry Lochhead was the surprise batting star for the Spiders, knocking in all four runs. The score was 4-4 after nine. In the tenth inning, though, with no one out, St. Louis shortstop Ed McKean took a bender of Carsey's to the fence in left center. McKean sped around the bases and beat the throw to home plate. After another bitter loss, the Spiders were 3-18. They had been outscored 33-13 by St. Louis. Of the Spiders' three victories, all had come at the expense of Louisville.

Curiously, *Sporting Life* reported that while Cleveland fans were staying away from the ball yard, the newspapers of the city were supporting Lave Cross and his Misfits (May 20).

Sat May 13 The Spiders traveled to the Steel City of Pittsburg, Pennsylvania to face the Pirates. Eighteen hundred baseball souls showed up at Exposition Park, so named as a site for circuses and tent shows (Reidenbaugh 218). Pittsburg manager Bill Watkins sent his lefthanded ace Jesse Tannehill to the mound against the Spiders' Jim Hughey. It was no contest. The Pirates blanked the Spiders 6-0, playing very organized, championship ball. It was Cleveland's second whitewashing of the season.

Tannehill was on the top of his game, limiting the dispirited Clevelands to three hits. Home town hitting heroes were centerfielder Ginger Beaumont and seldom-used shortstop Art Madison. Both men totaled three hits apiece against Hughey. The story of the game was the embarrassment of Louis Sockalexis. The former great outfielder twice fell down in the outfield with the ball in his hands, flabbergasting even the official scorer, who chose not to charge Sockalexis with any errors. One of the miscues became a three-base hit with two runs scoring. The *Plain Dealer* reported that Pittsburg grandstanders applauded Sockalexis running off the field, after the inning of one such outfield adventure. Sockalexis, apparently not wise to the sarcasm, simply doffed his cap on the way back to the bench. The *Pittsburg Post* described Sockalexis as "nothing more or less than a tobacco sign in right field. In fact, a tobacco sign could not have done the damage he did." (May 14). Manager Cross heard talk about taking Sockalexis out of the game, but did not. However, Sockalexis was not the only Cleveland player with egg on his face. As Soc stood for the fielding frustrations of the Spiders, Tommy Tucker chose Pittsburg as his venue to symbolize Spider baserunning blunders. The *Pittsburg Post* related, "In the second inning Tommy Tucker hit along the left field foul line for two bases. When Hughey was at bat Tannehill threw to second to catch Tucker but failed. Madison, who covered the bag, tossed the ball back to Tannehill, but remained on the bag. Tucker instantly took a lead, and instantly the ball went from Tannehill to Madison, and Tucker was caught. It raised a great laugh." (May 14). Besides providing description of Spider misfortunes, the *Pittsburg Post* was also kind enough to add a new nickname to the club: "Remnants." (May 14).

Sun May 14   For all of their troubles, the Spiders were off to Chicago for a game with the Cubs. In the occasional three-team doubleheader, the Cubs were also to play the Louisville Colonels, but both games were postponed by rain.

With the team idle, the *Plain Dealer* focused on two pitching prospects. In an attempt to strengthen the team, Cleveland management was speaking with 40-year-old Tony "The Count" Mullane, a career 285 game winner in the leagues (May 15). Nicknamed because of his elegant attire and handlebar moustache, Mullane had last pitched in "fast company" in 1894 in Cleveland. He had a spectacular career in the 1880s, pitching 500 innings in two separate American Association seasons. Mullane was noted for his unusual ambidextrous abilities. On occasion, he threw both left and right-handed in a game. The club was also trying to obtain the services of lefthander Fred "Cobblestones" Klobedanz, recently released by Boston after a 1-4 record. Klobedanz was 26-7 in 1897.

From Pittsburg came a very unflattering article on the Spiders from the *Pittsburg Dispatch* (May 15). The remarks concerned Saturday's game with the Pirates.

The Clevelands were a large sized, juicy cinch for the Pirates, and after witnessing their amusing exhibition one did not wonder that the people of Cleveland declined to patronize them. The team is a big joke. They have had a hard row to hoe this season, but yesterday they were up against it as never before. The unfortunate individual who chaperons the outfit decided that our old friend Coldwater Jim Hughey would be the proper person to take a fall out of the Pirates and the obedient James appeared on the rubber with the same old smile. Well, Jim's smile faded away long before the time set for ceasing hostilities, for the Pirates treated him shamefully, in which they were ably assisted by Hughey's own comrades.

Standing out in bold relief all by his lonesome, among offenders on this visiting team, was Sockalexis, the Indian. His Socklets must have been heap full of dope, for his efforts to take care of things that wandered into right field were as funny as a cage of monkeys. He was about as fast on his feet as a cow, didn't get within a mile of the drives to his garden and seemed to be dreaming of better days. In his slowness and bad judgement, Williams and Madison owe the three-baggers with which they are credited and which resulted in several runs. Several other members of the team played like amateurs and how they won three games this season is a mystery.

More talk continued to swirl around in league winds of a re-organization or reduction of the circuit. There were four clubs that many patrons of the game believed would be dropped. The teams were Louisville, Washington, Baltimore, and Cleveland. The *Plain Dealer* reported that the average attendance of these teams was "not visible to the naked eye." (May 15).

Mon May 15   After the Chicago washout and National League scheduling brilliance, the weary Clevelands headed back home to face the Cincinnati Reds. Braving cold weather before a full house of empty seats in League Park, the Spiders and Reds played a quick, 78-minute game. There were 150 people present. Said the *Cincinnati Enquirer*, the "men were on the lookout for Eskimos and Icebergs." (May 16).

Lave Cross summoned crowd favorite Jack Stivetts to the mound while the Reds countered with righthander Pink Hawley. Both pitchers appeared up to the task. In a close-to-the-vest, low-hit affair, the teams were tied at two entering the ninth inning. Cincinnati shortstop Tommy Corcoran led off with a walk and second baseman Bid McPhee sacrificed him to second. First baseman Jake Beckley singled. With Corcoran heading for home, the outfield throw mysteriously bounced over Cleveland catcher Zimmer's head. The Spiders went down meekly in their half of the inning, continuing their incredible streak of bad breaks. It was their 11th defeat in succession. The bad bounce loss was especially disheartening for Zimmer. The Chief was criticized a few weeks earlier in a Cincinnati newspaper for his poor throwing arm. He had gotten his revenge against the Reds, throwing out four would-be basestealers as he "nipped 'em all a mile or two from the base." (*SL*, May 27). For the third time in four games, the Spiders had lost in the final frame. For the first time in a long while, the *Plain Dealer* praised the umpiring work of Gaffney and Andrews. But, perhaps, Cross and his bunch could take solace in the fact that in Cincinnati, a local ball team called Blystone's Rough Riders defeated Bell's Lobsters in a close shave score of 62-0 (*TEC*, May 15).

After watching ancient Tony Mullane warm up in Chicago, manager Cross was not satisfied and Mullane did not make the team. The *Plain Dealer* asked as to the whereabouts of the much-ballyhooed Charlie Knepper, now that Mullane had failed.

Tues May 16   The Reds-Cleveland game was rained out so the *Plain Dealer* devoted their day to baseball gossip. One such item came from the traveling correspondent of the *Cincinnati Enquirer*:

The Cleveland games are being patronized by small but select audiences these days. The spectators treat the players kindly and are most fair minded withal.

"I have never played before nicer audiences in my life," said Joe Quinn this afternoon. "True, the stands are not filled at every game, but the people who do come out are most kind to us."

"Yes," chimed in Lave Cross, "We ought to take our hats off to them every time we come out, and mark my words before the season is very far advanced, we will give these faithful supporters occasion to be proud of us." (May 17).

Another reporter had less flattering things to say about Cleveland fandom: "The players are doing the best they can and only ask that the spectators use no fire arms." (*TSN*, May 13).

The statements made by Quinn and Cross showed their modesty and loyalty.

Meanwhile, there was a story of a shakeup on the Cleveland team. Spiders' management released catcher Jack Clements, who had caught in only four games and was nearing the end of his National League career. Speculation was rife that utilityman Suter Sullivan was going to Washington, pitcher Jim Hughey to Kansas City, and Harry Maupin and Louis Sockalexis to the dogs. The *Plain Dealer* still believed that George Bristow could do the job, after his ankle injury had healed (May 17).

Sockalexis, though, was another story entirely. Instead of going to the dogs, Louis went to the theatre on Monday evening to view a performance of "A New Year's Dream." The play so enchanted Sockalexis that he was soon fast asleep and snoring loudly. His heavy breathing created such a ruckus that patrons were disturbed and a policeman had to be summoned to wake him. Thinking Sockalexis inebriated, the policeman took him to the central station (*CPD*, May 17).

Wed May 17 For the second straight day, rain and wet grounds postponed the Cleveland game with the visiting Red Legs. Seizing upon the opportunity, the *Plain Dealer* treated the non-event with sarcasm. They said that Cleveland's good luck was continuing and that two days had passed without a defeat. Since the Spiders didn't draw flies, the tacky newspaper continued, the games might as well be played (May 18). *Sporting Life* added that the Cincinnati team profit was less than $100, owing to the postponements (May 27).

Newspaper sports editorials appeared around the country about the dangers of syndicate ball. Most were in agreement that the plan aroused suspicions with a top team and bottom team. However, despite the Lave Cross/Tebeau story, Sockalexis' poor play, and the trials of the Spiders, the *Plain Dealer* went on record as saying the situation in Cleveland was not due to syndication.

Having little choice, Lave Cross released Louis Sockalexis. The Indian's downfall was his tragic game in Pittsburg, the incident at the theatre, and his incessant drinking habit. Sockalexis played in only seven games.

Thur May 18 The rain fell again in Cleveland. As ballplayers loved to read about the sporting fortunes in the papers, they probably got a chuckle out of this item. A team from Boston defeated a team from Rushville, Indiana by 6-5. Nothing amazing here. Except, the Boston Bloomers were women (Phillips).

Fri May 19 Another day of rain and cold weather stalled the Cleveland season. It was the fourth time in a week that weather had postponed ball games. Manager Lave Cross met with Manager Billy Shettsline of the Philadelphia club at the swank Hollenden Hotel in Cleveland to discuss the postponements and baseball in general.

Sat May 20 After looking to the standings and the heavens for a miracle, the chilling rain finally dissipated for the Spiders. The slugging Philadelphians must have forgotten their raincoats and their bats. The team from the City of Brotherly Love brought their 17-10 powerhouse to face the woeful 3-20 Clevelands in Cleveland. When it was over, the fanless wonders walked off the field with a 10-4 victory. The disgrace of the defeat was not lost on the *Philadelphia Enquirer*. Their headline muttered, "This is sad, very. To think that those Phillies of ours should drop a game to the tail-enders." (May 21). It was the Spiders first of the year against a team outside of Kentucky, snapping an eleven game loss string. The triumph was Cleveland's second of the month.

Mr. Silent William Hill pitched marvelous for the hometown happiness boys against Wiley Piatt for the Phillies. Piatt was anything but Wiley to the Clevelands. His control was nonexistent as he surrendered eight walks and hit two batters. Behind him, Philadelphia exhibited poor fielding and "resembled a team of overgrown schoolboys." (*CPD*, May 21). When Piatt did throw one over the plate, Lave Cross and Joe Quinn found his offerings to their likings. Catcher Zimmer's 4th inning home run drive into the lattice work in left field knocked Piatt from the game. Incredibly, it was Cleveland's first four-base hit of the year. For once, luck was on the Cleveland side.

Sporting Life printed this short article about the contest (May 29).

A young man who made something of a reputation as a "sure-thing" plunger stood in front of a downtown hotel Saturday afternoon and offered to bet $100 against $25 that Philadelphia would beat Cleveland. A half-dozen printers, who had just been paid off, held a hurried conference across the street, and decided to take the bet. The money was placed in the safe of the hotel, and the young man started for the ball game. "That $25 will buy me a light overcoat," he shouted as he boarded the car. But, it didn't. Instead, six linotype operators sat down to a feast with champagne and 40-cent cigars on the side, and never left their chairs until the $100 was gone.

Sun May 21 With their spirits buoyant, the Spiders "dashed from the diamond to the depot," catching a train to Louisville to play the Colonels (*SL*, May 27). On a sloppy, rain-soaked field, Cleveland managed to defeat the Clarke Men.

The score was 4-3. Said an astonished *Plain Dealer*, "They seem to have won two games in succession." (May 22). For several hours though, the game was in doubt. Originally scheduled as a doubleheader, heavy precipitation kept the crowd down to two thousand and cancelled one of the games. But, to make the Spiders' $300 travel costs worthwhile, a "large force of men and boys were put to work with brooms, rakes and drags as soon as the rain had stopped." (*LCJ*, May 22).

It was a comical contest, especially for the Colonels. Louisville managed the worst against the elements of infield mud and outfield puddles. Again, the *Plain Dealer* referred to the Spiders' opponents as "school boys." (May 22). Deacon Phillippe went for Louisville against Jim Hughey. Both pitchers were strong but critical Louisville mistakes were the difference. Colonel's shortstop Tommy Leach committed four errors that helped the Spiders. "Buttermilk" Tommy Dowd led the visitors with four hits. Honus Wagner splashed a home run in inning five. In the ninth inning, with the Spiders on top 4-3, Wagner made a game ending base running blunder. With one out and Wagner on second, the next batter popped to shortstop. Wagner inexplicably headed for third. Harry Lochhead promptly threw to Joe Quinn and the game was over. The Spiders were 5-20, fourteen games behind St. Louis.

With two straight victories under their belts, the Misfits probably had a little reason to smile. Lave Cross insisted that perfect harmony existed on the ball club (*SL*, May 27). But certainly, with umpire woes and other circumstances beyond their control, Cleveland players could have found time to chuckle at this article printed in the *Plain Dealer*. It was called "An Old Time Trick." (May 22).

Several years ago, when the Pirates had the reputation all over the circuit for not being the fairest exponents of the game of baseball as it is written, they turned many a trick away from the green diamond that was never brought home to any particular player nor even was punished. One of the members of that old aggregation confessed that umpires were the particular prey of the old crowd- umpires who had not given the team what they thought was coming to it. "One way of getting even with umpires who did not please us was most amusing," said this player. "Umpires, you know, leave their uniforms in a dressing room at the park when they are officiating in a city. Well, when an umpire whom we disliked came along we would get some hot liniment and pour it all over those portions of the uniform that would be most liable to be rubbed when the umpire was in action. When the liniment got in its work by being warmed up, the umpire was a picture of misery that we players enjoyed immensely. It was our revenge. The greatest sufferer I ever saw from this treatment was the late Jack McQuaid. We put liniment in his trousers and his shirt one day when the thermometer was about 100 degrees. Say, Turkish dancers could not duplicate his performance when the liniment got to work. Players today have reformed and such tricks are no longer resorted to."

The *Louisville Courier-Journal* printed a goofy article on the same day entitled, "Kittredge as Kidder." Colonels' catcher Malachi Kittredge was the same man who seemed averse to third base (May 22).

Kittredge is the greatest joker on the team. He caught a "sucker" yesterday afternoon, and what he did to him was something fierce. The victim came in on one of the excursions from Indiana, and drifted over to the club-house while the players were waiting for the sun to come out. He examined Dowling's arm and swallowed the statement that it was encased in a plaster cast in order that it might not get broken. When he sat down by Kittredge, the players smiled.

Kittredge mentioned something about the bath-tub, and told the Hoosier that he should have been with him last winter when he was taking baths in the Appolinaris River. The stranger wanted to know where the river was, and "Kitt" told him it was up in Ohio, just beyond the Rhine, over which people sometimes go when they are in Cincinnati.

"And say," continued Kittredge, "you ought to see my father's cheese mines out in Kansas. They had 60 men to work out there, and all they have to do is dig the cheese out of the mines and put it in boxes."

The Hoosier stood for this all right. He observed that it was wonderful, and said that he would like to visit the place, as cheese and crackers were bully when one was hungry. But, "Kitt" went a little too far when he mentioned his father's vinegar wells.

"On my father's place are nine wells of pure vinegar," said Kittredge. "He has planted acres of cucumbers all about these wells and the vinegar overflows on them and all the men have to do is pick the ready-to-eat pickles and ship them away."

The stranger arose, sighed, stretched his arms and said he thought that he would walk around for awhile, and he passed sadly away.

This story got President Dreyfuss started, and he perpetuated one that will carry off the laurel. He stated that in Berlin, Germany, there was a sausage factory which contained a wonderful machine. The machine was such a perfect mechanism that whole pigs could be put in at one end and they came out sausages packed in a box at the other. But the marvelous part of the machine was seen if a sausage was found to be bad, it was placed back in the machine and came out a pig at the other end.

Then the players went out to practice in the mud.

Mon May 22　After their one game fling in Louisville, the Spiders returned home. There, in front of 200 souls against an awful Washington team, the Clevelands were demolished 14-3. Willie Sudhoff pitched, a word used liberally, for the home towners. Manager Arthur Irwin's Senators team countered with slender Gus Weyhing. The *Washington Post* related that the Senators "piled up runs so fast that there was never anything to it thereafter." (May 23). The Spiders were back in form. "Before Sudhoff got a chance to catch his breath, Washington cut in and had all kinds of fun. They simply used the ball for a lawn mower, and cut the grass all over the park with it. The Cleveland fielders chased after base hits, single and plural, until they were tired and then contributed a couple of errors to increase the score." (*CPD*, May 23). The *Washington Evening Star* was no kinder about Sudhoff saying the "Senators saluted him as if a long lost brother was found." (May 23). After the first inning, the Senators led 8-0. But, Sudhoff stayed gallantly in the game, walking one batter, hitting two others, and watching the Senators make runs. He pitched until the eighth inning, surrendering a double and a home run to Washington right fielder Buck Freeman. The right field homer, landed "on a porch on the other side of the street." (*WP*, May 23). Harry Maupin added some relief. Only three ninth inning runs scored off his tosses.

Despite the loss, *Sporting Life* praised the Spiders work ethic at morning practices. "Cross generally finds eight or ten of them working away as if for dear life when he reaches the grounds at 10am. They go after everything and there is no suggestion of the take-it-easy style of play which some top-notch clubs have attempted to popularize." (May 27). Specifically, the shortstop play of young Harry Lochhead was singled out. To everyone's surprise, he was "handling the hardest grounders cleverly and getting the sphere over to Tommy Tucker like a shot." (May 27).

Tues May 23   "Energetic enthusiasm" from the "game lot of ball players" turned the tables on the Senators (*CPD*, May 24). For the third time in four games, the Clevelands won. This time it was 4-3. It was a wondrous game for cranks who liked to come out to the ballpark and yell themselves hoarse at the umpires. Old Cleveland nemesis Burns was in top form.

The Senators let Kirtly Baker pitch while the Spiders put in an improving Bill Hill. The *Plain Dealer* picks up the story with commentary on umpire Burns (May 24).

All the hard luck there was in the game went against the Clevelands, and as to the umpires! The vernacular of the fans, strong as it is, fails to contain language capable of explaining the kind of work that was done by "sloppy" Burns. The laws regarding the obtaining of money under false pretenses must be exceedingly narrow or this man Burns would be open to conviction; he pretends to be an umpire and he draws his salary. Burns' nickname "Sloppy" as faintly expresses the quality of his work yesterday as it does the condition of certain Cleveland highways after a hard thaw. Burns, it is alleged, has earned his right to be an umpire by his past services in the game, but if he is entitled to any consideration from the National League he better be pensioned and put where he can do no more harm to baseball.

Specifically, the Burns controversy went like this. On one occasion, shortstop Lochhead threw to first baseman Tucker and received a "safe" call for his efforts. Burns made the call. It led to an early Washington run. In the second inning, Lochhead apparently beat out a bunt, but was declared out by

Burns. McAllister was called out trying to steal third base and an argument ensued from Cleveland. Lave Cross hollered that McAllister was never tagged. Burns then changed his story and said that McAllister went out of the base line. In the fourth inning, Hill was charged with a balk by umpire Smith. Hill protested to Smith but Burns butted in. Hill invited Burns to a tete-a-tete after the game. The vocal Tommy Tucker then took up the Cleveland banner against Burns. Tucker and Burns spent the remainder of the afternoon howling at each other. The Cleveland fans spent the rest of the game siding with their favorite first baseman. Before it was all over, Cross had a running home run to right-center, McAllister made two running grabs in the outfield, and the Spiders were winners.

When the contest had finished, Cross said that the crowd should pay a second admission to see Tucker and Burns duke it out. The crowd probably would have. It was a costly win for Cleveland, though. Gentlemanly fan-favorite Dick Harley was spiked by second baseman Dick Padden as he tried to steal in the first inning. He was replaced by Suter Sullivan. Doctors remarked that Harley would miss several weeks of action.

Wed May 24   The final game of the Washington series was an almost for the Misfits. With the usual sparse of about 250 looking on, the Senators got the better of Cleveland by 8-6. Big Bill Dineen twirled for Washington versus Kid Carsey. Neither pitcher was particularly impressive. The game was highlighted by the infield play of Washington second baseman Frank Bonner. Bonner seemingly spent all afternoon robbing the Misfits of hits. His play and a trio of Senatorial triples by Buck Freeman, Jimmy Slagle, and Win Mercer, were too much to overcome. But, the Spiders tried and they almost did it. Trailing 8-3 in the ninth, Cleveland managed to load the bases for Lave Cross. Smart fans, mindful of Cross' home run the day before and starving for hero worship, got excited. Cross singled and later in the inning Tommy Tucker batted with the sacks jammed. But, there was to be no superman. Tucker grounded into an infield force play and the rally was over. Tommy Dowd had three hits for the losers. Unlike the day before, umpire Burns did a good job. There was no boxing match with the boisterous Tucker.

According to a Baltimore sportswriter who had been keeping track, the Spiders home attendance stood at 3179 for 9 dates through games of May 9. In contrast, Philadelphia was 94 thousand, St. Louis-83 thousand, Chicago-74 thousand, Brooklyn-73 thousand, and Washington-17 thousand (*SL*, May 27). The Senator's owner Earl Wagner offered a solution to M. Stanley Robison and the lagging attendance in Cleveland: "Engage a posse of cowboys who are expert with lassos, locate them along Superior Street and request them to lasso the floating population and bring 'em to the ballgame." Robison's reply? "They would sidestep the lasso, sneak home and engage in such hilarious pasttimes as pinochle, blindman's bluff or lawn tennis." (*WP*, May 29).

President Ebbets of the league leading Brooklyn club was in town discussing baseball matters with Senators' President Wagner. Ebbets was interested in Joe Quinn and Lave Cross of Cleveland. No deals were made, however.

Thur May 25 The *Plain Dealer* called it the most exciting game played on the home grounds on the young season. "The Forsakens gave a surprise party" and the guest was the Baltimore Orioles. Not many present in attendance could guess that a "crack layout" like Baltimore could have any trouble with the Spiders. But, in a baseball show punctuated by an amazing unpredictability, the Clevelands recorded yet another sweet victory. Jim Hughey took the slab for Cleveland while the undistinguished Ralph Miller started for John McGraw's Orioles.

From the start, the umpiring was horrid, but incompetent in such a way that it favored no team nor altered the outcome. It was umpire Smith's turn to be vilified. Second baseman John McGraw led off the game with a double, stole third to great Cleveland protest, and was singled in by Jimmy Sheckerd. Cleveland's modest attack of singles, sacrifices, and fly balls, netted four runs in the third. By the 5th, the Spiders were sitting on a 6-1 lead. But, Baltimore tallied three times in the next inning, helped out by Harry Lochhead's wild throw. Center fielder Tommy Dowd killed any further run producing with a fine grab. In the top of the eighth, the Orioles tied the game. After two were out, Miller, McGraw, and left fielder Ducky Holmes smashed consecutive doubles. Not to be dismayed by the Baltimore rally, Lochhead started the Spiders' eighth with a bunt single. Tucker was hit by a pitch and Sullivan flied out. But, on a poor throw, Lochhead headed home. He arrived at the plate just as a grandstand photographer was snapping the picture. In a jumble of arms and legs, the developed photograph looked like one man with multiple appendages. It was to be the winning run. Later in the inning, Tommy Tucker scored an insurance tally on Jim Hughey's base hit. As he crossed the plate, Tucker whooped and hollered like a kid at Christmas, ecstatic over the Spiders' fourth victory in six games. Eight to six final. The Clevelands were 7-22.

The *Plain Dealer* had this to say about the umpiring.

Umpire Smith showed his weakness in yesterday's game when he allowed O'Brien to deliberately foul every ball that came over the plate.

He could find at least two rules to cover such action if he could get the price of a rule book and hire someone to read it to him.

Smith and Burns are the rankest propositions that have been seen in this neck of the woods, and if they remain on the league staff, it will be another proof that Nick Young needs a guardian.

Fri May 26   Fresh from their emotional win over the Orioles, The Spiders once again met the McGraw Men on the Dunham Avenue Grounds.   Their hopes were dashed to earth.   The Lord Baltimore's, led by righthander Frank Kitson's six hitter, shut out Cleveland 12-0.   Altogether, the Orioles piled up 21 safe hits, 13 off the slants of Wee Willie Sudhoff and eight more from the debut of Charlie Knepper.   Said the *Baltimore Sun*, "Sudhoff was sent to the barn," Knepper was "big and dark," but "they (Orioles) did him too.   They all look alike." (May 27).   Knepper entered the fray in the 7th inning, long after the game was lost.   Mgr. Cross wanted to give the lad a trial.   Said the *Plain Dealer* of Knepper, he "seemed rather stiff," giving up hits to first baseman Candy LaChance, massive catcher Wilbert Robinson, and pitcher Kitson.   McGraw was then hit by a pitch, stole second, while Knepper was "in a trance."   It was an inauspicious debut.

The umpiring in the game was given mild criticism.   Smith called Wagon Tongue Keister safe at home, after he slid in on his keister.   Orioles catcher Wilbert Robinson was hurt in a slide of home in the seventh inning, his keister being considerably bigger than Wagon Tongue's.   Robinson was replaced by Pat Crisham.

Following the affair, the *Plain Dealer* commented on Knepper.   "He looks big and strong enough to pitch a ball through a plank, but he was easy.   He evidently thinks he is Samson, with his strength in his hair, for he is in great need of a hair cut.   Knepper has a good drop ball that should be troublesome, but he could not control it." (May 27).

The *Plain Dealer* also printed a challenge from the Chagrin Falls Misfit Juniors.   The Chagrin Falls baseball team was interested in playing any club averaging 19 years of age.   The professional Misfits were not contacted.

Mon May 29   The Saturday contest with Baltimore being rained out and an off day Sunday gave the Clevelands plenty of time to pack for a short trip to Philadelphia.   There they were met with open arms by the revenge-minded Phillies.   Billy Shettsline's squad had been humiliated 10-4 on May 20 at League Park.

For the Phillies, the homecoming was very easy.   It was played at the Huntingdon Grounds, a.k.a. Baker Bowl, known for its railroad tunnel underneath the outfield and sheep that would chomp grass between games (Lowry 70).   In front of 3355 spectators, the Phillies waltzed 7-1.   Lave Cross, the ex-Philadelphia favorite, led his charges, which were being used "to keep the National League and American Association Base Ball Clubs going." (*CPD*, May 30).   Phillies Righthander Red Donahue kept the Spiders in check, allowing only five hits.   Taking a prosaic tip from Homer, the newspaper referred to Donahue as "he of the auburn tresses."   Smiling Jim Hughey was greeted by the home towners who "connected with his delivery with delightful regularity." Hughey surrendered fourteen hits in all. The Phils hit parade was led by rightfielder Elmer Flick, who hopped a train barefoot to begin his professional career as a 15-year old. Catcher Klondike Douglass was also a standout. Flick flicked four safeties while Douglass icily added three singles and a double.

Tues May 30   With the entire National League involved in traditional Memorial Day festivities, the Spiders traveled north to Boston. It was their first visit to Beantown. Morning-afternoon doubleheaders were the order of the day in six cities. St. Louis was in Baltimore, Cincinnati at New York, Chicago in Philadelphia, Louisville in Brooklyn, and Pittsburg at Washington rounded out the schedule. The league reported over 87 thousand watched the National Game on this day.

The early game was blessed with glorious weather. A crowd of 2500 spectators showed up at the lovely South End Grounds. The park was famous for its twin-spire grandstand turret. Considering the attraction, Beantown cranks were in full force. Lave Cross started a sentimental choice in Jack Stivetts. Wrote *Sporting Life*, "Old Jack will put many a pennant-aspiring club to sleep before the ides of October." (Jun 3). Stivetts had spent the last seven years in Boston, going 35-16 with two no-hitters on the 1892 champions. The big Cleveland lefthander was welcomed by friends and admirers. Boston manager Frank Selee countered with lefty Frank Killen. It was a pitching battle of Pennsylvania natives. But, the battle lasted about as long as it took for the home club to take the field. Killen was masterful, not giving up a hit until the eighth inning. The *Boston Globe* commented on Killen being "cheered vigorously by the crowd." (May 31). Jack Stivetts' homecoming was much less successful. The once great Stivetts was wilder than a hawk, allowing six bases on balls, a hit batter, and a wild pitch. By the time he departed in the fifth inning, behind 6-0, the *Globe* said he "looked tired and anxious to retire." (May 31). Cross replaced Stivetts with Still Bill Hill. Despite its one-sidedness, the game was punctuated by some fancy fielding. Both teams contributed three glove gems. The left side of the Boston infield robbed the Spiders of two hits. Jack Stivetts' blast into the left field corner was snared by the acrobatic Hugh Duffy. The newspapers reported the leaping grab as one of the best ever made in Boston. Cleveland also displayed some fielding prowess by rightfielder McAllister, shortstop Lochhead, and third baseman Cross' breakneck catch of a Jimmy Collins foul pop. It wasn't until the last inning that the Spiders could claim a batting hero. Again, the *Globe* takes up the narrative:

Chief Zimmer, an old Indian fighter and a good one, too, discovered that Killen was dropping them up close, having lost his cue about the left field fence. Swish! went the club, and all eyes were turned to the west where the ball went, taking its merry flight as the big catcher went jogging around the path like a six-day walker with first money in sight. (May 31).

The final score was 7-3, Boston.

The home team boys fully expected to win the afternoon game also. Despite threatening weather and a dust storm that bothered spectators in the front seats of the pavilion, the contest began. As the crowd swelled to over six thousand, Boston sent their star pitcher Kid Nichols to the mound against the maligned Willie Sudhoff. Righthander Nichols had been a thirty game winner in each of the last three seasons and a main cog in the championship team of 1898. Sudhoff had been complaining about a lack of support by his teammates when he pitched (*SL*, Jun 3). Baseball, though, was a perilous game to predict.

With a slim chance of a Spiders victory, the Boston fans spent game two applauding the Clevelands every movement. It was as if the home city was Cleveland and not Boston. Spurred on by this pleasant surprise, the Misfits rose to the occasion. The game was scoreless in frame one. "In the second inning the orphans discovered the combination and poultised the leather for four lovely singles, the work of McAllister, Lochhead, Tucker and Sudhoff. Three large, juicy runs were chalked upon the blackboard and the Boston boys realized they had good, hard work ahead." (*BG*, May 31). The Beantowners never recovered. Nichols was totally outpitched by Sudhoff who had "elegant command of the ball and his curves puzzled the champions." (*CPD*, May 31). For good measure, Sudhoff went 2 for 2 at bat, driving in two runs. Lithe Willie also fielded well, "throwing Bergen out in the eighth on a perfect bunt that was as pretty a bit of work as one wants to see." Besides Sudhoff, Cleveland had other heroes. Normally light-hitting Harry Lochhead contributed three safeties against the mighty Nichols and Tommy Dowd played a fine game in the center garden. Interestingly enough, the *Plain Dealer* described Dowd's work as "marvelous" while the *Globe* called him a showman. "Sir Tommy played for the gallery and drew applause." (May 31). Six consecutive Boston fly balls settled safely into Dowd's glove at one stretch. The Boston's had little to cheer safe for Hugh Duffy's fourth inning home run over the left field fence. The score: Cleveland 6, Boston 3.

Wed May 31 Nothing that happened in the day's previous doubleheader could have prepared 1800 baseball patrons for the next Boston-Cleveland affair. A smug Boston paper said, "Following the Clevelands, we will have the Cincinnatis, and then there will be fun." (*SL*, May 27). The fun came early. In the wackiest, wildest, and craziest tilt of the season, Boston hammered Cleveland by the football score of 16 to 10. Obviously, pitching played little part in the game. The batters of both teams gleefully racked up 34 hits. Among them were five triples, but no doubles or home runs. The *Boston Globe* described the aptly named Beaneaters starter Piano Legs Hickman as giving the "most wretched exhibition ever seen at the South End Grounds. He had no control and seemed like a man laboring under a bad case of stage fright." (Jun 1). Incredibly, the Spiders scored seven first inning runs, and had the bases loaded with one out before Quinn and Cross were retired. The *Globe* didn't realize that their description was apt for several other pitchers. Still Bill Hill started for Cleveland and promptly gave up two singles, two triples, and three runs. He lasted one inning. Jack Stivetts, no better than the day before, was touched for five more tallies, three bases on balls, and two wild pitches. His misery also lasted one inning. In just two frames, the Spiders' seven run lead evaporated. Then, Lave Cross drew straws and tried Jim Hughey. He lasted the rest of the contest to the tune of eight runs. The game's only effective hurler was Boston's Ted Lewis, who surrendered only one run in six innings of relief.

The batting stars were too many to count but Boston outfielder Chick Stahl led all players with six hits in as many tries. All were clean singes. Beantown first baseman Fred Tenney had three its, including a triple. No less than nine others had multiple hit games.

Besides the slugging, fielding played an important part in the outcome. Lack of fielding would be a better description. Sport McAllister chose a bases loaded situation to muff a fly ball. All runners scored.

As far as umpiring went, "Smith was weird on balls and when he called Zimmer out in the sixth on a ball fully two feet wide of the rubber, the crowd fairly shrieked." (*CPD*, Jun 1). But, in the fourth inning, with Boston ahead 10-9, one of the strangest occurrences of the season took place. The *Boston Globe* narrates:

Stahl was on first when Long hit to center. Chick kept right on for third and got there by a fine slide, Tommy Dowd playing the ball to Cross in fine style. Dowd was disappointed at not getting the out and went after umpire Burns, who put a small fine on him. This so enraged Dowd that he called Burns a few pet names and was ordered out of the game. Manager Capt Cook and bottle-washer Lave Cross had a hand in the abuse and was fined and finally ordered out of the game for his poor English. The air was full of blue holes during this little trouble, and Mr. Lochhead declared himself in. He offered to perform a few sleight-of-hand tricks for Burns' pleasure but Tom couldn't see it, so the shortstop was sent to the bench for a few days rest. As Hill and Stivetts already had retired, and Sudhoff was in his bicycle suit, the visitors could muster only eight men, and this was against the rules. Rather than disappoint the crowd, manager Selee allowed Hill to go into the game, claiming the privilege of a protest if the game were lost.

What happened next was rather riotous. Pitcher Hill wandered out into the outfield with no previous experience at the position. Gnarly-handed catcher Joe Sugden moved to third base. His big league resume read four games in 1894.

Pitcher Kid Carsey tried shortstop, where he had played two games in 1891. Despite the inexperience, only Sugden was suspect, committing two errors.

June

"Snowed Under Once More."

Thur June 1   As they had done the day before, the Spiders took an early lead over Boston at the South End Grounds. The result was the same, though, as Boston counted a dozen beans to the Misfits six. With 1500 people looking on, Frank Selee sent the reliable Vic Willis to the rubber against a tired Willie Sudhoff. Willis started shakily. In the early going, the Spiders managed four runs without the benefit of a hit or a Boston error. Simply put, Willis habitually hit batters and allowed free passes to first. All Cleveland had to do was make good on a few sacrifice bunts. Sudhoff, on the other hand, started strong, but was repeatedly hit hard after the second inning. He hurt himself by making a costly error. Wee Willie also did a poor job of holding runners on base, as Boston stole five for the game. It was an exasperating experience for catcher Joe Sugden. While Willie struggled, Willis made the "visitors easy mutton for his curves" and the rout was on (*CPD*, Jun 2). The Boston fielding support behind Willis was flawless. The hitting stars for the winners were shortstop Herman Long and third baseman Jimmy Collins, with three hits apiece. When it was over, happy Boston "straggled off to a hot dinner and a few steins." (*BG*, Jun 2).

In the aftermath, the *Globe* was critical of the Spiders' tactics for blaming umpires for losses. They said the rowdy Clevelands were hurting the sport. The *Globe* also blamed umpire Smith for giving leadoff hitter Jack Stivetts first base on balls after he had apparently struck out (*BG*, Jun 2). Stivetts was replacing Tommy Dowd in center field after the latter had jammed a finger. The newspaper seemed very happy to see the visitors leave town.

Spider frustrations continued to mount. Their pitching woes were all too evident as Boston scored 38 runs in the four games. The team appeared to be snakebit. As related in *Sporting Life*, "When fortune turns her back on a ball team, all is off. The Cleveland Exiles are not the greatest players in the league, but they are certainly receiving no favors from the fickle dame." (May 20). Bad umpiring seemed to pack its bags and ride on the same train. The syndicate baseball idea was a disaster. Tommy Tucker was often barred from the coaching lines, probably because of his nasty reputation. It was a duty he really enjoyed and Cleveland fans appreciated his "lively" but "never offensive" encouragement. (*CPD*, Jun 2). When Tucker wasn't coaching, catcher Joe Sugden was piping to batters to "cut 'er through." (*SL*, Jun 3).

Fri June 2   On Wednesday, the Spiders held a 7-0 first inning lead over the Beaneaters in Boston. They lost 16-10. On Thursday, Cleveland had a 4-0 second inning advantage over Boston. They lost 12-6. On this forgettable day, the Spiders watched a 10-0 lead in the sixth inning evaporate. Their opponents were the front-running Brooklyn Bridegrooms. The *Plain Dealer* blamed the Cleveland performance on the syndicates saying the Spiders were "obliged to resort to extreme methods not to win." Since Brooklyn was the lead team in the Brooklyn-Baltimore contingent, the *Plain Dealer* reasoned, the Spiders "dare not win." The Clevelands also had no business in defeating teams friendly to the syndicate, "In other words, Cleveland will try to beat only Washington, Boston, Philadelphia, and Louisville." (*CPD*, Jun 3). It was the harshest criticism yet of syndicate ball from the Cleveland newspaper.

It happened this way. Brooklyn was host to a three game series at Washington Park. Twenty four hundred ball cranks were on hand. Lave Cross started old veteran Kid Carsey. Brooklyn manager Ned Hanlon summoned Brickyard Kennedy. He might as well have been throwing bricks. In no time at all, he let the Clevelands begin scoring. Returning Tommy Dowd singled and Cleveland had two in the first. When Brooklyn batted, first baseman Tommy Tucker shoved third baseman Doc Casey off first and Carsey picked him off. It was just the kind of roughhouse tactic that Tucker was famous for. When Cleveland batted, "Pop flies began dropping safely in all directions." (*BDE*, Jun 3). Kennedy let a runner reach on his errant throw. It was 3-0 Cleveland after two innings. In the third, Sport McAllister's hot smash to the box almost "tore Kennedy's hand off." (*CPD*, Jun 3). The Spiders continued to score and by the middle of the sixth inning, Cleveland had a ten run advantage. Chief Zimmer was on his way to a four hit day and every member of the Cleveland outfield had solved Brooklyn pitching for two hits. In the sixth, the Bridegrooms began to time Carsey's slowball. They got a single run and two more in the seventh. With two innings to play, it was 10-3 Cleveland.

Many fans actually left the park disgusted at this juncture. The Spiders didn't score in their half of the inning and "Carsey began the eighth inning with a smile as long as one of his native Staten Island mosquitoes." (*BDE*, Jun 3). Then came trouble. Left fielder Joe Kelley started fouling off Carsey's pitches. After a dozen or so, Carsey weakened and Kelley coaxed a base on balls. When the Cleveland pitcher questioned home plate umpire Lynch, he was rebuked and ordered to continue. Shortstop Bill Dahlen followed Kelley and drew another walk. Inexplicably, Carsey could not throw the ball over the plate. He quickly lost his nerve, and crumbled like a cookie. Run after run trotted home. A frustrated catcher Chief Zimmer went to the mound to try to bring order to Carsey's eroding confidence, even refusing to let Carsey grab the ball back to pitch. But, the determined Carsey grabbed the ball from Zimmer, and proceeded to throw two more wide ones (*BDE*, Jun 3). Before it was over, ten men had walked. Manager Cross was fit to be tied. Jim Hughey was summoned into the spectacle. As the walking rally intensified, the crowd was "waving hats, scorecards, and any old thing that was at hand, many accompanying this performance with a jig step or two to reveal their overwrought feelings." (*BDE*, Jun 3). Seven runs scored and the game was tied. The ninth inning was anticlimactic. The Bridegrooms, who must have all been feeling like it was their wedding night, scored the winner on a sacrifice fly. Brooklyn won 11-10. Wrote *Sporting Life* of the Spiders: "the club is not of the fighting kind" and President Stanley Robison was a "good loser." (Jun 3).

Sat June 3 After his humiliation of the day before, Brickyard Kennedy begged Brooklyn manager Ned Hanlon for another chance to pitch against the "transfers." The request was granted. Bill Hill didn't have to beg. In fact, he may have been rather reluctant to go against the Bridegrooms. At any rate, it was another Brooklyn-Cleveland affair at Washington Park.

A big gathering of 6700 showed up to watch several attractions. Their Brooklyn team was leading the league. The Cleveland Spiders were dead last, but providing a brand of ball not seen in many years. Cleveland's *Plain Dealer* called them the "team that does strange things." (Jun 4). The game of the day before had been a raucous victory for the home towners. Lastly, Tom Tucker was becoming quite an attraction himself, with his foghorn coaching voice and rowdy comicality. As the large crowd was settling into their seats, Tucker's pre-game antics gave arriving spectators some chuckles.

It wasn't much of a contest. For a man that some league observers said had "more speed than Rusie," Hill was totally ineffective (*BDE*, Jun 4). Wild Bill surrendered nine bases on balls, 13 hits, and committed two throwing errors. Perhaps, catcher Zimmer should have set himself up two feet outside home plate. Behind Hill, the support was ragged enough for three more miscues. Doc Casey and Joe Kelley contributed three hits apiece. Outfielder Wee Willie Keeler did "hit 'em where they ain't;" twice, in fact. Brickyard Kennedy pitched very well, avenging himself from Friday's disaster. The only noise from the Spider bats was from the two Tommys. Dowd, who was under rumor of release, had three safeties. Tucker had two (*SL*, Jun 10). Behind Kennedy, the fielding was excellent, especially Doc Casey's catch of a Joe Quinn liner, "straight from the bat and hot as pepper." (*BDE*, Jun 4). It added up to a 13-4 loss for Cleveland.

Sporting Life related that baseball sentiment in the city of Cleveland was mixed. Should the editors swear allegiance to Tebeau, root for the Spiders, or pull for the Cleveland team to get into the Western League? (Jun 10). Either way, baseball followers in Cleveland appeared in a quandary.

Mon June 5   There was no contest on Sunday, so both teams traveled to nearby Weehawken Field to watch the New York Giants and Louisville Colonels play. There was no contest on Monday either, although league rules stipulated that both teams be on the field at the same time and commence some sort of game.

A desperate Lave Cross named Jim Hughey as his designated losing pitcher against Jack Dunn of the Bridegrooms. Interestingly, Brooklyn had acquired a new nickname of late; the "Superbas," named after a vaudeville troupe called Hanlon's Superbas (Reidenbaugh 58). Since Ned Hanlon was the manager of Brooklyn, the name fit. The Superbas were indeed, a superbly talented aggregation. The Spiders, on the other hand, more closely resembled a vaudeville act.

"The Cleveland team can't win without pitchers," penned the *Plain Dealer* (Jun 6). And so it went. Coldwater Jim Hughey was touched for 19 hits, 14 runs, and 32 headaches. In describing a long Brooklyn scoring rally the *Plain Dealer* mocked, "There was murder in the sixth." (Jun 6). The *New York Times* speculated: "at some times it fairly rained base hits, and the Cleveland outfield earned their pay, for after the third inning they no sooner had taken their positions than they were compelled to chase after the ball." (Jun 6). Commentary by the *Brooklyn Daily Eagle* was no more sympathetic, "Will somebody please tell the Clevelands that fly balls knocked up in the air are intended, according to the rules of the game, to be caught. It would make their game more interesting." (Jun 6). The Brooklyn batters weren't particular about their hitting. Fielder Jones hit a home run to center. Catcher Farrell knocked two triples and Willie Keeler put on a special bunting clinic. In contrast, Brooklyn righthander Jack Dunn gave up only four singles from his mixture of curves. The only real Cleveland highlight was the reprieve given catcher Chief Zimmer. Joe Sugden took a turn trying to catch Cleveland pitching. The final was 14-2. The Spiders were 8-30.

The New York Times reported that Frank Robison of St. Louis had acquired manager-third baseman Lave Cross and pitcher Willie Sudhoff for his number one team. In exchange, Robison was sending pitcher Frank Bates and catcher Ossee Schreckengost to Cleveland (Jun 6). Bates, an ex-Dayton minor leaguer, had pitched in only two games with St. Louis. The year before, Bates signed near the end of the season as new "twirling timber" for Cleveland (Phillips). Bates defeated St. Louis' Harry Maupin 3-2 in October of 1898.

Schreckengost's distinction was his reputation as a big eater and a name so long he often appeared in the box score as merely "Schreck." Frank Robison was attempting to prop up a sagging St. Louis squad, which had just lost to Washington and was now in fourth place.

Perhaps no man was more affected by the dismal Cleveland showing than Lave Cross. Put in the unenviable position of managing an out-of-shape, castoff ballclub, the loyal Cross did well to endure. The home towner was the only man who brought the team a "certain measure of support." (*SL*, Jun 17). Constantly, Cross was defending his team against the slings and arrows of outrageous fortune, not to mention reporters. Cleveland was beset with almost laughable pitching, little teamwork, horrendous bad luck, and umpires that seemed to have a personal vendetta against them. All of his managing occurred against the ugly backdrop of the St. Louis/Cleveland syndicate.

Once Cross reportedly said to Frank Robison, "I need about five players to have a pretty good team, Mr. Robison, a couple of pitchers and a shortstop would help. Give me these and even with the other Misfits we'll win some games."

"I am not interested in winning games here, play out the schedule. That's your job." (Lewis 31).

Those statements appear contrived. There was even a newspaper controversy over St. Louis manager Patsy Tebeau telling Cross which pitchers to start. Though Cross was an exemplar athlete, abstaining from wine and tobacco, there was every reason to start vices after being around these Spiders. Louis Sockalexis couldn't abstain and he became another sad chapter. Despite it all, Cross managed a respectable .286 batting average. He was always a vital cog in offensive rallies, driving in runs, playing every game, and standing out like a "chalk mark on a blackboard." (*SL*, Jun 3). According to many observers, he was the best fielding third baseman in the league. His transfer to St. Louis must have filled him with mixed emotions, knowing he failed in Cleveland, but relieved over his new job with Frank Robison's club.

Righthander Willie Sudhoff compiled a tough luck 3-8 won-lost record while with Cleveland. He defeated Louisville in Cleveland on successive days to begin May, the first game going 14 innings. But, after those victories, he suffered two heartbreaking losses. On May 8, Harry Wolverton's 3-run 9th inning home run beat Sudhoff in Chicago. Three days later, Louis Sockalexis' muffs afield did Willie in against St. Louis. Lave Cross lined out with the bases loaded to almost pull a game out for Sudhoff. Sudhoff's last win occurred May 30 in Boston as he defeated Kid Nichols, 6-3. It was thought that Sudhoff would do much better with a stronger team.

Tue June 6 Without Cross and Sudhoff, the Spiders continued their New York odyssey at the Polo Grounds against the Giants. As related by the *Plain Dealer*, the players "filed solemnly out from their clubhouse today prior to the melee and devoted their time to pounding the ball over the lot in a melancholy sort of way, bemoaning the fact that they had been deprived of their stars." (Jun 7).

"But we've still got our bats," said Jack Stivetts.

"Yes, and our uniforms," said Chief Zimmer.

Joe Quinn added, "And pay days keep coming until we're bounced. And that makes life a great deal easier to be home in hot weather."

It was an ironic statement from Quinn, who was playing so well that he could be expected to be released (*SL*, Jun 17).

The Spiders still had a sense of humor but the game wasn't funny in the least. The only reason New York won was that someone had to, and Cleveland rarely did. Only 300 fans showed up for the contest, the smallest crowd to ever see a game in New York (*CPD*, Jun 7). Manager John Day of New York started lefthander Ed Doheny. The rudderless Cleveland's decided it was Kid Carsey's turn. Both pitchers could have sued their own teams for lack of support as eleven errors were committed; two by Doheny. Lave Cross' replacement at third base, the versatile Sport McAllister, fumbled two himself. Though affected by a lame back, McAllister would make no excuses for his play (*SL*, Jun 10). The only highlight was second baseman Kid Gleason's catch of a Joe Quinn liner. Gleason leaped at least three feet in the air to snare the ball. When it was over, the New Yorkers had it won, 9-6.

More sarcasm came from the *Plain Dealer* indicting syndicate baseball. The Cross and Sudhoff transfers were not popular in Cleveland, especially after management had said they would never occur.

Wed Jun 7 With Cross gone, second baseman Joe Quinn took over as manager of the Misfits. Quinn named newly acquired Frank Bates as his pitcher. The Giants countered with Doughnut Bill Carrick. It was unknown how Carrick acquired his gastronomic nickname, but possibly it came from pitching against the Spiders. Doughnuts were all the Spiders seemed to put on the scoreboard, losing 7-1. Again, a crowd of only 300 "wilted rooters" were on hand for the game played on a hot summer day (*NYT*, Jun 8).

Frank Bates' debut was as good as could be expected. It would have been better had the 4th inning not been part of his ledger. In that frame he surrendered five walks, three stolen bases, and five runs. Later, he was almost whacked in the head by a ball off the bat of centerfielder Foster. The *Plain Dealer* said that Bates could round into a winner before the season was over (Jun 8). Giants' curveballer Carrick gave the Spiders only eight hits. Big first baseman Tommy Tucker smacked three hits. Besides Carrick, the star of the game was Giants' third baseman Parke Wilson who sparkled afield and contributed three hits.

With all the rumors of league reduction and more releases, Cleveland players fully expected that the end of their team was near (*CPD*, Jun 8). But, when magnate Frank Robison was telegrammed about the disbandment, he issued a flat denial (*SL*, Jun 17).

The release rumors were real. Pitcher/outfielder Jack Stivetts, catcher Chief Zimmer, and pitchers Bill Hill and Kid Carsey were all given their walking papers. It was a ten-day notice of release. The current issue of *Sporting Life* called it an "heroic use of the pruning knife." (Jun 3). The *Plain Dealer* blasted upper management, writing, "The manner in which the team is conducted is a travesty on sport and no good to the league at large." (Jun 8). Reasons for the releases were not given, but poor play and economics were probably factors. "Any player who draws a $2000 salary can expect to be released," chimed the *Plain Dealer* (Jun 8).

Sporting Life commented: "For once there is not the slightest doubt that Frank Robison made a mistake. His own intimate friends in the National League are criticizing him for the action taken, and have said openly that if he doesn't want the Cleveland franchise he should sell it." (Jun 7).

Righthander Carsey was 1-7 in nine games, but may have been better suited to the infield. He would have been more effective had he not been taken out after 5-6 innings (*SL*, Jun 17).

Lefthander Hill was only 2-5, but that was a good record on the Spiders.

Chief Zimmer hit .342 in 20 games and played his catcher position ably. He was in his 15th season and had played in Cleveland since 1887. In his heyday, Zimmer was known as the leading catcher of mechanical ball playing in the league.

Eleven-year veteran Jack Stivetts, who was in Cleveland "attempting to pick a few games," appeared washed up (*SL*, May 13). He was winless in four decisions and ineffective in every start.

Thur June 8   For the third game of the series at the Polo Grounds, Joe Quinn struggled with a makeshift lineup composed of to-be-released players and Misfits out of position. It didn't work. For obvious reasons, Still Bill Hill didn't really care to pitch, and didn't. Chief Zimmer was forced behind the plate and Jack Stivetts took up residence at shortstop. Because of Hill's ineffectiveness, Stivetts also pitched. Two catchers, Joe Sugden and Ossee Schreckengost, found themselves in right field, and "Schreck" even wound up at shortstop. The Cleveland Spiders were a bad situation getting worse. Joe Quinn was the unfortunate inheritor of the great National League mess.

The usually small New York gathering watched their boys win easily 14-5. At least fans could sink their teeth into a new ball park concession, 'red hots', later to be known as hot dogs (Flexner 188). New York scored early and often. The Giants sent Cy Seymour to the mound to rub salt in the Misfits' wounds. Backed by superb infield play, Seymour and the "locals simply enjoyed a practice game." (*NYT*, Jun 9). The Spiders did manage to tie the game at 5-5 in the fourth inning, but New York was no match after that. The *Times* also remarked that the visitors were "at present in no condition to be in the league and will win very few games." (Jun 9). Hadn't the *Times* been paying attention? The Spiders had won but eight of 41 games.

The *Plain Dealer* showed their allegiance by doting on variations of Ossee Schreckengost's name, calling him "Shreik," "Mr. Ghost," and "whipping post." The newspaper even said that Schreckengost caused many a telegraph operator aberrations (Jun 9). Ossee had three hits, though it was not known if they caused Seymour any aberrations.

Fri Jun 9   The finale of the Spiders-New York series was an exciting affair, played before the proverbial 300 fans. All four games of the series had reported three hundred in attendance, perhaps due to the fact that all of them fell asleep, as did the ushers, during the three games. However, this contest may have woken them up.

Again Joe Quinn experimented with his charges, putting Jack Stivetts at third base, Ossee Schreckengost behind the bat, and Harry Lochhead back at shortstop. Once great righthander Jouett Meekin started for the New Yorkers while Quinn sent lame duck Kid Carsey to the rubber. As they did the day before, the New Yorks jumped on top with a four run first inning. The Spiders were shut off in their first when center fielder George Van Haltren caught a fly and threw a man out at the plate. But, Dick Harley "sent one over the ropes in right field for the circuit" in the third inning with two men on and the Spiders were only behind 5-3 (*CPD*, Jun 10). Cleveland pestered away to tie the score in the eighth 6-6, but a double, a passed ball by Schreckengost, and a sacrifice fly by Kid Gleason won it for New York. Meekin was a bit weak on the mound, but helped himself with a single, double, and triple at the bat. For the Spiders, it was "as near as they have come to victory since the have been in this part of the United States." (*CPD*, Jun 10). Cleveland was now 8-34 and oh for New York.

Rumors continued to fly concerning the released players. Chief Zimmer was to go to Louisville, Stivetts to Washington, and Carsey to Boston or Buffalo of the Western League.

Sat June 11   Saturday being a travel day, the Clevelands journeyed to Cincinnati for a Sunday game with the Reds. Sunday ball in Cincinnati was an event in itself because in 1881 the Reds were kicked out of the National League for their beer and Sunday ball playing (Reidenbaugh 84). The ban lasted ten years.

Buck Ewing's men had defeated the Louisville Colonels in the first game of a three team doubleheader, 8-2. The Spiders were next. A big gathering of 8000 showed up at Redland Park for the affairs between the Reds and the league's two tail-end teams.

Lefthanded rookie hurler Noodles Hahn started for the Cincinnati Porkopolitans while Frank Bates was slated for Cleveland. Hahn allowed the Spiders very little, save for a triple by right fielder Joe Sugden and a run scoring single by Bates. Cleveland also managed to shoot itself in the foot with poor baserunning. On the mound though, Bates was a different story. Exclaimed the *Plain Dealer*, Bates "pitched as if trying to secure his release," sulking over his misfortune of being a Spider after his transfer from St. Louis (Jun 12). He seemed to just float the ball in the vicinity of Schreckengost the catcher. A recap of Bates' work: In the first inning left fielder Kip Selbach walked, but Bates retired the next two on flies. Selbach was then caught off base. When Bates fired to Tucker and Tucker to Quinn, reliable Joe missed the tag. Quinn then committed an infield error, unnerving Bates. The pitcher plunked second baseman Harry Steinfeldt on the arm, forcing him out of the game. Charlie Irwin's single scored three runs. In the second inning, another hit batsman, a walk, and two hits meant three more runs. In the third, Bates' wild ones forced in another run and in the sixth three more tallies were made with free passes, singles, and an outfield error by Dick Harley. "Bates didn't seem to care if he was pitching or bowling." (*CPD*, Jun 12). The *Cincinnati Enquirer* was no kinder saying, "nothing like him has been seen in these parts since the days of Schmit." The reference was to an obscure, old time pitcher, Frederick Schmit. In all, Bates allowed nine walks, including five to Kip Selbach. The Reds breezed 10-1. It was the Spiders' eleventh straight defeat, all on the road.

Mon June 12   Upon their return home to League Park, the Spiders were greeted with less than overwhelming support. Playing before more empty seats, the *Plain Dealer* sarcastically commented, "those present were in no fear of a panic." (Jun 13). Later, *Sporting Life* reported the gathering to be exactly fifty-eight. It was not known if the figure included players, umpires, and reporters (Jun 13).

The Pittsburg Pirates provided the opposition and the game was close and tense throughout. Righthander Tully Sparks and the Spiders' Jim Hughey matched pitches for the better part of six innings, while Coldwater Jim was being eyed by Pittsburg management (*SL*, Jun 17). The Pirates scored two cheap runs in the first two frames while Cleveland baserunning woes were again evident. The Quinn Men allowed no less than four players thrown out at second. In the third, Quinn's bases loaded single provided two tallies and in the fifth "Buttermilk Tommy" Dowd, Quinn, and Suter Sullivan singled to tie the game at 3-3. In inning six, Pittsburg manager Patsy Donovan replaced Sparks with "The Goshen Schoolmaster," Sam Leever. The mild-mannered Leever had taught seven years before his baseball career.

Tommy Tucker singled, Schreck flied out, and then Hughey struck out into a double play; Tommy being Tuckered out. The game winning rally occurred in the Pirates' seventh. Both Hughey and first baseman Tucker were paralyzed by three Pittsburg bunts for two runs. School was out. It ended 5-3, Pittsburg. It was the Spiders' 12th consecutive loss. Umpire Gaffney, sans his partner Andrews, umpired the contest alone.

Of the recently released players, Cleveland catcher Chief Zimmer came to Cleveland to pack his bags. Bill Hill received an offer from Boston and "Happy Jack" Stivetts was planning to join Hill in Beantown. Kid Carsey, meanwhile, quit baseball for the present as he had "both an opportunity and a disposition to get mixed up with the running horses in the east." (*CPD*, Jun 13).

Tues June 13 Venerable baseball writer and scorer Henry Chadwick once said, "Skillful fielding is by all odds the most attractive feature of the National Game." (Curran 3). Luckily, Chadwick was not in attendance. Pittsburg won 10-6, due to "many cases of stupidity and blundering" by the Spiders (*CPD*, Jun 14). The Spiders committed seven infield errors. Four of them were made by shortstop Harry Lochhead, who insisted on throwing the ball nowhere near a lunging Tommy Tucker at first base. When Tucker did manage to get into a position to catch the ball, he botched two himself. Third baseman Suter Sullivan also added a bobble. Keeping an historical perspective, the *Plain Dealer* called it "the worst fielding on record." (Jun 14). This mayhem of miscues offset the fine pitching of Charlie Knepper, a ground rule Tommy Dowd home run to left field, and a fine ninth inning batting rally. Pirates Pitcher Billy Rhines just had to show up to get the easy victory. Again, umpire Gaffney went it alone.

The Pirates of Pittsburg were also depressed. The June 17 *Sporting Life* tells the story:

A forlorn set of men went aboard the train yesterday for Cleveland at 9 A. M. Four days in that town will take all the energy out of any club. Secretary Ballet has made full preparations for the sad journey, round trip tickets and a wad of cash for hotel bills, for there was almost a certainty that the club's share would not exceed $100 for the four games...

Fourteen men made the journey. For once, the stay-at-homes smiled.

Wed June 14 Jesse Tannehill, who one month before had manhandled the Spiders in Pittsburg, again set them down. Seldom seen Harry Maupin and Frank Bates split the pitching duties for the Clevelands. Neither Maupin nor Bates were effective, surrendering 16 hits while the Spiders managed only half a dozen. In inning seven, shortstop Art Madison and catcher Frank Bowerman hit triples against Bates. Then Tannehill drove one to the short fence in right field that Sport McAllister caught. Umpire Gaffney, having charge of the field decisions himself, was screened on the play. He gave Tannehill a double and the Clevelands screamed. It really didn't make a difference as the final was 10-1, Pirates. The Cleveland highlight consisted entirely of Tommy Tucker bellowing from the coaching box with his lively banter (*CPD*, Jun 15). Gaffney had afforded Tucker the privilege many other umpires in the league did not. The loss string was now fourteen.

Boastful Pat Tebeau made an apology through the newspapers on the collapse on his team. He offered all manner of reasons why St. Louis had tumbled from their early lofty perch. Tebeau also predicted that the pennant was still in sight.

Thur June 15 Only one hundred people showed up for the finale of the Pirates-Spiders series in Cleveland. The small group was treated to the "eighth wonder of the world." (*CPD*, Jun 16). Finally, after a terribly long losing skein that began with Lave Cross and continuing into Joe Quinn's tenure, the Spiders won a ball game. They did it with ease, playing a championship style ball game that would have beaten many teams in the league. The final score was 6-2; Joe Quinn's first as manager.

Still Bill Hill started for the Spiders in his last game before his release. He pitched marvelously. The Pirates could secure only seven hits off Hill. Behind Still Bill, the Spider defense played errorless ball, catching every fly and grounder. They were led by an improving Suter Sullivan, who made a fine tag of catcher Pop Schriver's attempted steal of third base. The two scuffled over the play, but Sullivan held his ground. For the Buccaneers, Sam Leever was Patsy Donovan's choice. The Spiders' five run fifth inning did Leever in.

The contest started with a very odd play. With one out, Dick Harley singled and Quinn hit a sinking fly ball to right field. Harley, thinking it impossible for the outfielder to make the catch, sprinted towards second. But Donovan did make the play and instead of throwing the ball to first to double off Harley, Patsy headed for the base himself. He beat Harley back to the bag for an unassisted double play. It was the first such play in memory (*CPD*, Jun 16). The game went to the fifth with Pittsburg holding a 1-0 lead. Then the Spiders tallied five times with Sport McAllister providing a bases-loaded single. Hill won his game despite the Pirate players taunting him; "They won't let you get away after this game. Better unpack your trunk." (*SL*, Jun 24).

A small controversy over Hill's release was reported in the *Plain Dealer*. According to the newspaper, Still Bill was now being offered another chance with the team. After all, his victory was his third of the season, and he was the only Cleveland pitcher to win a game in the last fifteen. But, Hill declined the overture, thinking that it was not in good faith. He was expected to sign with

Baltimore (Jun 16). Kid Carsey, meanwhile, had reportedly received an offer to pitch with Boston and he was heading that way. Perhaps, he wasn't interested in horse racing after all.

After the series, Pittsburg President Kerr conferred with club secretary Ballet about financial returns. "We did well over there. Ballet has just told me he got an average of $16 per day as the Pittsburg club's share. Great, isn't it?" Kerr joked further on the 58, 73, 84, and "about 100" turnstile counts (*SL*, Jun 24).

Fri June 16   With no game scheduled and the Spiders five games out of eleventh place, the *Plain Dealer* devoted its lead article to "The Situation in Baseball." (Jun 17).   They reported a complicated financial theory that Cleveland was being used as a lever to pry the Washington franchise out of the league (Jun 17).

The *Plain Dealer* was also astounded that all the games were going on as scheduled, despite the lack of fan support.   They inquired aloud about the intentions of the owners of the Spiders and why games were not transferred, even when the Pirates offered to move them to Pittsburg where money could have been made (Jun 17).

The weekly magazine *Sporting Life* disagreed with the sentiments of the *Plain Dealer* saying that baseball was alive and well in Cleveland, though it wasn't manifesting itself in the National League. *Sporting Life* cited the crowds that showed up for amateur, college, and back lot exhibitions around the city that would number 12,000 on a Sunday.   Few fans passed through the Dunham Avenue turnstiles because of the Sunday ball controversy, transfer rumors, and the rowdyism of Tebeau and his "pink tea with umpire" bouts that repulsed many Clevelanders (Jun 24).   Eight or ten years ago, the paper lamented, there was no better baseball city in the United States.   Fans had to buy their tickets early and catch trolleys to the ball yard.   Four to seven thousand people routinely were present throughout the city for the games (*SL*, Jun 24).

Sat June 17   After the Spiders' surprise win over the Pirates, both teams traveled to Steeltown to play a contest at Exhibition Park.   As they had Monday, the teams started the same pitchers.   Jim Hughey went for Cleveland while the Pirates gave Tully Sparks the ball.   The pitching choices could not have been better.   What ensued was an old-fashioned pitcher's duel in front of over 3000 fans.   The crowd size was large in contrast to the neighborly gatherings at League Park.

For the fifth straight game, umpire Gaffney had to work alone and that may have worked against Cleveland.   Tired 1-1 in the eighth, Pirate second baseman Art Madison singled to right.   Sport McAllister misjudged the ball and Madison made second.   Player-manager Patsy Donovan then drove Madison home with a hit. The Spiders trailed 2-1. In their half of the ninth inning, Spider third baseman Suter Sullivan reached first on a balk by Sparks (rules of day). McAllister then ripped a scorcher to Willie Clark at first base. Clark's throw to try to force Sullivan was ill advised and all runners were safe. Tommy Tucker grounded to the infield weakly and the play was made on Sullivan at third. Harry Lochhead singled to score McAllister and tie the game. The throw from the outfield came home late but an aggressive Tucker raced for third. Catcher Frank Bowerman's throw nailed Tucker. "The decision looked a little raw." (*CPD*, Jun 18). What followed was another of boisterous Tommy's dirt kicking and screaming exhibitions at umpire Gaffney. The colorful first baseman "hunted sympathy from the bleacher and got it." (*SL*, Jun 24). The exhausted umpire, who had just run up and down the baseline from home plate, would have none of Terrible Tommy's antics. Gaffney's decision stood. Lochhead then stole second and Ossee Schreck walked. But Hughey made a weak out and the rally was over.

In the Pittsburg ninth with one out, center fielder Tom McCreary singled. Tucker, still fuming from Gaffney's earlier decision, stalked to the mound. Tommy took out his frustration by saying "hot things" to Hughey (*CPD*, Jun 18). A bit rattled by his teammate, "Coldwater" then plunked Clark with a pitch. The aptly-named shortstop Bones Ely drove a single to right. McCreary scored and the game was lost.

Once again, sarcasm flowed from the ink of the *Plain Dealer*. "Cleveland played well enough to lay blame on the umpire," said a headline (Jun 19). Umpire Gaffney came "to the rescue just in time," as if a Cleveland victory were akin to a loss of life (Jun 19).

To reduce the monopoly of star players and teams, President Hart of Chicago proposed a time limit on player's services with one club to five years (*CPD*, Jun 18). There was no official comment from the Spiders.

Mon June 19 No game was played on Sunday in Cleveland. After the day off, the confident Brooklyn Superbas invaded League Park and "started in a half-hearted sort of manner, just as if winning the game was a foregone conclusion." (*CPD*, Jun 20). It might as well have been, as games with the Forsakens and the Bridegrooms were easy victories in Brooklyn. The Spiders couldn't beat Hanlon's gang with a ten run lead on June 2.

Righthander Jack Dunn, who had pitched so well against the Spiders at Washington Park, took the rubber for Brooklyn. Frank Bates was the choice for Joe Quinn's squad. The game began with Tommy Tucker making a first inning unassisted double play. In the second, Cleveland's alert fielding resulted in shortstop Bill Dahlen being thrown out at the plate. Second baseman Tom Daly's bonehead baserunning led to his being erased on a run down. Dunn had

Spiders' batters at his mercy. In inning three, catcher John Grim's double sparked a two run rally for the Bridegrooms. In the fifth, Bates had problems throwing and walked the bases loaded. Then, miraculous fielding shut off any Brooklyn runs. At the end of six innings, the score was 2-1, Brooklyn. Bates then allowed the front-runners some breathing room in the seventh. Grim, Wee Willie Keeler, and Fielder Jones all hit safely and Bates hit third baseman Doc Casey with a pitch. Three runs resulted. In the last frame, Bates was involved in a nifty pitcher-catcher-first double play. The heroic fielding was too late. In all, the erratic Bates surrendered nine hits, seven walks, and three hit batsman. Jack Dunn tossed an easy five hitter at the Clevelands. The final was 6-1.

Tue June 20   Once again the Bridegrooms crossed bats with the gallant Spiders. The Brooklyn victory was not a walkover. No cigars were handed out to the Clevelands although they made it close and kept coming back from big deficits. Alas, the boys of Brooklyn won out, 9-7. What could one expect from a team that was making a mockery of the league race with a 42-12 record and the Misfits, who had won only nine of fifty contests?

It was a game predicated on hitting. Brooklyn secured 16 off Charlie Knepper and the Clevelands lashed an even dozen off Dr. McJames. Wrote the *Plain Dealer* of Knepper, he "had speed and he used it. If anything he used it to excess, for he seemed to be afraid of his slow ball that is usually effective, and would have worked well against the slugging Brooklyns." (Jun 21). Leftfielder Joe Kelley homered off Knepper, with the help of a crazy bounce past centerfielder Tommy Dowd. Rightfielder Willie Keeler knocked three hits and infielder Tom Daly had four.

The usually reliable McJames, "showed disposition to weaken at times, particularly when the accomplished rooters got at him, and had there been 150 persons present instead of 100, they might have rooted hard enough to win." (*CPD*, Jun 21). The comment may have shown the local newspaper to be just as victory-starved as the Spiders. Since the players rarely won, maybe the Cleveland ball cranks could cheer the team to success. Tommy Tucker touched McJames for two two-baggers and Knepper knocked a triple.

Wed June 21   A slugging contest took place at League Park, harkening back to "the kind of baseball that used to be played before the magnates did all in their power to take the life out of the game." (*CPD*, Jun 22). At least Tommy Tucker still had some life in him, indulging in "some most brilliant repartee" with umpire Hank O'Day (*CPD*, Jun 22). Luckless Jim Hughey went for the Spiders against Brickyard Kennedy for the Superbas. Neither was effective.

To begin the game, Brooklyn engaged itself in some sloppy fielding, handing the underdog Spiders a 2-1 lead after two stanzas. The Brooklyns caught up

69

and led 3-2 after six. In the 7th, Doc Casey tripled off Hughey and scored the fourth run off Wee Willie Keeler's out. The Spiders got one back in their half when manager Joe Quinn singled, went to third on outs and scored on Tommy Tucker's bloop past shortstop. The Bridegroom's Bill Dahlen was blinded by the sun as the pop landed just beyond his reach. Then came the fatal eighth inning. As was their custom, the Spiders disintegrated and allowed Brooklyn six runs on singles and amateurish play afield. The 75 to 100 rooters that constituted the audience must have nodded their heads in agreement. It always appeared that when the Misfits got close in a game, they would let the opposition score at will. For the Spiders' batters in the eighth, Schreckengost doubled, Hughey singled, and Quinn looped to the outfield for two runs. Another comeback fell short and the Spiders were losers, 10-6.

Afterwards, the *Plain Dealer* remarked that Schreck, who had four hits in the game, was playing to secure his release. His work was "so good that it could hardly be tolerated here." (Jun 22). The comment was ironic since Frank Bates was reported to be pitching to secure his release, a few days before. Only Bates' pitching was horrendous and catcher Schreckengost was playing a fast game. The Spiders could not win for losing.

Thur June 22 The last game of the Brooklyn-Cleveland series wasn't much of a game at all. In fact, it was a Brooklyn walkaway by 8-0. Little Joe Yeager had the honors in shutting out the Spiders while Harry Maupin absorbed the loss. Maupin, whose appearances seemed of a token nature, surrendered a dozen hits, committed two balks, and made an error to seal his doom. Yeager had no trouble with the home towners, scattering five safeties. The Bridegrooms were helped by some fancy fielding and double-steal baserunning. Wrote the *Plain Dealer*, "The good fielding, however, did not compensate for the lack of hitting and general stupidity of the game, and taken all in all it was just the kind of game not to see." (Jun 23). The Cleveland sporting populace did just that, and few showed up at League Park. The Spiders must have been happy to see the Brooklyns pack and leave town.

Umpire Tom Burns was released by the National League. He had been involved in numerous controversial decisions along with his partner Smith. Burns had officiated in several late May games with the Spiders. Said Burns to the *Cincinnati Enquirer*: (Jun 23)

I have umpired good ball, and I know it. I have never had the slightest trouble with any of the teams except the New Yorks and the St. Louis Browns. I cannot understand the way matters are run in the league. A lot of rules are passed, and then the umpire is instructed to enforce them. When I started out I was told that the rules are observed to the letter. I was told that under no circumstances no vulgar language, no obscene language be tolerated. I enforced the rules just as I was instructed. I put a number of players out of the game, but I never sent a player to the bench who was not guilty of indecent language. I don't object to a player protesting against a decision in a decent way. I wouldn't give a cent for a player that does not interest enough in the game to protest. The kind of kicking I objected to was of the vulgar and indecent kind. I never put a player out that did not break a rule ten times over. If I had killed some of the players for the language they used to me I would have been exonerated by any kind of jury. It was something awful.

When asked who Burns charged with his release, he replied:

The New York and St. Louis players. The last trick in New York was a deliberate attempt to injure me for life. In Philadelphia I gave a decision against the St. Louis team. Pat Tebeau walked in to the plate, and after calling me all kind of names told me he would have me out of my job in ten days. He has kept his word. He has gone out of his way to take a living from an honest man.

Fri Jun 23 With the Superbas gone, the other New York entry in the National League came to Cleveland for a series of contests. The Giants were "the latest team to find an easy thing." (*CPD*, Jun 24).

As the newspaper reported, the "standing room only signs were not overworked, and neither were the turnstiles." Both managers could afford a pre-game chat (*CPD*, Jun 24). Both John Day of New York and Joe Quinn jokingly agreed that any ball hit in the crowd should account for four runs. Including foul balls. The intimate gathering numbered only 125.

Frank Bates took the call for the Quinn Men against New York lefthander Ed Doheny. Bates was wild as always, giving the Giants nine walks and took his usual battering as an assortment of base hits whizzed past his ear. Three stolen bases were also rung up by the visitors. The unfortunate Ossee Schreckengost chased after Bates' tosses all afternoon and committed two errors in the process. New York waltzed, 8-2.

With umpire Burns griping to the league about his release, Smith now teamed up with Andrews and "showed marked improvement. In fact, on yesterday's form Smith should become a star allowing for the same improvement- if he only stays in the business long enough. It might take several hundred years, but a little thing like that will never discourage a man of Smith's propensities." (*CPD*, Jun 24). *Sporting Life* also praised Smith for his home plate work. The weekly said that despite the occasional calling of a ball for a pitch "square across and waist high" and a strike "two feet wide and over the batter's head," Smith was convincing players and spectators alike of his earnestness (Jul 15).

The Spiders secured another pitcher for their team to go along with Hughey, Knepper, Bates, and Maupin. He was Eggleberth from Brockton, New York.

Eggleberth was expected to report in a couple of days. "Who recommended him or by what right he assumes to play in the big league has not been learned." (*CPD*, Jun 24). In other player developments, catcher Joe Sugden was suffering from an attack of malarial fever, leaving the Spiders with only Ossee Schreckengost behind the plate. Sugden would probably not be able to play for some time.

Sat June 24   The *Plain Dealer*'s lead paragraph to describe the conditions of Saturday's affair with the New York Giants went like this: (Jun 25)

Cleveland had a narrow escape yesterday. For some time it looked as if another day would go without their meeting their customary defeat, and there was great anxiety felt by the friends of the players. There is no telling what effect such an accident would have on them, and they might not be able to survive it. It looked so much like rain shortly before the game that there seemed little hope of getting in the daily beating. Secretary Muir, however, was speedily reassured. The game was played and as it resulted as usual the nervous systems of the players and audience sustained no shock.

Despite the weather, a significant crowd of 300 watched the New Yorkers defeat the Spiders by 7-2. However, the contest proved to be less of a baseball game than a track meet for New York. No less than ten stolen bases were made off the righthanded motion of Charlie Knepper and his befuddled battery mate, Ossee Schreckengost. Leftfielder Tom O'Brien swiped five by himself, including second base three times, third base, and home plate. O'Brien's steal of home occurred when Schreck threw to second base to try to nab Parke Wilson. Seizing opportunity, O'Brien raced home and scored on the double steal. Since O'Brien was given three free passes to first by Knepper, he decided to work up a sweat by running. The other five steals came from every member of the Giants infield. Most of the pilfering played a significant role in the run making.

Cleveland native Bill Carrick pitched for the Giants and was welcomed by the fans with a bouquet of roses when he came to bat. It was the "first bunch of fragrance that has scented the atmosphere at League Park in many a day. The bouquets thrown at the players lately have not been of the tangible variety." (*CPD*, Jun 25). Actually, there was little for Carrick to do except toss a few leisurely balls to home plate. The Giants' righthander committed two errors in the field to help Cleveland avert a shutout. The only Spider threats occurred in the 4th and 7th innings. In the 4th, the bases were loaded with none out. However, the Clevelands then contrived to hit weakly three straight times and no runs could score. In inning seven, Knepper placed one down the left field line for a double. "A hay wagon drawn by lame horses could have reached third, but Knepper is no hay wagon and had no lame horses to assist him." (*CPD*, Jun 25).

Cleveland management continued their efforts to secure pitchers. Handsome Eggleberth arrived from Brockton; a "big, strong, clean cut young fellow and looks every inch a ballplayer." (*CPD*, Jun 25). A.B. Smyth of Oberlin College was also being sought and arrangements were made for the collegian to meet with M.Stanley Robison in Cleveland (*SL*, Jun 25).

Another player, lefthander Fred Schmit of the Chicago City League, signed a contract fresh from his remarkable 21-0 record. It was the same Schmit whom Cincinnati had compared the horrendous pitching of Frank Bates. Now, Schmit was coming to Cleveland.

Known for eccentricities and thick German accent, Schmit kept track of opposition batters' strengths and weaknesses in a little notebook that he pasted in his cap. Schmit once delayed a game for several minutes while he went searching in the clubhouse for his diary that noted the weakness of all the hitters in the league. The notebook supposedly listed one Adrian Constantine Anson's weakness as a base on balls. The first time the German faced the legendary Anson, he walked him (Aug 18). Dubbed "Crazy" by the players, Schmit had previous league experience, going 1-9 with a sorry 1890 Pittsburg National League team. The Pirates that year won twenty-three out of one hundred thirty six games.

Two years later, Schmit pitched with Mobile of the Southern League. One day, after a good performance, he got into a scrap with a "fresh young guy" and "hammered him pretty badly." Only the "guy" turned out to be a prosecutor and Schmit was arrested for hitting the man with a brick. The case went to trial and incredibly, the justice was an inveterate ball fan who once commented that Schmit's pitching was such that he could kill a man if the ball got away from him. When asked by the judge who would defend him, Schmit calmly pleaded, "Yer honor, with my well-known speed and command, do you suppose for one moment that if I'd hit a man with a brick he'd be here to tell the story?" Mr. Schmit was immediately discharged (*TSN*, Apr 8).

Schmit also pitched briefly with New York and Baltimore in 1892-1893. But, before 1899, Schmit had been out of action since 1894. He had suffered an injury in a "collision with a seltzer bottle and his arm." (*CPD*, Jun 28). Said *Sporting Life* on his signing; "He will persist in breaking into the big leagues from time to time." (Jul 8). Schmit harangued the umpires when they didn't call his pitches a strike and yelled at his teammates when they committed errors behind him. Earlier accounts called him a "well-looking German boy" who "talks intelligently" but his tongue was a strange mixture of English and German. Older veteran players caught on to his tricks and kidded him at every turn (*PP*, May 24, 1890).

73

In his first year with the Pirates, Schmit shut out the Reds 4-0 and then proceeded to lose his last nine decisions. In the midst of the streak, Pirate management fined Schmit for "indifferent pitching." (*SL*, Jun 28, 1900). It was a bizarre decision on a team that boasted hurlers like Kirtly Baker (3-19), Guy Hecker (2-9), Bill Sowders (3-8), Dave Anderson (2-11), and Bill Phillips (1-9). One week after his only victory, Schmit was beaten badly. The *Pittsburg Dispatch* simply wrote, "Mr. Schmit hadn't his notes." (May 20, 1890).

Sun June 25 After 13 losses in a row to New York-based teams in the month of June, the Spiders were in no mood to be around the Superbas or Giants. Unfortunately, the company of the Giants would linger. Both teams boarded a late Saturday train from Cleveland to St. Louis for a doubleheader. Because some cities still banned Sunday ball, "teams where it was banned went to play where it was allowed." Hence, the three team doubleheader (Hurlbert 132).

Before a large crowd of ten to twelve thousand rooters, "Pat's Peaches" were beaten 5-3 by the Giants. The game lasted ten innings. A local newspaper sarcastically referred to the Giants as "Pygmies." (GD, Jun 26). As cranks sensed an imminent St. Louis loss in the waning stages of the Giants game, they began to disfavor the home team. It wasn't long before one profanity led to another and the gathering became somewhat like vultures descending upon carrion. As the second game was about to begin and the Spiders took the field, a crowd chorus screamed, "Now, we will get our money's worth." (*GD*, Jun 26). As Cleveland fans had cheered their old heroes in the Forest City, St. Louisians were now supporting the Spiders. The headline in the *Plain Dealer* read, "Forsakens Not Forsaken." (Jun 26). Turnabout was fair play, even in the maddening world of syndicate baseball.

Few contests played by Cleveland were as exciting. Tebeau started diminutive righthander Nig Cuppy against Joe Quinn's Coldwater Jim Hughey. From the start, both hurlers put on a fine exhibition of twirling. The score was knotted 1-1 after six. In Cleveland's turn at the plate in inning seven, Sport McAllister singled and Tommy Tucker reached on Ed McKean's error at first base. Then came Ossee Schreckengost, the catcher Tebeau had annexed to the Spiders. Earlier in the game, Ossee had doubled. After fouling off several of Cuppy's best pitches, Ghost belted one near the left field bleachers. Both runners scored. In his zeal, Schreck attempted to stretch his long triple into a home run. A shrieking Schreck was declared out at home plate. In the St. Louis eighth, Cuppy and Burkett hit safely. Second baseman Cupid Childs bunted down the first base line but as pitcher Hughey and first baseman Tucker chased the ball, they collided with Childs running to the base. Umpire McDonald, viewing the action from home plate, declared Childs out for interference and the runners back to their bases. It was, to say the least, an unpopular ruling.

Manager Tebeau and Childs "registered severe kicks." (GD, Jun 26). The audience howled at the spectacle but no runs were scored. Trailing 3-1 in the ninth, the home towners tried one more time against Hughey. Shortstop Rhody Wallace was hit by a pitch and then Quinn fumbled ex-teammate Lave Cross' grounder. Catcher Lou Criger sacrificed and centerfielder Harry Blake walked to load the bases. Tebeau then called on Jack O'Connor to bat for Cuppy. The decision was questionable since Cuppy had hit safely twice and was robbed another time on a one-handed stop at third by Suter Sullivan. O'Connor popped weakly to Sullivan and Burkett grounded out to end the game. Hughey and the ebullient Spiders were winners 3-1. Miraculously, Cleveland had defeated the #1 syndicate team.

There were several interesting occurrences in the contest. Three times Spiders' third baseman Sullivan popped up balls in the direction of first baseman Ed McKean. The first time a swirling wind caught the ball and it landed untouched in front of an embarrassed Ed. The second pop was dropped in the catcall din. When a third lazy fly was actually caught, the crowd roared in mockery. By then, even McKean could see the humor in the situation and he smiled along (GD, Jun 26). Besides the McKean razzing, the partisans singled out Burkett and Childs for roasting. Burkett, hitting .379 at the time, was greatly disturbed and addressed the stands from his outfield position when opportunity arose. "Childs made known his displeasure by booting the ball all over the field between innings, turning cartwheels, throwing his heels in the air, and performing other like contortion feats." (GD, Jun 26).

Mon June 26   Believe it or not, after the Spiders and Giants played their single contest in St. Louis, both teams tramped back to Cleveland for a short series. By train, of course. It was the kind of scheduling snafus that had taken place in the National League all year long. The Clevelands were in the midst of a one game winning streak.

Charlie Gettig made his 1899 debut for New York. Frank Bates went for the Spiders. The small scattering of fans were treated to a rather lively ball game. In the second inning the Giants scored two runs but Cleveland came back with four in the third, putting together a batting streak of five hits and a walk. In the Giants third, Bates sent outfielders George Van Haltren and Mike Tiernan to first on balls. He then hit first baseman Jack Doyle. Infielder George Davis then walked to force in Van Haltren. Two singles followed, a wild pitch, another walk, a Bates error, and a short pop that dropped at the young pitcher's feet. Catcher Schreck could only sigh. Five runs were on the board and the Giants led by 7-4. In the Spiders fifth, Joe Quinn beat out a bunt to third but Wilson's erratic throw lodged under the scoreboard located in foul territory. In the confusion of the New York infield chasing after the ball, Quinn came all the way around the bases and raced home with a run. In the seventh, Quinn dusted one down the left field line for a double. The ball struck the chalk line, but shortstop George Davis and catcher John Warner protested to umpire Smith in language not generally heard at weddings. Smith would have none of it. Sullivan flied to Van Haltren who erred and McAllister sacrificed. Tucker then popped a little one between pitcher and first base. Gettig ran into the ball, and managed to kick it towards the grandstand. It was a comedy befitting P.T. Barnum. When it was over, the Spiders were losers 10-7, despite outplaying the Giants in the field and at bat. The unsteady Bates was the primary scapegoat, surrendering nine hits, nine walks, three hit batsman, one wild pitch, and committing an error. The *New York Times* reduced the game to a single sentence writeup: "The wildness of Bates lost the game for the home team." (Jun 27).

Tue June 27 The league re-incarnation of Chicago City League phenomenon "Flying Dutchman" Schmit was decent. He outpitched his rival Bill Carrick at League Park. In all, only five singles were made off Schmit but he gave the Giants fivers in walks and stolen bases as well. The Spiders hit and fielded well, but the scoreboard did not lie and showed the Giants as winners 6-1. Something was rotten in the state of Cleveland. The Spiders occasionally outhit and outfielded the opposition and still lost overwhelmingly. Actually, there was little chance for the Spiders to win so soon after their St. Louis miracle on Sunday. "That's enough to hold them for awhile," penned the *Plain Dealer*, although it was unsure if "them" was Cleveland management, players, or fans (Jun 28).

Until the third inning, the game was scoreless. Outfielders Dowd and Harley led off with hits but both were caught trying to steal second base. The decisions were made by umpire Andrews. The volatile Tommy Tucker objected, grabbed Andrews by the throat and was about to punch when Dowd and Quinn pulled him away. Tucker was fined $5 and removed from the game. He was replaced by Joe Sugden. Again, it was a case of an aggressive Tucker standing up for his team, and umpires "abusing him beyond the limit of endurance." (*CPD*, Jun 28). In the New York half of the third, Andrews gave a few close calls to the visitors. Schmit walked Parke Wilson and then catcher John Warner's single and errors by Harry Lochhead and Ossee Schreck led to four runs. Cleveland managed to avoid Carrick's shutout in the ninth on Sugden, Schmit, and Dowd singles.

On the umpire situation, the *Plain Dealer* wrote afterwards, "If a well organized combination were working against Cleveland it could do no better work that is being done right along. The Forsakens are certainly getting the muddy end of the stick with discouraging regularity." (Jun 28). Specifically, the newspaper spoke of the Tucker-Andrews incident. "If there were a few more

Tuckers and a few less of the Andrews type in the league it is safe to say that baseball would be a better paying investment." (Jun 28).

Early fears of the Spiders being put out of the league due to failing finances were ending. However, the *Plain Dealer* reported on the systematic transferring of games after July 1st. Apparently, the plan had been arranged at the last league meeting, but it was hushed over by the magnates. Officials of the Spiders were convinced that baseball could not gain a foothold in Cleveland (Jun 28).

Wed June 28   With rain forestalling the first game of the Boston-Cleveland series at League Park, the owners Robison took time out to speak to the *Plain Dealer* about the Spiders situation. Cleveland President M. Stanley Robison denied transfer rumors to Indianapolis and spoke of financial woes. "I cannot keep running a club with a salary list of $30,000 for an attendance of 100 a day. And if I could, the other clubs would not stand it. I have been notified by several clubs that they will not return here, but I do not know what to do with the scheduled games." (Jun 29).

A clever writer of the *Plain Dealer* pointed out that National League rules stipulated that teams must report according to the schedule or face a fine of $1000. Since many clubs were now refusing to come to Cleveland, the Spiders could technically await them in Cleveland and win games by forfeit (Jun 29). It was probably the Spiders best chance to get back in the pennant race. But, Frank Robison, who was really interested in Cleveland as an experimental farm team for St. Louis, answered: (*CPD*, Jun 29).

Under the present rules that would be well and good. But, it would take the members of the league about twelve hours to call a meeting and rescind that rule. Clubs that come here take away about $20 for the games they win are not going to stand for a rule that will cost them a $1000 and a game as well.

If the clubs will come here, we will play our games as scheduled. If they will not, I cannot see how I can be expected to maintain a team here.

Two and one-half months into the season, few visiting teams were willing to pay "expenses out of their own treasuries for the pleasure of stopping a few days in the village by the lakeside." (*CPD*, Jun 29). An important announcement on the situation of transfers was to be made on July 4. In an attempt to diffuse the situation the Spiders club was petitioning the league to transfer the Saturday Boston-Cleveland affair to neutral New Castle, Pennsylvania.

Thur June 29   "The sage philosopher who remarked that even a blind dog can pick up an acorn once in a while probably had no thought of the Cleveland

77

baseball team, but that institution gave an example yesterday that proves the allegory." (*CPD*, Jun 30). With the transfer specter hanging over the players' heads and a large crowd on hand, the Spiders beat the Bostons 7-2. The "large" crowd size was only relative to other Cleveland games on the Dunham Avenue grounds. But, it was a vocal bunch and their enthusiasm rivaled that of the first St. Louis game in Cleveland.

Joe Quinn sent the longhaired Charlie Knepper against Boston's Ted Lewis. Boston took a quick 1-0 lead in the second inning. Then, "Cleveland went to work just as if they were playing a team their own class and before they got through they had the Rev. Mr. Lewis thinking things that he had never learned at the Howard Theological School." (*CPD*, Jun 30). Rambunctious Tucker went out but then Harry Lochhead bunted safe, Schreck was hit by a pitch, and Knepper walked. With the bases loaded, Tommy Dowd drove home a pair with a single. Boston outfielder Charlie Frisbee, who pre-dated the pie-pan craze, threw wild to home and the runners moved up. A shaken Lewis walked Dick Harley and Quinn popped a sacrifice fly to the outfield, scoring his pitcher. Suter Sullivan singled for two more tallies before Sport McAllister grounded out. The long rally produced five runs. Knepper was sharp and scattered a few hits to the Bostons.

Due to an unmentioned technicality, the transfer of the Boston-Cleveland Saturday game to New Castle was rejected. Instead, two games were to be played to make up for the Wednesday rainout.

Fri June 30 Buoyed by their great victory over tough Boston, the Spiders again played a worthy game. But, as was the usual case, they played just well enough to lose.

Beantown manager Frank Selee called on newly acquired Harvey Bailey to pitch while Quinn gave the ball to Jim Hughey. From the beginning, the Bostons tried to take advantage of Hughey's inability to field bunts. In the first inning, rightfielder Chick Stahl walked. First baseman Fred Tenney bunted the ball a trifle too hard to Quinn at second base. However, umpire Andrews, sadly out of position, bumped into Quinn as he was trying to field the ball. Andrews ruled Tenney safe. Bob Stafford bunted to load the bases. Then, Jimmy Collins dropped one in front of Hughey. Smiling Jim smartly threw home to get Stahl and Ossee Schreckengost fired to first for a double play. Incredibly, Hugh Duffy then bunted to Hughey, who lost control of the ball for a minute, and then threw to Schreck who tagged Tenney at home plate. No runs scored. In the second, Boston scored once. The Spiders' Sport McAllister singled and Bailey hit the loudest first baseman in the league, Tommy Tucker, with a pitch. But Bailey, pitching in his first big league game, snuffed out the rally. Boston began the fifth with a 1-0 lead. Catcher Boileryard Clarke grounded to Harry

Lochhead at shortstop but the young infielder kicked it. Clarke then stole second but Schreck's effort to throw him out was so poor that the ball sailed somewhere into the nether reaches of the outfield. Before it could be tracked down, Boileryard raced home. In the sixth, Suter Sullivan's muff of Stafford's pop up gave the Beaneaters another gift. The lone Spiders tally resulted from a Lochhead single and a Schreckengost double. Bailey and the Bostons squeezed 3-1.

National League President Nick Young made some radical decisions about his umpiring crews. All season long, Young and his umpires had been criticized by players and managers for their decisions in games. "Uncle" Nick had been quite good to his men, treating their mistakes as a "general frailty of human nature." (*Chicago Times-Herald*, June 30). Now, Young's move was to shift umpiring teams around. He split up the pair of Emslie and McDonald who had received few complaints. McDonald now became a partner of Smith. McDonald moved from his calling decisions on the bases to behind the bat. Smith, who earlier had made several bad calls against Cleveland, stayed on the bases. The other pair was to be Emslie, who remained in his capacity as home plate umpire and the re-instated Burns, who was reduced to the flying dirt and dust around the sacks. Burns re-instatement caused a controversy on its own and did Young's bold move to split umpiring duos.

"Like a lot of wild men."

Sat Jul 1   With Cleveland transfer talks continuing, several small miracles occurred at League Park. The largest crowd of the season, 1500 souls, showed up at the ball yard for the Boston doubleheader. Many rode the Robison trolley line to get to their destination. It seemed as if a full-scale revival of baseball was taking place in Cleveland. They came to show their sympathetic support for the Misfits. Many of the fans who hadn't come to see a game since the Old Clevelands left town, now appeared in droves (*CPD*, Jul 2). Even the umpiring in the game took a back seat to the fans, since arbiters were not likely to commit open robbery with so many Cleveland faithful on the scene (*CPD*, Jul 2). Just what they witnessed was the kind of event that makes grandfathers happy to sit children on their knees and explain.

In game one, Vic Willis started for the visiting Bostons while Frank Bates was fodder for Quinn's men. From the beginning, Willis handled the Misfits with ease, surrendering only three hits after eight innings. The Beaneaters, meanwhile, built a 7-0 lead against a hopeless Bates who pitched "with about as much heart as that which a rabbit would tackle a ferret." (*CPD*, Jul 2). Bates made a circus-like assortment of pitching mistakes. When they weren't hitting him, Bates continually hit batters and let runners steal bases. The lone Spiders' highlight was the fervor of Tommy Tucker coaching from the lines and the bench. Mr. Boisterous came close to blows with Boston players. He was not playing first base due to his arm swelling after being hit by Boston's Bailey the day before. Schreckengost took Tuck's place on first.

The Rabbits trailed the Ferrets 7-0 as they took their last at bats in the bottom of the ninth. Bob Stafford booted Dick Harley's grounder at second base. Quinn smashed a hot one to third. Jimmy Collins couldn't handle it and all were safe. Suter Sullivan grounded out to move up the runners. Outfielder McAllister punched one up the middle of the diamond and two runs were in. The shutout was averted. Ossee Schreck flied to Charlie Frisbee. With two out and the Spiders still five runs behind, little Harry Lochhead singled and so did catcher Joe Sugden. Willis then walked his rival Bates to force in the third run. Centerfielder Buttermilk Tommy Dowd smoked a clean drive to score Lochhead and Sugden. The score was now 7-5 in favor of Boston. The large gathering squirmed in their seats. Harley then singled to score Bates and reliable Quinn doubled in Dowd to tie the score. The crowd hollered like mad. Sullivan drove one deep to center, but Frisbee tracked it down to keep Quinn from the winner. After nine innings the score was deadlocked at seven.

Neither club scored in the tenth. In the eleventh, the Bostons pulled ahead. Jimmy Collins doubled and Hugh Duffy was hit by Bates. Busy Frisbee sacrificed and Bobby Lowe gave the Beantowners a two run lead with his single to right field. The runs seemed to let the air out of the big audience. Bates bore down and retired the next two hitters. Trailing 9-7, the Spiders gave it one last try. Bates solved Willis for a single. Dowd then singled to knock an embarrassed Willis from the game. Manager Frank Selee replaced Willis with Ted Lewis. A wild Lewis promptly walked Dick Harley to load the bases. Lewis then wild pitched Bates home. It was 9-8. Quinn's grounder forced Dowd at home plate but then Joe boldly stole second base. Sullivan roped a shot to the outfield. Harley and Quinn raced home. Bates and the Misfits were astonished winners by 10-9. President M. Stanley Robison personally shook all the hands of the victorious and said the season would be played out in Cleveland (*SL*, Jul 8). On the stunning victory, the *Plain Dealer* remarked: (Jul 2).

The scene that accompanied this finish can only be imagined. Those who know Hugh Duffy, and Tenney, and Bill Clarke, and know what kind of losers they are, can form a slight idea of their actions.

The Cleveland players were like a lot of wild men. When Joe Quinn came in with the winning run the players gave a pretty good imitation of a school let out for recess, and the audience was as wild as the players. Sullivan, whose single scored the last two runs, was surrounded, and cheered, and hugged. Everybody seemed to be suddenly possessed of the irrepressible desire to pound the nearest person to him and break somebody else's hat. The demonstration lasted fully five minutes and only ceased when exhaustion set in.

Another Cleveland paper offered this panegyric to support Cleveland's great victory: (Jul 2).

It is no exaggeration to say that the club that was soon to be cast adrift to become a barnstorming band displayed more genuine ambition and pluck in Saturday's great game than any home team has exhibited in 10 or a dozen years. There were no snarling remarks about the left field bleacherites, no talk about getting down to the Hawley for supper, no loafing, no grand stand bickering with the umpires. Instead, Quinn's men simply played ball. This is what the people like. It may be observed in this connection that while the Cast Adrifts were thus making the champions look like cancelled postage stamps, the ex-Clevelands were sassing the umpires, quarrelling with the audience and- incidentally- getting a beautiful walloping at the hands of the rejuvenated Orioles down in St. Louis.

Misfits Win a Game
Cleveland Press

Artist: Michael D. Arnold

Even *Sporting Life* was taken by the great Cleveland victory, saying with a considerable degree of civic pride, "you can go up the street exultantly and tell everybody the story." (Jul 22).

The *Boston Globe* headline, "Misfits, eh? Well, they're good enough to trim Boston." (Jul 2).

The second game didn't seem to matter much for the Spiders or their delirious fans. Another game like the last would probably cause collective crowd heart failure. Nonetheless, the contest went on with the frustrated Bostons taking it out on the Clevelands. Frank Selee's bunch beat Germany Schmit and Harry Maupin to a bloody pulp, 14-0. Piano Legs Hickman was in tune for the visitors and allowed the home boys only two singles. So ludicrous was the Cleveland effort that once with two Boston runners on base and first baseman Joe Sugden playing well off the bag, Schmit zipped a pickoff throw to first. The ball sailed down the right field line. Both Bostons scored and Schmit said, "Vy Joe, vere vas you? You vas dere a moment ago. Don't you know a lefthander never looks vere he throws?" (*TSN*, date unkn). After six innings the game was called so Boston could catch a train.

In four games at League Park, the tail end Spiders had played the second place Bostons even.

A special National League meeting was to be held in three days to consider the Spiders' transfer of games from their city. "We are floundering around in the choppy sea of uncertainty. We haven't any compass and we can't see the stars," commented *Sporting Life*, quoting no one in particular (Jul 15). Manager John Day of New York said that his club and Boston would oppose such a move and try and help the Clevelands (*CPD*, Jul 2).

Mon July 3   After their series of wonders with Boston, the Spiders traveled to Pittsburg. There, in front of a large Monday throng of 2500, they faced Jesse Tannehill and his elusive curveball. Christy Mathewson would later say of a pitcher's reputation, "All he's got to do is throw his glove into the box to beat that club." (50). Tannehill threw his glove into the box. On this day, the great Tannehill made mincemeat of the Misfits, winning handily 7-1. The Spiders "brought exactly seven bats to the grounds, no more, no less," and made six hits (*PP*, Jul 4). Charlie Knepper was Jesse's mound opponent who "will develop into a good winning pitcher and be of use to Robison's Perfectos but today he got a little wild now and then and when he did timely hits were made." (*CPD*, Jul 4). The *Plain Dealer* hinted of Knepper's removal to St. Louis as soon as he improved.

Besides the hurling of Tannehill, the Pirates' hero was third baseman Jimmy Williams who was solid afield and at bat. In the sixth inning, Williams ran out a home run that "was the cleanest made on the grounds this season." (*PP*, Jul 4).

So impressive was Williams' performance that two National League umpires, viewing from the stands, lauded Williams' efforts after the game. The *Pittsburg Post* account of the game featured a little kid cartoon brandishing a bat and pointing, as if in mockery to the Cleveland contingent. The caption read "dead easy." (*PP*, Jul 4).

The contest was umpired by Ned Swartwood and his new assistant Arlie "The Freshest Man on Earth" Latham, former major league funnyman. The comical Latham was taking over after Swartwood's partner Warner had resigned.

Tue July 4   It was a sweltering hot day in Steeltown, the kind that prompted players to place cabbage leaves under their caps to avoid sunstroke (Schlossberg 75).   The Pirates and Spiders played a holiday morning-afternoon doubleheader. The more than ten thousand who showed up for the two matches could not have been treated to more exciting baseball. Their home town heroes had won seven straight games.

Game one started promptly at 10am in front of over 4500 people. Bill "Wizard" Hoffer, who piled up impressive statistics for the 1895-1897 Baltimore club, went for Patsy Donovan's Pirates. Donovan had replaced manager Watkins in mid May. Joe Quinn countered with the well-liked Jim Hughey. Neither side scored a run in the opening stanza. In the Spiders' second with one out, Tommy Tucker, who "would play the best he knew how for a sandlot team," raised a few eyebrows by socking a triple (*SL*, Jul 8). Harry Lochhead grounded to his counterpart at shortstop, Bones Ely. The slender Pirate threw home to get Tucker but catcher Frank Bowerman dropped the ball. Cleveland led 1-0. In the third frame, the Spiders scored two more with the help of Tucker's timely two-run single. Said the *Pittsburg Post*, "The Misfits scored three runs before the Pirates got the smell." (Jul 5). Jim Hughey controlled the game until the Pittsburgers batted in the wacky sixth inning. Donovan popped one down the left field foul line. Dick "Harley went after it, got his hands on it and forced it into foul territory." (*PP*, Jul 5). Umpire Swartwood ordered Donovan to second base for a double. Catcher Joe Sugden screamed that the ball was foul while kicking up dirt. The umpire stuck to his guns. Outfielder Jack McCarthy took advantage of Hughey's weakness by bunting safe and Jimmy Williams' double along the left field line scored two runs. Williams then attempted a steal of third base. Catcher Sugden threw him out. Speedy bunting specialist Ginger Beaumont dunked his way on. When Beaumont tried to steal the next base, he was caught by the strong throw of Sugden. First baseman Willie Clark struck out. After six innings it was 3-2, Cleveland. Hoffer and Hughey matched pitches until the Pirate ninth (*CPD*, Jul 5). Ely singled and Bowerman eventually drove him home for the tie. The luckless Spiders struggled against Hoffer, unable to score since the third. In the Pirate 10th inning, McCarthy singled but was forced at second base by Williams. Ginger Beaumont then dribbled to Quinn whose throw to Tucker was perfect. Except...Tucker muffed it and Beaumont was safe. Clark forced Beaumont at second base while Williams trotted to third. The skeletal Bones Ely then singled in Williams for the winning run. Hughey and Cleveland were defeated 4-3 but they "went down kicking like steers." (*PP*, Jul 5). The Pirates had their eighth consecutive victory.

As the second affair began, an even larger gathering settled in for the holiday festivities. More than six thousand spectators jammed into the ball yard to see their beloved Pirates and Cleveland. Righthander Tully Sparks assumed the pitching chores for the home towners against Frederick M. Schmit. Early on, the Pirates rattled the German forcing him into an error, a hit batsman, and a key Donovan double that gave Pittsburg four runs. In the sixth, the Spiders awoke against Sparks. Ossee Schreckengost tripled and with one out "Pink Coat" Tommy Dowd walked and stole second. Harley, Quinn, and Sullivan singled in succession to produce three runs. The visitors took the lead in their half of the eighth with the help of Dowd's double and Sullivan's safe blow. It was 5-4, Cleveland. Pittsburg tied the score at 5-5 with a solo tally in their half of the inning. Neither team could score in the ninth but Art Madison pinch hit for the struggling Sparks, who gave way to Jesse Tannehill. Both Schmit and Tannehill were invincible until the 13th inning, a "number sure to be a Jonah for one of the teams." (*CPD*, Jul 5. Tannehill, who had already beaten the Misfits three times on the season, was aiming to do it again.

In Cleveland's 13th, Harley drove one just beyond the reach of shortstop Ely. Quinn bounced back to Tannehill who threw to Ely for the force on Harley. Ely threw wild on the attempted double play relay to Clark at first. The ball skirted down the right field line and Quinn raced all the way to third base. Sullivan smoked a liner to Clark who caught the sphere, held Quinn on third and then proceeded to throw the ball over catcher Bowerman's head. The throw was so poor that Quinn had time to tag and score the go-ahead run. Tannehill's anger at the gift could not be controlled and he gave an "awful exhibition of insulted majesty," slammed him uniform cap on the ground, and yelled at Clark (*PP*, Jul 5). When the ball rolled back to Tannehill from Bowerman, he kicked at it in frustration. Not pleased at the unsportsmanlike demonstration, the crowd screamed at Tannehill who promptly gave four wide ones to McAllister. The Spider outfielder, trying to take advantage of Tannehill's irritation, attempted to steal second base. An alert Bowerman nabbed him. As the Pirates headed toward the bench, Tannehill stayed clear of Clark (*PP*, Jul 5). The Spiders led 6-5. Colorful Schmit went to work. The first batter, Bowerman, singled. Tannehill bunted safe and then manager Donovan bunted to Schmit who erred on his toss to Tucker. All hands were safe and the bases were loaded. McCarthy then squibbed to Tucker who instinctively threw home to get Bowerman. The runner appeared to be out but the umpire ruled in Bowerman's favor, saying Schreckengost did not tag Bowerman. Mr. Schmit then let loose with a verbal string of German-English invectives that few on the field could comprehend. Schmit threw up his arms and played to the crowd. For an instant the score was tied at 6-6. Schreckengost then threw the ball back to Schmit who "evidently did not know a game was going on. He was excited and the ball went to center field, while Tannehill walked home with the winning run." (*CPD*, Jul 5). It ended 7-6 Pittsburg. The Spiders had found an innovative, new way to lose, though many observers thought they had exhausted all previous efforts.

Thur July 6 A travel day occurred on Wednesday. The Exiles boarded a train westbound for the 600-mile journey to St. Louis. In those early days of baseball rail travel and Pullman car bunks, "star players had lower berths, average players the uppers." (Schlossberg 103). So, where did the Misfits sleep? For the long trip, there was plenty of time for the Wanderers to chat, play cards, snooze, drink, pull pranks, and raise hell. In St. Louis, the Tebeauites were still smarting from the June 25 loss to the #2 syndicate team. The Perfectos were looking to regain their fan base.

The contest took place in League Park, so renamed from Sportsman's Park, by owner Frank Robison at the beginning of the 1899 season. It was a smallish but fun-loving bunch of ball cranks, who divided their enthusiasm between their two "home" teams (*GD*, Jul 7). Indeed, all of the players on the Cleveland team had done duty in St. Louis except McAllister and Lochhead. Righthander Jack Powell went for the Perfectos against Frank Bates. Neither pitcher was particularly sharp, though Powell exhibited a "fair amount of speed and perfect control." (*GD*, Jul 7). Five double plays, three by the Spiders, and fine fielding by Lave Cross on foul flies, kept the score down. The much-maligned Bates, on a one game winning streak, returned to form. Several costly errors were committed behind his back. Bates' misery began in the St. Louis second. Five runs tallied due to four bases on balls and a Joe Quinn miscue at second base. Cleveland put together a nifty batting streak to get to within 5-4 in the third. Dick Harley's triple and Suter Sullivan's double were the big blows. Despite the unexpected flexing of the Misfits' muscles, Tebeau stayed with his pitcher. In the St. Louis third, easy Ed McKean was safe on another Quinn error and manager Tebeau doubled to score his second baseman. Two batters later, pitcher Powell collided with the irrepressible Tommy Tucker at first. The close decision went against the Misfits. "Tucker got gay with umpire McGarr," kicked up a storm, and used language unbefitting a gentleman. McGarr was prompt and ordered the loud mouth to take a seat on the bench. Joe Sugden took

Tucker's place. Powell injured his foot slightly on the play and limped for the rest of the game. It didn't matter, though. The St. Louis pitcher blanked the Clevelanders for the rest of the contest. In the seventh, Ed McKean lifted his second home run of the season into the right field bleachers. Both his homers had been against the Misfits. St. Louis won 9-4.

The inexperienced outfielder Charlie Hemphill was rumored to be heading to Cleveland. In the "exchange," if it could be called that in syndicate terms, Dowd and Harley were to report to St. Louis.

The *St. Louis Globe-Democrat* printed a blurb about Cleveland's pitching rotation. They cited Hughey, Knepper, Bates, and Schmit as the hurlers. Catcher Joe Sugden singled out Schmit as a winner.

Sat July 8   With Friday's game being postponed due to wet grounds, the Spiders and Browns continued their St. Louis series with a doubleheader. Once again the crowd favored the heavy underdog Quinn contingent. The Tebeauites were left to wonder how their home town fans could cheer for an opponent that had won a dozen games out of sixty-five.

Between four and six thousand persons attended the contests in Missouri, depending on which newspaper one wanted to believe. The *Plain Dealer* reported the smaller turnstile count while the *Globe-Democrat* beefed up the total. In the first game, Cy Young took the rubber for the home boys against Joe Quinn's man Charlie Knepper. The Browns scored a solo run in the first. Swift outfielder Jesse Burkett stole third when Suter Sullivan dropped Ossee Schreckengost's throw. Burkett came around with the run. In the fourth inning the Spiders startled Young and put three tallies on the chalkboard. Old Reliable Joe Quinn singled to left. Young balked Sullivan to first. With two on, Sport McAllister sacrificed and Charlie Hemphill erred on Terrible Tommy Tucker's long drive. Quinn scored. Shortstop Harry Lochhead grounded weakly to Lave Cross at third. Cross threw to home plate to get Tucker but catcher Jack O'Connor missed tagging Tommy. Lochhead was caught stealing, but Ossee Schreck doubled and later scored. St. Louis added two in their fourth with the help of John Heidrick's triple and Lave Cross' double. The fifth inning featured a few more prize fielding goof-ups by St. Louis. Buttermilk Dowd singled and waltzed to second when Hemphill had trouble fielding the ball. Catcher O'Connor let a pitch get by him and Dowd went to third. A disgusted Cy Young walked Dick Harley and watched as O'Connor threw the ball into center field on Harley's steal of second base. At the end of six innings the score was even at 4-4. In the seventh inning Tebeau and O'Connor were on base with one out. The *St. Louis Globe-Democrat* picks up the description: (Jul 9)

With Young at bat O'Day called "ball three" on what the home players claimed was the fourth. Every member of Patsy's band rushed at O'Day and registered a

87

complaint. O'Day might have been wrong, but whether he had erred or not, he stuck to his decision. Finally, he pulled out his watch and told the home players to resume playing within one minute or he would declare the game forfeited to Cleveland. The men took fifty nine seconds of the time allowed them, and the game proceeded. It was two and three on Young, when he foul-flied to Schreckengost. As soon as the leather had sunk into "Schreck's" glove, the locals again raised a howl. Burkett then walked, filling the bags, but Hemphill's fly was caught by Dowd, ending the inning.

In the Cleveland ninth, Schreck again lashed a double but was left on base by the crafty Young. With a chance to win the game in the last inning, Knepper apparently hit O'Connor with a pitch but O'Day refused to allow it saying O'Connor had purposefully stood over home plate. O'Connor's frustration boiled over. He jawed at O'Day to no avail and was assisted ably by the "anvil chorus." (*GD*, Jul 9). The Browns did not score and the game went on. The Spiders failed to sore in the tenth and the St. Louis team took another turn at Knepper. All game long they had bettered Charlie to the tune of fifteen hits. The *Globe-Democrat* reported that the St. Louis players "ran the bases with more than their ordinary alacrity." (Jul 9). Knepper registered five walks and four steals against. But Young, who was working on a seven hitter, had been poorly supported by catcher O'Connor and outfielder Hemphill. In the St. Louis 10th, the great Jesse Burkett started things with a single. Hemphill sacrificed Jesse to second. Heidrick skied to Dowd in center. Then, shortstop Rhody Wallace bashed a long one over Dowd. "Tom tried for an impossible catch but missed connections with the ball by several yards." (*GD, Jul 9*). The Spiders were losers 5-4.

The second game packed far less drama; a word seldom used to describe Cleveland baseball. The ex-Spider, diminutive Wee Willie Sudhoff, took the mound for Tebeau. Joe Quinn countered with Jimmy Hughey. St. Louis began the run getting in the second inning as Cross scored. In the third, Cleveland tied the score. "Peanut Hands" Sugden walked and was sacrificed to second by Hughey. Sudhoff wild pitched the catcher to third and Sugden scored on Dowd's sacrifice fly to Burkett. The Tebeau Men took the lead right back in their third inning. Sudhoff singled and Burkett bunted him to second. Hughey, a bit rattled at teams who loved to bunt on him, hit Hemphill. A distracted Hemphill was "caught a block off first" but umpire McGarr ruled him safe and saved the young outfielder from a managerial tongue-lashing (*CPD*, Jul 9). Heidrick flew to Harley in the left garden. Wallace hit back to Hughey but the pitcher's errant throw to Tucker trickled into foul territory. As Tucker chased the ball, Sudhoff scored but Hemphill was thrown out in his eagerness to add another run. In the St. Louis fourth inning, Cross went down pitcher to first. McKean singled and scored on Tebeau's triple and Criger knocked in Tebeau with a safe hit. Errors by Harley and Sugden helped St. Louis to two runs in the sixth, cementing a 6-2 St. Louis win. Sudhoff was clever against his former teammates while Hughey was "one of the easiest things the locals have faced in weeks." (*GD*, Jul 9).

Sun Jul 9 One of the league's other poor teams made their way to St. Louis to face the Perfectos in a three-city doubleheader. The Louisville Colonels were demolished in the first game by 11-4, Jack Powell vastly outpitching Deacon Phillippe. The game's highlight occurred when Jesse Burkett caught up to a long fly by Honus Wagner and made a circus catch. Burkett's acrobatics prevented three runs and on the way back to his position, Jesse doffed his cap numerous times.

Cleveland's effort was no better. The contest was played before an overflow gathering of 11,000 well-behaved customer's who gave both clubs the "glad hand" for good playing. They squeezed into the grandstand, pavilion, field seats and deep center field area. Fully 1500 cranks viewed from the edge of the playing field. Ropes were used to prevent trespassing and balls hit beyond the periphery were considered ground rule home runs (*GD*, Jul 10). Highly charged by the huge audience, the dynamic Frederick M. Schmit took the mound for the Spiders. He was in his element, ready to entertain what he thought to be his congregation, and did so with an ear-to-ear grin. Tebeau sent Nig Cuppy, "the man with the perennially bad wing," into the breach (*CPD*, Jul 10).

The Misfits drew first blood in the initial inning on key blows by the two Tommy's, Dowd and Tucker. Schmit controlled the Perfectos for two innings until the third. Jesse Burkett bunted safe and Heidrick dribbled to the German pitcher who threw to Harry Lochhead at second. The little shortstop dropped the ball and all were safe. Rhody Wallace also bunted, taking advantage of Schmit's weakness to get off the mound. With the bases loaded, Lafayette Napoleon Cross took a liking to one of Schmit's curves. The St. Louis third baseman homered for four runs. The blast "drove the grin off his (Schmit's) face, and from then on his slants were driven to every corner of the field." (*GD*, Jul 10). Patsy's gang tallied two more in the sixth and five more in the eighth. The runs scored primarily on bunting and a McKean home run to the right field bleachers. The McKean blow was his second in four days and his third of the season, all against Cleveland pitching. The final was 11-4.

Despite the amateurish glove work in the error columns for both sides, good fielding did occur. Cross robbed Lochhead on a hot smash. Tommy Dowd took away an extra base hit from Cross and Burkett returned the favor with a running catch off Dowd. The Spiders left prematurely after the inning eight to catch a train. It was their 8th loss in succession. Quinn's boys were happy to leave St. Louis. Sarcastically, the *Plain Dealer* commented, "Robison's team won." (Jul 10).

Sporting Life reported that Tucker and Harley were needed on the St. Louis team to keep the Perfectos "in the race 'till the finish." (Jul 22).

Tue July 11   Monday was a travel day for the Nomads who made the long train trek from St. Louis to Philadelphia's Baker Bowl. The Bowl was a strangely dimensioned ball yard with a bicycle track rimming the outfield. Flychasers were required to sprint up (and down) inclines when going after long flies.

Three thousand five hundred ninety four ball cranks witnessed a "distressingly orderly function, the Phillies going through their various parts, conscious of victory, and the Clevelanders playing theirs as though defeat was their certain portion." (*PE,* Jul 12).

Frank Bates pitched his best. He gave up only five runs on eleven hits and two stolen bases. His opponent, Red Donahue, who had no-hit the champion Bostons in 1898, was wild in the first inning. The Philadelphia righthander hit Sport McAllister and then Tommy Tucker with the bases loaded. Harry Lochhead hit a screaming liner to left field, but Ed Delahanty made a sensational catch to end the threat. Delahanty's star fielding and hitting would set the tone for the contest. Cleveland could score no more off Donahue and managed only seven hits.

It was a game of fielding superlatives. Both clubs played adroitly and not an error was committed. Philadelphia shortstop Monte Cross made the best play of all. In the fourth inning, he made a high-jumping catch of Lochhead's liner that "would probably have broken Sweeney's record had it been over a bar." (*CPD,* Jul 12). The Sweeney reference was for a popular track athlete. The *Philadelphia Enquirer*'s description of the catch was even better. They called the Cross catch a "lollapoloosisia," and remarked, "The proof reader is requested not to hunt this up in The New Century (dictionary). He will thereby save time and add to the reputation of the writer." (Jul 12). Cross and Donahue were not the only heroes of the day. Almost every man managed to distinguish himself with the glove. The entire Philadelphia outfield of Delahanty, Elmer Flick, and rookie Roy Thomas made running grabs. Infielders Napoleon Lajoie at second base and Sir Richard "Duff" Cooley at first base were applauded by the faithful for fine stops. Third baseman Bill Lauder made a good catch on a foul fly. Catcher Klondike Douglass was singled out for his throwing. With names like Napoleon, Sir Richard, and Klondike, the Phillies sounded more like an expeditionary force than a baseball team. On the visitors' side, outfielders Dick Harley and Tommy Dowd ran down balls that looked like sure hits and the middle infield of Lochhead and Joe Quinn sparkled.

Wed July 12   It was the second game of the Quakers-Nomads series. Philadelphia manager Billy Shettsline sent Bill Magee, who earlier had pitched against the Spiders as a member of the Louisville club. Joe Quinn answered with big, strong Charlie Knepper. The game was a wondrous pitching and fielding duel, attended by precisely 3249 (*PE*, Jul 13).

Cleveland began the scoring in the first when gentleman Dick Harley politely doubled against the right field fence and scored on Suter Sullivan's single. The Phils Duff Cooley's "corking three bagger to left-centre" helped tie in the initial inning. "Quinn in the third made a hair-raising stop and throw of Delahanty's seemingly safe grounder." (*CPD*, Jul 13). Neither team could muster any tallies until the fourth when Philadelphia's Elmer Flick smashed one down the right field line and later scored on Bill Lauder's hit. It was 2-1 Phillies. The Misfits tied the score in their sixth on a McAllister single and a Schreckengost double. The Philadelphians then "proceeded to make things merry" in their half of the inning against Knepper (*PE*, Jul 13). Flick hit another double and with Lauder and Douglass following with singles and Magee's sacrifice fly, they took a 4-2 lead. The score stayed that way until the finish. Though Magee was hit hard, he was saved on several occasions by the smart moves of Monte Cross at shortstop, Nap Lajoie at second base, and Roy Thomas in center field. Tommy Dowd, Harley, Tucker, and Sullivan were the victims of Philadelphia's fielding prowess. The visitors had their heroes, too. Besides Knepper's fine twirling, Quinn had two hits and made "Magee visibly nervous by his actions on the base." (*CPD*, Jul 13). Dowd, Sullivan, and Lochhead excelled at their positions. But, once again, the Misfits lost.

Thur July 13   The skies above Philadelphia threatened rain before the game began. But, before 2565 ball cranks, the contest began. Chick Fraser was the starter for Shettsline's gang while Jim Hughey was summoned for the Wanderers. From the beginning, Quaker Fraser outpitched Misfit Hughey, "compelling the batsmen" to hit his pitches and let his fielders do the rest (*CPD*, Jul 14). Fraser surrendered only three hits, two by the light-hitting Harry Lochhead. Hughey, on the other hand, let the Phillies whack his slants for twelve safeties. Smiling Jim did manage to put a frown on the great Delahanty's face by striking him out.

It was a clever fielding game. Fraser's support was excellent behind him. Like Lochhead on Tuesday, Sport McAllister fell victim to fine Phillie fielding. Catcher McFarland made a nice running catch of Mac's pop in the second and Nap Lajoie at second speared a hard grounder that seemed headed for right field. Monte Cross and Roy Thomas also turned in good glove work. For the visitors, Dick Harley robbed Elmer Flick of a hit in the fifth inning and the outfield was splendid.

In inning seven, amid darkening skies, umpire Gaffney said he could not see low balls go over home plate and he called the game. It was 5:20pm (*PE*, Jul

13). The Misfits accepted the loss as their resigned fate but had the home club been behind in a similar fashion, they would have surely raised a "runction." (*PE,* Jul 13). Despite the 5-1 loss, the Spiders played very competitively against the Phils, who moved into second place.

Two simplistic blurbs ridiculing the names and German ancestries of two Misfits players somehow found their way into the *Enquirer*'s pages. "Schreckengost! That would be a nice name to take into a folding bed, wouldn't it?" The meaning of the comment is unknown. Another ridiculous ditty: "Schmit, Schreckengost, beimlaufs, dreislockers, wienerwursts. Ach! This may be a trifle to the reader. That being the case, it may be stated without any violation that the writer has nothing on the reader. It's all even." (Jul 14).

Fri July 14 From Philadelphia the Misfits chugged their way to Baltimore to take on the fiery John McGraw and his Orioles for three games. McGraw had said the day before that he would be "greatly chagrinned" if the Clevelands won any games with Baltimore (BTS, Jul 14). The *Baltimore Sun* warned that the Misfits could give the Birds a fight. The Orioles themselves were on the skids, having dropped four of six games to lowly Washington and Louisville. Perhaps the Orioles were spending too much time in the showers. A thermal bath cabinet had just been presented to the Oriole dressing room so the players could take "Turkish Baths." (*BTS,* Jul 14). The popular belief was that the steam could sweat the alcohol out of a player's system.

Three Misfits were given the "glad hand" as they appeared on the field. All had a bit of a Baltimore connection. Joe Quinn, a popular Oriole in '96-'98, was applauded. Tommy Tucker, a Baltimore player who led the American Association in batting with a .372 mark, was also treated nicely. Tucker's aggressive style of play seemed more suited to McGraw. Finally, Suter Sullivan had a small fan club in attendance, "who rooted manfully for him and his team." (*BTS,* Jul 15). Besides those polite displays of affection, there was one particular Cleveland crank who made such a ruckus that he made many Baltimore faithful upset and nearly got himself arrested (*CPD,* Jul 15).

Just over one thousand attended the contest at old Union Park. To try to shake up his team, McGraw had his men bat first and used a new lineup against Cleveland's Frank Bates. The Orioles pecked for one run. In Cleveland's half, they looked out to the mound and saw an old friend, Still Bill Hill. The first batter, Tommy Dowd, was safe on shortstop Topsy Magoon's error. Lefthander Hill, eyeing Dowd and wary of his speed, attempted to pick Tommy off base. Hill's throw bounded down the rightfield line, and into a tall, grassy area. Before the bumbling Orioles could locate the ball, Dowd flashed home with the tying run. Baltimore added two more in their second inning. For the Misfits, Lochhead reached on Magoon's second error and then Hill uncorked a wild ball that plunked batter Bates in the chest. Bates lay on the ground for some time and many feared serious injury. Manager Quinn summoned Crazy Schmit to run for Bates, an altogether different role for the pitcher. However, Bates recovered quickly and returned to the game. Bates should have stayed on the turf. The Orioles continued to score against Bates, who had seemingly patented the fine art of pitching ignominy. The hapless Bates surrendered 12 hits, six walks, four stolen bases, two wild pitches, and he hit a batter. The Orioles displayed "scientific team work at bat," bunted at will, and ran the bases with abandon (*BTS*, Jul 15). John McGraw was walked three times and scored three times. One occasion, wily McGraw scored from second on a groundout without the aid of a Cleveland error. First baseman Candy LaChance cracked out three hits while Steve Brodie, Jimmy Sheckerd, and Hill had two. One of Brodie's hits was an inside the grounds home run that had Dowd chasing. So valuable was the bat that Brodie kept his eye on it throughout the game and secured it in his locker (*BTS*, Jul 15). Hill, meanwhile, handled his old teammates with ease, giving up only three hits with his speedy curves and pinpoint control. It ended 14-1.

The Brothers Robison were keeping a very low profile but had attended a Chicago conference probably making arrangements for the transfer of games. Frank Robison denied the story before he left for Chicago, and stated that all the games would be played as scheduled in Cleveland. However, later investigative reporting by the *Plain Dealer* and the *Sun* revealed that Robison had already transferred the Cleveland-Washington series to Washington and was about to do the same for a Baltimore series (Jul 15).

Sat Jul 15   To make up for a rainout in May, the Orioles and Misfits played two games for the price of one. Said the *Plain Dealer*, stealing a line from a rather famous British playwright, "As brevity is the soul of wit, the most commendable feature of the doubleheader today between the Orioles and the listless Outcasts was the shortness of the two games." (Jul 16). The newspaper could have easily quoted Shakespeare's Sonnet 29, "When in disgrace with fortune and men's eyes, I all alone beweep my outcast state." The Spiders hadn't won since their "Midsummer's Night's Dream," the 10-9 July 1st victory over Boston.

Game one was played before 2436 fans. It lasted only 105 minutes while rookie Joe McGinnity tossed a four hit shutout. "Schmit was in the box for Cleveland. A good many years ago Schmit pitched for the Orioles. He was a circus then and the rooters enjoyed him today. They found enjoyment in the way he rejoiced in his own performance and the way he pitched into the fielders whenever an error was made or a chance lost." (*CPD*, Jul 16). What happened was the usual parade of hits, errors, walks, and daring baserunning by Misfits' opponents. Ducky Holmes homered and threw Suter Sullivan out at the plate so convincingly that kicks were ignored by the unlucky Clevelands (*CPD*, Jul 16). The only bright spot for the Nomads was the play of veteran catcher Joe Sugden who "stood his ground firmly as the young and frisky Orioles came dashing into him." (*CPD*, Jul 16). In all, there were ten young and frisky Orioles.

Game two was no better. Righthander Frank Kitson, who had blanked the Spiders in May by 12-0, did it again. This time the score was 5-0 because the "Orioles didn't try very hard after the fourth inning" and "took pity on their opponents and helped to end their troubles as quickly as possible." (*CPD*, Jul 16). Kitson's five-hitter easily beat Charlie Knepper, who hit two batters in the first inning, and allowed the rambunctious McGraw to steal four times. What little scoring opportunities the Misfits had were blown by the inopportune bat of Sport McAllister. In the first with two out and two on, he grounded weakly to Bill Keister at second base. In the ninth, McAllister struck out with Sullivan on second.

Thus far in the series the Spiders had been outscored 29-1, with their only tally a gift from Magoon and Hill. With the double loss, the Misfits' new string reached fourteen. Curiously, a pants manufacturer released a big advertisement on trousers going for .99 a leg, two for $1.98 in the sporting page. But, the Spiders hadn't a leg to stand on.

Mon July 17 The Baltimore and Cleveland teams were idle Sunday after "Saturday's double picnic" but resumed their series on Monday (*BTS*, Jul 18). Due to a scheduling misfortune, the weary clubs played another doubleheader.

Before 1561 paid, Baltimore summoned lefthander Jeremiah Nops to the mound for game one. In recent outings, Nops had pitched badly for the Orioles and was teetering on McGraw's brink. For the Clevelands, it was Jim Hughey's turn. Buttermilk Tommy Dowd led off the game with a smash that bounded away from outfielder Steve Brodie for a three-bagger. Harley was hit by a pitch and Joe Quinn's hit to right center scored Dowd. Suter Sullivan stroked a hard one to second that McGraw couldn't handle and was safe on an error. McAllister sacrificed and it was 2-0. Tommy Tucker then bounced to shortstop Topsy Magoon whose play was at home plate. Magoon's throw was wide. Quinn scored for 3-0. Harry Lochhead drove in the fourth tally with an infield out. The maligned "Jerry" Nops wasn't exactly getting solid infield support. Baltimore came back to slice the Misfits' lead in half; scoring on two sacrifice flies. But, with two out, Joe Quinn caught a Pat Crisham pop to end the threat. Said *Sporting Life* in hyperbole, "When Captain Quinn starts for a fly ball the scorers mark an out, re-light their cigars and settle back for a rest. The sphere never wriggles out of Joe's horny hands." (Jul 8). The Orioles wasted a Magoon triple in the fourth and neither team did much until the sixth. In that frame, Cleveland's batters went to work. Nops hit Lochhead with a pitch, Schreck sacrificed, and Hughey hit a short pop to Nops. With two out, Dowd singled in Lochhead. Manager McGraw fumed from his second base position. The next hitter, Dick Harley, sent a Nops' delivery against the right field fence. Dowd scored on Harley's triple. When sliding into the base, Harley sprained his ankle and was replaced by Crazy Schmit. McGraw raced to the mound screaming at his pitcher and told Nops to have a seat. Frank Kitson was brought in to finish. Meanwhile, gallant Hughey was near unhittable, the Birds making "their favorite mistake of trying to break the ball instead of appealing more to the science of the thing." (*CPD*, Jul 18). Smiling Jim and the smiling Misfits were victors by 7-2. McGraw was greatly chagrinned, so much that he picked Nops as the natural scapegoat, and suspended the Baltimore pitcher for 30 days without pay. Nops was probably hung over at the time, allowing for his poor showing (Alexander 65).

A jubilant Hughey said of his victory, "I am glad that they did not bunt on me as they did on the other pitchers. If they had I should have had a hard time of it, as I have a bad leg and could not have fielded bunts." Part of the credit for Hughey's win could also go to Suter Sullivan, who played a tight third base and dared the Orioles to bunt. Sullivan had begun to round into form after listening to the advice from veteran Quinn on where to play each man and how to field each kind of ball (*WES*, Jul 19).

As they had done on previous occasions, the Misfits merely showed up for the next game of the doubleheader. Righthander Handsome Harry Howell was McGraw's choice in the box. The Misfits were stuck with Frank Bates, a 14-1 loser the previous Friday to these same Orioles. By coincidence, the *Washington Evening Star* sports page printed a large Hecht Co. advertisement that read "a merciless slaughter of prices."(Jul 18). Ladies $1.00 white duck shirts were going for 49 cents, $2.00 washable shirts were on sale for 98 cents and $2.98 muslin garments were as low as 98 cents. Another merciless slaughter was taking place about 85 miles northeast of Washington at Baltimore's Union Park. The victim was Frank Bates. In only four innings of work, Bates, who was said to resent his veteran teammates advice about his temper and fielding bunts, turned a "batting matinee" into "burlesque." (*CPD*, Jul 18). The Orioles stockpiled enough hits and runs for a week. With Bates hitting five batters with his wild west shooting, the Lord Baltimores sent 18 men across home plate. To add to the fun, Magoon and Candy LaChance bounced three-baggers over the befuddled Misfits' heads. Fifteen of the runs came in the third and fourth innings. Manager Quinn finally removed young Bates and replaced him with Crazy Schmit, who was patrolling the left field garden for the injured Harley. Bates repaired himself to left field. Schmit took advantage of an 18-5 deficit, and played with the partisan Baltimore crowd by gesticulating and yelling like the nasty uncle in The Katzenjammer Kids comic strip. When it was over, the Orioles had a laugh by 21-6.

After witnessing the series, Frank Patterson, a reporter covering Baltimore for the *Sporting News*, implored the National League to drop Cleveland immediately and annex a minor league team such as Milwaukee, Buffalo, or Toronto to transfer into the league. The weekly also remarked about Hughey's surprise victory that the Misfits could not beat the Orioles another game in 500 and that another loss would drive Baltimore rooters to drink (Jul 22).

Mr. H.R. Vonderhorst of Baltimore completed arrangements with M. Stanley Robison of Cleveland to have games originally scheduled in Cleveland in late July switched to Baltimore.

A Washington newspaper reported that ex-Misfit Jack Clements, still on the bulky side and at home in Philadelphia, wanted $2400 to play again. An unnamed manager said, "Baseball players are like nothing else on earth." (*WES*, Jul 18).

The writer covering baseball for *Sporting Life* magazine, Elmer E. Bates, came up with this tongue-in-cheek gem on the rationalization of losing (Jul 22).

There is some satisfaction in being in twelfth place. You have everything to hope for and nothing to fear. Defeats do not rack your nerves or disturb your sleep. An occasional victory affords both surprise and delight. You are in no danger of being displaced by some team that has been designated by the critics as no good; especially are you in no danger when the next nearest club in the race is .167 percentage points ahead of you. You are not asked fifty times a day: 'What's the score?' People take it for granted that the club was defeated and do not bother the sporting editors.

Tue July 18   From Baltimore the Misfits took the short trip to Washington. Once again, two games were scheduled to make up for the lost games in Cleveland. In essence then, it was a double series. The Misfits were to play the Senators seven games in four days. What better way to play than a doubleheader with "Joe Quinn and brother tourists who were being footballed to the various angles of the major league map?" (*WP*, Jul 19).

The 3500 in attendance were treated to a fine contest for the National Park opener. "In concurrence with the old adage 'misery loves company' the Washington fans were exceedingly generous towards the travelers who have no home but like nomads of the desert are roaming at large." (*CPD*, Jul 19). Senators manager Arthur Irwin started the erratic righthander Bill Dinneen while Charlie Knepper took his turn for the Exiles. With Schreckengost again behind the plate, the *Plain Dealer* made this quirky comment. "The aroma of wienerwurst and bock exudes from those titles, and in the event of an international rift in the diplomatic relations 'twixt America and Germany, Joe

96

Quinn suggests that his Teutonic battery be appointed on the arbitration board." (Jul 19).

"The Human Mosquito" Jimmy Slagle led off the first inning with an infield hit. Jack O'Brien bunted safe and then Knepper uncorked a wild pitch to move the runners. Third baseman Charlie Atherton scored Slagle on a short outfield fly. Buck Freeman ran out a triple to plate O'Brien. The Senators led 2-0. Big Bill Dinneen held the Misfits down until the sixth when Washington had built a 4-0 lead. In that inning, Crazy Schmit singled to center but was forced at second on Joe Quinn's bouncer to shortstop Dick Padden. A Suter Sullivan base hit sent Quinn to third. Sport McAllister drove home Joe with a hit. It was 4-1. Knepper, the "stalwart youth with cyclonic speed and a sharp-shooting curve," began to dominate the Senators' hitters (*WP*, Jul 19). In the Spiders seventh, the bottom of the order loaded the bases on hits. Lochhead poked an infield hit and Schreck put a Dinneen toss between second and first. Pitcher Knepper then bunted right in front of the mound. Catcher Malachi Kittredge, recently signed with Washington after a bout with Louisville management, bumped into Dinneen who was also going for the ball. The two tumbled to the ground and all hands were safe. The remarkable Tommy Dowd then tripled to tie the game and scored the go ahead on Schmit's groundout. Seeing this, the crowd shifted their allegiance to the visitors. The *Plain Dealer* commented on Dinneen's sudden loss of effectiveness. "Two singles in the seventh sent his wheels to whirling and before he set his brake four runs had crossed the plate. When the going is easy Dinneen can pitch a lot of batters to a standstill, but let him strike a snag and up he goes." (Jul 19). Knepper remained courageous in his uphill struggle and despite a late Washington rally, the Misfits held on for a 5-4 victory. The *Washington Evening Star* said of Cleveland, "When the cherry pie was offered them in the seventh inning in the shape of the slovenly hurling by Dinneen, they woke up." (Jul 19).

Game two was typical of so many Misfit losses. Righthander Win Mercer, whose nickname was a bit of a misnomer, started for the Senators. Frank Bates, who'd been blasted the day before in Baltimore, this time chose Washington for his beating. In only two innings of work, Bates surrendered five runs and was dismissed. In the first inning, Washington scored twice as Bates was busy balking runners around the basepaths and making errors. In the second inning, first baseman Dan McGann, traded from Brooklyn, walked. Catcher Jim Duncan bunted near the mound but Bates' throw eluded the reach of Tommy Tucker. McGann scored and Duncan went to second. Pitcher Mercer, seizing the moment, did the same. His bunt was fielded by Bates but the throw was even wilder and Tucker had to chase the ball down the right field line. Duncan scored and Mercer moved to third. As the second inning ended, it was 5-0 Washington. An exasperated manager Quinn summoned Sport McAllister in from right field and Bates went to the outfield. The Misfits now had their rightfieder pitching and two of their starting pitchers in the outfield. Crazy Schmit was playing leftfield for the still hobbling Dick Harley.

With the Senators not used to McAllister's delivery, they took two innings without a score. Then, five runs resulted in the fifth as McAllister allowed an assortment of hits, bunts, and wild pitches. Mercer, meanwhile, easily controlled Cleveland batting and when the lead reached 10-0, he lobbed balls to the plate (*CPD*, Jul 19). All the Misfits could do was score four meaningless runs. The Senators waltzed 11-4 for the doubleheader split.

It there was a highlight for the Misfits, it was the presence of Schmit, "the energetic German with a boiler-shop voice that was employed in disturbing the peace from the coach line whenever the vocal valve of his brother soloist, Tom Tucker, was short on basso notes. Schmit was allowed to proceed with his solos by umpire Gaffney. He is longer on wind and more vociferous in pipes than the emotional first baseman, who must remove the cobwebs from his valves ere he trots in the same melodic class as Schmit." (*CPD*, Jul 19). An analytic *Sporting Life* added: "Bellowing and baseball are alliterative, though not necessarily synonymous terms." (Jul 22).

After the contest, Schmit was quoted commenting on his illustrious career. "All this warm atmosphere talk about minor league players being colts makes me giggle out of the corner of my mouth. Why, I have played with every bunch of minor league clubs, including the Alkali circuit in Arizona, the Gas Belt League, and the watermelon, in Georgia, when the vind fell off, and I guess I played in the Epworth League, whatever that is. I never kept a tab. But, here I am with the legits, as they call the Frohman actors. I'm in the big league and they call me a kid. If they looked me up in the Family Bible they would find I'm old enough to know." (*CPD*, Jul 19).

A bit strange was the Schmit reference to the "Epworth League." Did he know that this was a religious group in no way affiliated with baseball? (Phillips).

Dick Harley, ankle still on the mend, was seen working the turnstiles and visiting with friends from Georgetown University who had come to see him play.

Wed July 19

And so it fell out that the homeless tribe of Quinn tapped at the door of the Senators. And these same statesmen straightaway applied the pull-back action to the latch string; and the lookout at the portals spake unto Wise Guy Irwin: 'Here cometh the lobsters. Let's receive them as one Dewey greeted the demolishers of the hot tamale.' And the tribe of Irwin, as per cue from their sheik, went forth and contributed further woe unto the outcasts by compelling them the aforementioned troupers to osculate the dust of defeat. And so the Quinn tribe fell twice before the Senators yesterday. (*WP*, Jul 20).

With references to an American general in the Philippines war with the Spanish, the *Washington Post* began its column.

A crowd of three thousand gathered for the opener. Senators' manager Arthur Irwin started the "Lithe Caledonian" Dan McFarland against the Misfits' Jim Hughey (*CPD*, Jul 20). From the get-go, Hughey was a "lazy-don't care sort" and the Senators found his pitches ripe and juicy (*WES*, Jul 20). Washington led 1-0 after two innings. In the third frame with one out, Hughey walked and Tommy Dowd fouled to catcher Malachi Kittredge. Leftfielder Schmit was given a pass to first and Kittredge then committed a passed ball. Hughey ran to third but Kittredge's throw bopped him on the back. Hughey ran home. Schmit then scored on Quinn's single. The *Washington Post* called McFarland's performance in the inning "slightly tinged with saffron." (Jul 20). Cleveland led by 2-1. In the Senators' third, four runs resulted. During the proceedings, "Padden and Sullivan did a grand and lofty tumbling act. The Senators captain slid into third and upset Sullivan, who dropped the ball on the throw. Sullivan sat on Padden, but Kittredge, who was coaching, pulled him off and Capt. Dick scudded to the plate. It was a very ludicrous happening." (*CPD*, Jul 20). The Senators scored single tallies in the seventh and eighth off Hughey's slants and untimely errors by shortstop Harry Lochhead and the weary Ossee Schreckengost. Schreck had caught several games in succession due to Sugden's malaria. The Misfits made a gallant try to tie in the ninth inning. Sport McAllister, Tommy Tucker, Lochhead, and Schreck all singled for two runs. However, the rally fell short and the Misfits went down again, 7-4.

In between games pitcher and part-time outfielder Crazy Schmit philosophized with teammate Tommy Dowd on being a ballplayer. "Oh, but this barnstorming life with a big show in the big League is killing me. We go on at 2 p.m. and knock off about 4 p.m. with this club. I guess the union will put us on the scab-list for working overtime at the same salary. It's like Healy and Biglow's Medicine Show. In this troupe the leading heavy actor doubles in the band and makes a spiel to the Rubes before the show." (*WP*, Jul 20). Schmit actually fancied himself as the leading actor of the Misfits after only three weeks with the team. The Wanderers themselves were like a medicine show, treating their patients with pills of victory.

Game two was a real treat for Washington crowds more tuned to comic opera than pure baseball. Kid Carsey, who couldn't quite make a go with the Misfits or the racehorses, started for Washington. In his early days, Carsey pitched in the capital city and was considered a star. Crazy Schmit started for the Misfits. In his early days he was also considered a star, though his fan club included only one member- himself. On this day though, Schmit pitched well over his head, grabbing the headlines and the attention of the Washington faithful.

The game remained scoreless after four innings, with Carsey palming off his slow ball and Schmit off his curve (*CPD*, Jul 20). In the fifth Cleveland scored twice on a McAllister three base hit, Jimmy Slagle's misplay of Tucker's fly ball, and a Lochhead single. The Senators tried all kinds of tactics to score off Schmit like waiting for walks, bunting, and sacrificing, but nothing worked. Schmit handcuffed the Washingtonians on two hits through seven innings. "His grotesque antics, eccentric coaching, and witty sallies won the favor of the fans and he was constantly cheered even when it looked like he had the home team badly beaten." (*CPD*, Jul 20). "There is considerable shrewdness behind Schmit's funny tactics. He creates the impression that he is easy to hit, makes the batter feel good with a little praise, and then hugs himself when the ball is hit to the outfield for an easy out or a strikeout is recorded." (*WES*, Jul 20). In the eighth inning, though, Schmit's "heart or arm flickered and he commenced to pitching a slow, straight ball." (*CPD*, Jul 20). Schmit's opposite number, Kid Carsey, banged one off Lochhead's mitt. Five hits and a base on balls followed to the tune of six runs. The Senators had caught up with the mercurial German wunderkind. Schmit, despite one of his best major league efforts, was a 6-2 loser. He took the defeat to heart and slunk back to the hotel. The Misfits were 14-66.

After the games, the *Washington Post* was so enamored with Schmit's Gemütlichkeit personality that they printed this story: (Jul 20).

'This boy Schmit is one of the most original characters that ever broke into the League,' says Joe Quinn. 'He's so full of ginger that it oozes out at the pores. He's the first man out to practice in the morning and the first to dress on the trip. In St. Louis a few weeks ago he was out with Burkett in the morning practicing batting. 'Just give me a few tips on binging out those singles, Jesse, and I will be one of the star aces in Nick Young's deck next fall.' That was Schmit's request of Jesse. When we were warming up for our first game in Baltimore, Schmit asked McGraw for tips in batting, and Mac, who is somewhat on the string, gave the boy the information, coupled with a few hints about holding the bat. After the twin bill in Baltimore on Monday, Schmit confided to me that he had mastered Burkett and McGraw's style of batting. Dick Harley's leg was bad, and so I told Schmit he had to play in Washington. But, I advised him not to take Burkett's or McGraw's tips, or he might get mixed.

Thur July 20   Thursday was Ladies Day at Washington's National Park. Of the 1800 or so in attendance, about one quarter of that figure was the fair sex. The girls were dressed head to toe in resplendence and waved their fans coyly at the two handsome attractions on the pitching mound. Tiny righthanded veteran

Augustus Weyhing went for the Senators. Muscular blond Charlie Knepper twirled for the Clevelands. The ladies may have preferred Knepper, but home towner Cannonball Weyhing was in top form.

The game was scoreless in the fifth. Knepper was "propelling the ball to backstop Schreckengost at a Rusie rate of speed." (*WP*, Jul 21). With the Misfits' batting, Weyhing's support crumbled a bit behind him. The usually sure-handed Jimmy Slagle muffed Tommy Tucker's fly. Schreck singled and Knepper's grounder was botched by shortstop Dick Padden. With one out, Tommy Dowd strode in to try to break the deadlock. Weyhing, who some said would pitch anywhere or anytime, struck out Tommy and got Dick Harley to ground to first base. It remained scoreless until the Senators seventh. Fist baseman Dan McGann led off with a single. Second baseman Frank Bonner drew a walk. Outfielder Buck Freeman sacrificed and Padden tripled in two runs. Third baseman Charlie Atherton's long outfield fly plated Padden. The Senators led 3-0. Cleveland continued scoreless as Weyhing "toyed, flirted, dallied, monkeyed, and coquetted with the Quinn flock of Exiles." (*WP*, Jul 21). In the eighth, the Washingtonians scored once more as Bonner singled in Jack O'Brien. The doomed Knepper, masterful himself with errorless support, was simply outpitched by a veteran performer. The contest ended 4-0 for Washington. In all, Weyhing's curves and drops allowed only five hits. He struck out six Spiders hitters who "contracted asthma and breathed like winded porpoises." (*WP*, Jul 21). The ladies had their hero and it was Weyhing.

Afterwards, umpire Arlie Latham received praise from Senator's manager Arthur Irwin. "When ball players agree unanimously, and agree that an umpire such as Latham is competent, then I will doff my hat to him." (*WP*, Jul 21).

Fri July 21   The Senators-Misfits marathon series concluded with another doubleheader on Friday. Dick Harley had suggested to manager Joe Quinn that he give a 30-year old Washington native a chance to pitch for Cleveland. Quinn, realizing his Misfits were short on quality arms, took Harley's advice on the condition that a contract for the new man be negotiated afterwards. The new man was Harry Colliflower, wiry of build and medium in height and weight. Colliflower was a friend of Harley's and an amateur with the Eastern Athletic Club.

Game one started with Win Mercer on the rubber for the Senators against Colliflower, who was making his major league debut. The first inning was scoreless. In the second, the Senators' Buck Freeman was hit by a pitch and later scored on catcher Duncan's sacrifice. Pitcher Mercer helped himself with a base hit just past a diving Quinn for two more tallies. It was 3-0 Washington and looking rather easy for the Senators. Colliflower's fan club was undaunted and somehow, the Misfits started pecking away at Mercer, who was being "freely dallied with." (*WP*, Jul 22). They scored single runs in the 3rd, 4th, 5th, and 6th innings and another in the eighth. In each of those frames, the Misfits' leadoff hitter contributed an extra base blow. Tommy's Dowd and Tucker doubled, Quinn and Schreck tripled, and even Colliflower contributed with a two-baser of his own. Quinn's smash to deep rightfield provided a few hi-jinks for third baseman Charlie Atherton, Quinn, and the Washington ball cranks. "The ball was returned to Atherton and deflected off Quinn. Athy transformed Quinn into a cushion, and Joe, as a reward for serving as seating capacity for the burly third baseman, was permitted to score by umpire Latham." (*WP*, Jul 22). It was another slap in the face to the maligned third baseman who had been roasted all series for his infield deficiencies. In defense of Atherton, he was nursing a sore hand and a wrenched ankle (*WES*, Jul 22). Colliflower, more pitcher than vegetable, shut down the Washingtonians after the second. He did it with major league control, speed, and the "requisite nerve" required of successful pitchers (*WP*, Jul 22). In all, Colliflower surrendered only six hits. The Senators did their part, performing like a "band of headless players." (*WES*, Jul 22). Manager Irwin was sick at home with a cold. The jubilant Misfits were 5-3 winners.

The weather was clear and warm for game two. The Cleveland spirits were soaring after their opening game victory. However, Frank Bates took the mound for the Wanderers and soon all optimism was lost. Bates was opposed by Bill Dinneen, who had the misfortune of losing to the Misfits on Tuesday. In the first inning, leftfielder Jack O'Brien hit safely and Bates bopped first baseman Dan McGann with an errant toss. With two out, the leading home run hitter in the National League stepped to the plate. Buck Freeman "laced a terrific liner to deep left, the ball bounding behind the red board near the hospital fence." (*WP*, Jul 22). The blast gave Freeman a dozen homers on the season. Early on, it was 3-0 Washington. The game ended there. The Misfits played listless ball and the Senators maintained their lead due to the fine twirling of Dinneen and his battery compliment Malachi Kittredge. The final was 5-3. The only bright spot for the visitors was the fielding excellence of player-manager Quinn and the coaching of the insouciant Mr. Schmit, who kept the Washington crowd in stitches with his antics and funny remarks.

Afterwards, Quinn and Colliflower had a misunderstanding over the money offered the new pitcher. Colliflower was soon off the team. The rest of the players sided with Colliflower. The *Plain Dealer* reported that "a promising amateur gets away with a good game and then he gets away from the team." (Jul 22).

Another newspaper, the *Cleveland Press*, commented on the contract of pitcher Bates. "It would be interesting to note what sort of contract exists between pitcher (?) Bates and Brother Stan's team. Although, the ex-Daytonite succeeds in turning almost every game into which he participates into a howling farce, he is sent into the box in his turn, only to bring ridicule upon his unfortunate associates." (Jul 22).

Wed July 26 After their exasperating series in Washington, the Misfits traveled to Atlantic City, New Jersey for three exhibitions. They won two of the three games against an amateur team representing the city; 10-3 on Saturday and 6-5 on Monday. Tuesday's game was lost 12-8 with Crazy Schmit performing before New Jersey fans not quite sure how to react. Unfortunately, neither Nick Young nor the National League would recognize the victories in the standings. Wednesday was a day of rest for the weary Clevelands, their scheduled being juggled to the transfer of games. Next stop: Baltimore.

Thur July 27 With all their recent traveling, the Misfits season was beginning to resemble the French Foreign Legion. However, unlike the Legionaries, the Clevelanders rolled over dead in battle. The *Baltimore Sun* called it a "Slaughter of the Innocents." (Jul 28).

The first game pitted Harry Howell for the home boys against Charlie Knepper. Howell, feeling a bit sick, pitched like it, and after giving up three runs in the fifth inning, McGraw replaced him. The Baltimore crowd supported Howell's plight and urged their manager to keep the pitcher in the game. But, McGraw, always a man who considered himself to have the last word, stuck to his decision. With the bases loaded, Joe McGinnity appeared and shut down the rally. On occasion, McGinnity would toss the ball below his hip to fool batters (Thorn 6). It was the move of the game. Cleveland manager Joe Quinn had no reason to replace Knepper. When he wasn't walking the sharp-eyed McGraw, Charlie offered up fat peaches for the Baltimoreans to bash around the ball yard. The contest was for the Birds at 8-5. The only highlight for the Spiders was the play of catcher Joe Sugden. Joe shook off the cobwebs of inactivity and punched three doubles.

The second game was no closer in the final tally, but the Misfits did actually lead 3-2 into the sixth inning. Ex-Misfit Still Bill Hill did the twirling for the McGraw Men while Quinn resorted to his newcomer, lefthander Harry Colliflower. Quinn and Colliflower had since patched up their contract differences. The Birds had single tallies in the first and second while Hill checked his old teammates in the shutout hotel. In the fifth though, some of the Hill magic dissipated. With two out and two on, Tommy Dowd's grounder was scooped by shortstop George Magoon. Magoon's throw to first was wild. Dowd was safe but Hill had cleverly backed up the play behind first. Dowd, unaware of Hill, raced toward second. Hill retrieved the ball and threw to second to get the sliding Dowd. But, somehow, either the Baltimore fielders were napping or Hill's toss was bad, or both. The ball dribbled into left field and before the Birds could recover, all the Misfits had scored. With the visitors holding a 3-2 lead, the Orioles batted in the sixth against Colliflower. Harry was no stranger to Baltimore as he had pitched there with the Washington Y.M.C.A. team. In the sixth inning, though, Harry might as well have been a stranger. Colliflower was as wild as the vegetable in his name. He walked three, hit one, and surrendered three solid hits. Five runs scored and the inning wasn't over until fireball McGraw got himself called out at third. As per usual, McGraw raised a terrible fuss and for his trouble, umpire Snyder removed him from the game. In the eighth, Baltimore got to Colliflower for four singles and a balk and two more tallies resulted. When it ended 9-4, there were "two more Cleveland scalps dangling from the Oriole wigwam." (*CPD*, Jul 28).

Fri July 28   As they had the day previous, the Misfits and Orioles played another doubleheader at Union Park. In earlier days of Baltimore baseball, fans could make their way across the street to an amusement park where they could wine, dine, and listen to band concerts (Lowry 34). With the Misfits not exactly providing a star attraction, only one thousand showed up for two scoops of baseball ice cream.

In the opener, the pitching matchup provided much interest. Righthander Frank Kitson tossed for the Orioles. He had already shut out the Misfits twice on the season. Jim Hughey was on the mound for the Spiders. "Coldwater" had shocked McGraw's Baltimores twice with close victories. Something had to give. It did. The something was Cleveland. Their downfall for this game actually occurred after Hughey's victory over the Orioles two weeks previous. Hughey commented then that the Orioles did not bunt on him when he had a sore leg. But, Orioles skipper John McGraw, with his ears perked, took advantage of Hughey's failings and bunted him silly. With his fielders providing five errors, including three by catcher Schreckengost, Hughey was doomed. Schreck was charged with a passed ball and two poor throws to second base. Kitson, on the other hand, used his dominant curve ball against the lowly Clevelands. Schreck and manager Quinn took out their frustrations at bat, each stroking three hits off Kitson but the "others he had on his list." (*BTS*, Jul 29). The Orioles played with "dash and brilliance not only in the field but on the bases and at bat, and their team work was brainy and clever in every way." (*BTS*, Jul 29). It was an easy 6-1 crab cake walk for Baltimore.

For game two, McGraw pitched Harry Howell, who didn't really get a chance the day before. The Spiders trotted out Frederick Schmit. Howell, prone to tossing a "saliva sling," seemed a bit punch drunk in the first and gave the Misfits an early lead. Schmit's first inning was a bit worse. The result was five singles, two bases on balls, a hit batsman, and five runs. After the inning a frustrated Schmit yelled at McGraw, "You fellows don't play ball; there is too much bunteration and such foolishness with you." (*BTS*, Jul 29). The Misfits scored another in the third and Baltimore answered with three more in their half. This time Schmit let pitcher Howell and newcomer Chick Fultz bash three-basers. With the score 8-2, the teams played two more innings to make it an official five inning game. Then, the contest was called so both teams could hustle off the field to catch trains. In all, the Orioles swiped six bases. Howell redeemed himself by giving up only two hits.

Sat July 29   From Baltimore, the Misfits' express train snaked its way across Maryland, West Virginia, Ohio, and Kentucky. It stopped in the horse racing city of Louisville where Quinn's boys played a doubleheader against Clarke's Colonels.

For game one, the "Wanderers presented a giant named Knepper to toss the balls." (*LCJ*, Jul 31). The Colonels sent in righthanded veteran Bert Cunningham. Cunningham had the distinction of being the losing pitcher in Cleveland's first victory of the season. Knepper had the distinction of being the losing pitcher in almost all his games. With a big Kentucky crowd of 9624 filling every nook and cranny in the park, the contest began (*LCJ*, Jul 31). From the beginning, it was another Cleveland disaster. The fielding behind Knepper was atrocious. A case in point was Harry Lochhead, who botched two plays from his shortstop position. Once Lochhead booted a grounder. Another time he threw far over a leaping Tom Tucker at first base. The miscues came in succession. Catcher Ossee Schreckengost added to Knepper's misery by committing an error. However, it wasn't only Cleveland's fielding that did them in. The Colonels put on a monstrous power hitting display. In the first inning, rightfielder Honus Wagner poked a ball over the center field fence and duplicated the feat in the fourth by driving one over Tommy Dowd's head. Knepper was probably too aware of John McGraw's advice on how to throw to Wagner, "Just pitch the ball and pray." (Schlossberg 7). Centerfielder Dummy Hoy also wowed the crowd when he scored on a home run in the fifth inning. Meanwhile, Cunningham, with the help of ex-Misfit battery mate Chief Zimmer, puzzled the Cleveland batters and "pitched one of his old time games." (*LCJ*, Jul 31). It ended 9-2.

After the game, Ossee Schreckengost was told to pack his bags and catch the first train for St. Louis. Owner Frank Robison's team was in need of a backstop due to an injury. What Robison's team wanted, Robison got. Did it matter that Cleveland served as a major league farm team? Did it matter that they had only one other catcher named Joe Sugden? Schreckengost performed capably for the Misfits, hitting .313 in 43 games and providing a much-needed spark when he arrived from St. Louis. However, even the young and enthusiastic Schreck must have been bewildered by the Clevelands.

The second game of the doubleheader proved the old baseball maxim that anything can happen. "Anything," along with his fickle partner "Everything" did precisely that. Joe Quinn gave Harry Colliflower another chance to pitch. Fred Clarke gave the ball to lefthander Pete Dowling. Dowling had already defeated the Misfits twice on the season. The first time was in Louisville by 11-2. The next time Dowling did it was in ancient times when Cleveland played home games. Dowling was the Louisville pitcher of record when prankster Malachi Kittredge made his controversial running dash from second base by way of the League Park infield.

It started off tamely enough. In the second inning with Louisville batting, a Lochhead error and catcher Mike Powers' "corking drive to left field" led to a run (*LCJ*, Jul 31). Cleveland threatened in the third. Colliflower singled and Dowling walked Dick Harley. When Sullivan singled, Honus Wagner promptly threw Colliflower out at home plate. Louisville then turned a swift double play and the inning was over. After three innings, the score was 1-0. Then came a potent mixture of offensive firepower or horrendous pitching, whichever one prefers, and forgettable fielding. In the fourth for Cleveland, Tucker singled and Lochhead and Sugden were given free passes on the wildness of Dowling. With the bases loaded, Colliflower hit safely to drive in two runs and put his club in the lead. Tommy Dowd failed Colliflower and grounded into a double play to second baseman "Little All Right" Claude Ritchey. In Louisville's fourth inning, there occurred an almost comedic act of pitching and fielding blunders. A barrage of hits, walks, and hit batters muddied up the box score and Colliflower's pitching record. The Misfits conspired for several errors: Harley's misplay of Ritchey's single, Colliflower's bad throw on an attempted pickoff play, Tucker's fumble of a Tommy Leach grounder, Harley's muff of Mike Kelley's fly ball, etc. A home run by manager Clarke added to Cleveland's performance. Seven runs tallied. It was 8-2 Louisville. In the Colonels' sixth inning, after two were out, eight more runs scored off a succession of walks, singles, and Dummy Hoy's second home run on the day. By this time, Misfits' manager Joe Quinn might have been planning his own funeral, or at the very least the demise of one Harry Colliflower. The score stood at 16-2 after seven innings. In the eighth, Dowling's arm began to stiffen after spending so much of his afternoon on the bench watching his team parade around the bases. Two Misfit runs scored and with the chalkboard reading 16-4, a humiliated Dowling was relieved by manager Fred Clarke. Dowling's replacement was the seldom-seen Roy Brashear. Coming in with the bases loaded, Brashear promptly allowed Cleveland to hope for a miracle rally. Before the inning had ended, ten runs had crossed the plate with the "crowd jeering continually." (*LCJ*, Jul 31).

The only real Louisville highlight in the inning was Clarke's catch of a Colliflower liner. "Colliflower hit a low line fly over third. Clarke was after it like a flash. He ran about twenty yards and seeing that he could not reach the ball, he jumped horizontally about ten feet. He caught the ball as his fingers touched the grass, and rolled over and over, springing up with the white sphere in his hands. It was an electrifying catch- one of the greatest ever made by any player since baseball began." (*LCJ*, Jul 31). Finally, Brashear was replaced by Deacon Phillippe. Quinn made Colliflower and rightfielder Sport McAllister switch positions. After Clarke's catch, the excitement of the game ebbed and Cleveland was again a loser 16-13, despite outhitting their rivals 21-13. Both the *Cleveland Plain Dealer* and the *Louisville Courier-Journal* called the contest a "farce." (Jul 31). For his efforts, Brashear was rewarded with his ten days notice of release.

Back in Cleveland, the *Plain Dealer* reported on an amateur baseball contest between Pierce and Ottawa. The final score was 38-1. Perhaps, the Misfits could take solace in the fact that they were not the team with the 1.

The *Courier-Journal* also took time to print a statement from National League President Nick Young on the financial state of the league (Jul 31). The statement outlined all of the clubs in the league and speculated on how much profits they were sure to make by season's end. President Young mentioned that Cleveland was the only team not turning a healthy profit.

Sun Jul 30   Sunday and Monday were days of travel and rest for the ragged baseball minstrels from Cleveland. The relaxation was well deserved. The Misfits had just finished playing eight doubleheaders in sixteen days and eleven in the month of July. Almost all of the twin bills were due to the transfer of games, many of which were caught by Ossee Schreckengost, since removed to St. Louis. Cleveland's current loss string reached seven.

Of course, no other teams in the National League had to face such a makeshift, backbreaking schedule. But, then again, with the convenient exception of St. Louis, no other teams had the Robison Brothers as owners. *Sporting Life* reported that the transfer of games had made many fans distrustful of the sport of baseball and that magnates observed only the machinations of politics and greed (Jul 22).

"The Daily Downfall."

Tue Aug 1   In Philadelphia, the Phils and baseball's version of train hobos, played two on Tuesday. The *Cleveland Plain Dealer* newspaper, fed up with so many losses, began their lead article by reporting that $6800 was the gate receipt (Aug 2). Perhaps, it was a sign that attendance figures, wherever the Exiles went, were critical to the team's financial stability. This stability was already extremely tenuous due to the home game transfer plan, but the Brothers Robison believed it was the only way to recoup monetary losses.

Game one began in front of 6778 weekday ball cranks at Baker Bowl. Righthander Chick Fraser was slated for the locals. Jim Hughey took his regular turn for the Wanderers. In a previous start, Hughey had been battered 7-1 by Philadelphia.

The Misfits started fast. Tommy Dowd singled and stole second. With one out, manager Quinn hit to shortstop Monte Cross who caught Dowd in a rundown from second base. Dowd foolishly ran out of the baseline to avoid being tagged and was called out. On the play, Quinn alertly went to second base and scored on Suter Sullivan's single to center. In the second inning, the Misfits scratched for another run. Harry Lochhead was plunked by a wild Fraser toss and he too, stole second. Catcher Sugden's infield single moved Lochhead to third and when Dowd grounded out, Lochhead ran home for the second tally. There was no further noise until the fourth. Jim Hughey's pitching was speedy and accurate. In the Philly fourth, Hughey became unraveled. Phils' center fielder rookie sensation Roy Thomas walked and batting star Ed Delahanty singled. Elmer Flick hit a bouncer back to Hughey, but the Misfit pitcher exposed his fielding weakness and a throw to third base was wide of Sullivan. The bases were loaded. A ground out and a single tied the game at 2-2 for Monte Cross. He smacked a double and three runs scored. The inning ended with the home boys in front by 5-2. In the fifth, Duff Cooley smashed one over the right field fence. Misfits in arrears 6-2. The Phillies added another in the next inning thanks to a wild throw by Lochhead. But, the Misfits weren't quite finished with Fraser. Dowd singled, stole second, and scored on a Dick Harley hit to make it 7-3 in the seventh. In the eighth, Sugden led off with another cheap single and was forced at second by Hughey. Tommy Dowd stroked his fourth hit of the game. Harley was hit by a pitch and Sullivan's hot smash found a hole through the wicket that was third baseman Bill Lauder's legs. The Misfits had closed to 7-5. But, Fraser stayed on and shut the visitors down for the rest of the game. Yet another late inning rally had fallen short. The Exiles were losers once again. Recalled the *Plain Dealer*, "a pretty game to witness, bristling with clever fielding and hard hitting." (Aug 2). The Misfits had outhit their rivals by 11-7 but Philadelphia possessed the more opportune bats and Fraser pitched better in tight places.

The second affair was decided early on. Crazy Schmit was in the spotlight for the team representing Cleveland. The home pitcher was lefthander Bill Magee. The first inning was scoreless but the human comedy began in inning two. With the Misfits hitting, Sport McAllister bounced a routine grounder to M. Cross. He kicked it for an error. Tommy Tucker's solid drive put two Clevelanders aboard. Then, Lochhead lifted a soft outfield fly that somehow eluded Delahanty. First Delahanty caught he ball and then he dropped it. The Misfits led 1-0. Joe Sugden then topped a ball in front of home plate but catcher "McFarland made a mess of Sugden's little hit." (*CPD*, Aug 2). Pitcher Magee was bewildered. Four Misfits had come to the plate and three were safe on errors. The next batter Schmit must have figured he'd get on base too if he could hit a fair ball. However, Magee struck out the dynamic pitcher. Dowd then bashed a ball to center field to score Tucker and Lochhead but the wild throw in by Thomas enabled Dowd to take another base. Error number four. The Misfits led 3-0. Harley singled to score Sugden and Dowd but another wild throw from the outfield put Harley on second. The Phils had now made five errors in the inning and trailed 5-0. Quinn took advantage of the misfortunes of the Quakers and singled to score Harley. Six to zero. A fuming Magee was mercifully told to take a seat on the bench, Into the game came 28-year old rookie Strawberry Bill Bernhard, who proceeded to make the Misfits look as if they were hitting strawberries. No further runs scored for Cleveland. Schmit, meanwhile, twirled a "tantalizing slow curve ball" that had the Phillies flailing at air (*CPD*, Aug 2). He held the Quakers to two runs with help from sharp fielding by his infield of Tucker, Quinn, Lochhead, and Sullivan and the marvelous play of Tommy Dowd in center. In all, the crafty German struck out four Phillies, and seemed to revel in his performance with his "inane smile and unpardonable vanities." (*CPD*, Aug 2). It was nice to see the Misfits on the positive end of a final score. Schmit and the Clevelands were victorious 6-2.

As any loss to Cleveland was a major embarrassment for any team, the *Philadelphia Enquirer* called it "stupid work all 'round." The newspaper also made reference to the war in the Philippines; "Those Phillies of ours will never have their manly breasts decorated with medals on the strength of the game they put up against Cleveland yesterday." But, it was the following comment that really showed the Phillies as buffoons. "If Delahanty had caught Lochhead's fly, and if McFarland had handled Sugden's little drop in front of the plate, the inning would have ended for one run. That analogy is about as logical as that of a youngster who declared that if his aunt had worn trousers she'd be his uncle." (Aug 2).

The editor of the Philadelphia-based *Sporting Life*, Frances C. Richter, commented on the plight of the Clevelands, wondering how they could lose so many games to second division teams. Said Richter, "Without a home or manager; without newspaper support; without rooters; and without stimulus of incentive, the Cleveland team nevertheless strives hard. This in itself is quite an eloquent testimonial to the absolute honesty of the average ball player, of the interest he takes in his work, no matter how depressing or even repellent the conditions." (Aug 12).

Wed Aug 2　　What began as a scheduled doubleheader turned into an abbreviated single game. The reason for the short game was the cold and rainy conditions that postponed the game a few minutes.

Billy Shettsline's Philadelphias pitched righthander Albert Lewis Orth, known for his uncanny twirling and strange nickname, "The Curveless Wonder." Orth's nickname may have come from his ability to throw spitballs (Porter). The Misfits could counter only with the undistinguished Charlie Knepper; he of the Adonis build. From the beginning, the contest played out an all too familiar pattern. The home team was staked to a 5-1 lead after three innings because the Phillies applied their bats to Knepper's curves and straightened them out (*PE, Aug 3*). The Misfits were not so lucky against the man who tossed up spitters, and went out weakly. In the fourth inning, though, the Misfits put up a batting rally that befuddled Orth and tied the game. Tommy Dowd bopped a double and slow-footed catcher Joe Sugden stole second to lead a four run outburst. Phillie fielders didn't exactly help Orth as both shortstop Monte Cross and centerfielder Roy Thomas committed errors. It was 5-5 after four innings. Pitcher Orth gave way to Wiley Piatt, who set the Misfits down in the fifth. Then came the predictability of a counter batting rally from the Quakers. The unfortunate Knepper was pounded for three doubles, made an error on a pickoff attempt, and allowed three runs to score. The inning ended when Red Owens was hit by a batted ball while running the bases. The Exiles tried a comeback in the sixth. Tommy Tucker walked and was wild-pitched to second. Harry Lochhead struck out. Then, at precisely 3:30 p.m., umpire Gaffney "got himself disliked" and called the game due to darkness (*PE, Aug 3*). Phils 8, Misfits 5. Many irate Philly fans stood and howled at the umpire's decision, then rushed towards the gates to demand rain checks (*PE, Aug 3*). There was no such criticism of Gaffney's decision by the team it hurt the most. Joe Quinn and his Wanderers were resigned to their fate for the seventy-sixth time of the season.

From the Office of the Cleveland Base Ball Club in the Cuyahoga building in downtown Cleveland came a sensational announcement. The Misfits would play two series against New York and Boston- in Cleveland! The games would begin August 24. Perhaps, the Misfits would get a reprieve from their map hopping (*CP*, Aug 2). Both the Boston and New York clubs would not consent to the transfer of games scheduled to be played in Cleveland. Elmer E. Bates of *Sporting Life* said, "We shall have six more peeks at Joe Quinn's kicked and cuffed-about team of barnstormers." (Aug 12). President Soden of Boston was taking a "manly stand against this tampering of the schedule, this switching of games hither, thither and yon, wherever there is a dollar in sight." (*SL*, Aug 12).

Thur Aug 3   More than five thousand Philadelphia ball cranks showed up at Baker Bowl for Thursday's doubleheader. In the opener Harry Colliflower dueled Wiley Piatt even for six innings. Then the Misfits hurler crumbled under the strain. The 1-1 tie became an easy 6-1 Quaker victory as they scored three times in the seventh and twice in the eighth. Mr. Colliflower helped the home boys along with two errors. The late Philadelphia hitting barrage was led by Ed Delahanty and Monte Cross. "Iron Man" lefthander Piatt was supported very capably by the fielding exploits of Roy Thomas in centerfield and Delahanty, who gunned down a Clevelander at home plate with a strong throw from left field.

For game two, Joe Quinn sent the beleaguered Jim Hughey to the mound against Philadelphia righthander Red Donahue. Again, the Misfits' bats fell silent, whispering only five hits off the slants of Donahue. The veteran Donahue was masterful and with Monte Cross playing another brilliant game at shortstop and Delahanty in left field, the Phillies were winners 4-0 in a snore festival. Hughey pitched good enough to win and the Misfits were sterling on the diamond, catching all flies. But, a double and a triple by the Phillies' Elmer Flick and five stolen bases did in Smiling Jim.

The *Philadelphia Enquirer* bit hard into the "Wandering Willies," when actually the only Willie (Sudhoff) the Misfits did have wandered off to St.Louis some time ago (Aug 4):

Ye Rooter sought the bosom of the family- or any other old resting place that may have been his lot- with one of those old tired feelings about six and a half bells yesterday eve. When mamma berated him he denied it was the wine which made him weary, and explained that a brace of bum ball games he had been up against.

There were 5508 of these unfortunate babies. They had sat through a four hour session at the Philadelphia ball yard and seen the local lords waltz away with a pair of Cleveland scalps in about as uninteresting games as you can imagine. One run in eighteen innings- yes, that was the Wanderers record. No wonder they have been kicked out of home. What a pity it is that we got the dose. As an old timer sat and pondered on the errors of things in general he longed for a return to League vs. Association days. Certainly, tail-enders of minor league caliber like the Clevelands do the game no good.

Father Shettsline did his prettiest yesterday by gluing his two prettiest to the slab. His managerial syringe injected Piatt into the first game and Donahue into the second. Now, this is the best pair the Phillies have to draw to, and when they are stacked up against Rubes, as was the case yesterday, they are pretty nearly sure to cop the pot.

While the *Philadelphia Enquirer* suffered no lack of words on the visitors, all the *Plain Dealer* could say about their efforts was that the boys from Cleveland were playing "clean and good ball." (Aug 4). The Misfits generally acted as gentleman, except for the occasional offensive coaching of bellowing Tommy Tucker. But, Cleveland's relative attention to manners may have been one of their weak points in the ruffian-like sport of baseball.

After the game, the *Plain Dealer* reported another player move. Rookie outfielder and ex-Saginaw and Grand Rapids player Charlie "Eagle Eye" Hemphill was released from St. Louis to Cleveland after a brief stay with the Tebeau Men. The left-handed batting Hemphill was to replace Sport McAllister in right field, sending the latter in back of the plate to occasionally spell Joe Sugden. The Hemphill acquisition was not without controversy. St. Louis manager Tebeau had to order the young outfielder to join Cleveland or quit baseball. Of Hemphill, the *Plain Dealer* remarked that he was a "fast fellow, a good hitter, and a clever fielder. His tendency towards physical and mental inertia is his only drawback." (Aug 4).

The news prompted more rumors about high-salaried Tommy Dowd's status with the Ohio team. It was reported that Dowd could be sold or traded "as the Cleveland club is not drawing enough people to pay for a bean stew." (*CPD*, Aug 4).

Louis Sockalexis was back playing ball for Waterbury of the Connecticut State League, still trying to reform his chronic alcoholism.

Sat Aug 5 On Friday the Wanderers took their show from Philadelphia to the Windy City. They had spent the last month on the road. Pundits would agree that the Misfits had traveled more miles than scientists from the fledgling National Geographic Society.

Saturday's festivities were to involve two games but due to a sodden field, only one contest was played. A sparse crowd of 2700 was on hand in Chicago's West End Grounds. Righthander Nixey Callahan started for Tom Burns' Chicago Cubs. Joe Quinn's Misfits relied on Charlie Knepper. Like Sudhoff, Knepper was always being touted as a future star, providing he play for a stronger team. There were reports that Knepper was on his way to St. Lou. "Well, if Patsy wants the others, all he need do is ask for them." (*CP*, Aug 5).

There was no scoring in the first two and one half innings. Then, in the third frame, Chicago catcher Frank Chance fouled to Sugden. Pitcher Callahan hit a single in front of rightfielder McAllister. "While Knepper was holding the ball in a sort of trance, Callahan made a dash for second. He was there before the Clevelands knew what happened and not a move was made to prevent the steal. To make the discomfiture of the Cleveland battery more complete, Callahan stole third on the next play." (*CPD*, Aug 6). It was a shocking occurrence to have the opposing pitcher steal two bases, but Cleveland seemed used to such behavior:

Knepper, disconcerted by the dashing work of Callahan, grew wild, and gave both Ryan and Green bases on balls, (umpire) O'Day miscalling at least one ball to Ryan. Wolverton followed with a line drive over second, and Callahan walked home, but Ryan, in turning third, fell in the mud, and when Dowd picked up the ball, Ryan was wallowing in the muck and Green was perched on third. Dowd fired the sphere to the plate, but Sugden backed away, and before he could get back to the plate, Ryan had scored. Everitt smashed a hit past Tucker, and two more tallies counted, settling the game for all time. (*CT*, Aug 6).

It was 4-0. Despite Knepper's performance the rest of the way, the score held up. Pitching Callahan was a "lurid jest, for his shoulder was so sore he merely lobbed the ball in and let them hit it." (*SL*, Aug 12). With the Misfits lacking inclination to hit and Chicago fielders intent on catching the ball, no runs resulted. The sleeping Misfit bats had produced only one run in their last 27 innings.

With the exception of the mildly exciting third inning and Tommy Tucker's vocal ministrations, the game was rather dull. However, during the course of the action, police arrested a bleacherite who failed to return a foul ball (*CT*, Aug 6).

In light of the recent misfortunes of the Misfits, the *Cleveland Press* reported, "The wonder is not that Joe Quinn's team has won only 16 games, but that a club that has played second-fiddle to another should have won any games at all." (Aug 5).

Sun Aug 6   Much unlike Saturday's mundane affair, the Sunday baseball doubleheader in Chicago saw a huge gathering of 14,000. People had come from all around the Windy City and environs. Once they had settled into their seats, all would agree, it was a day of wondrous sport.

Joe Quinn sent Chicago native Crazy Schmit to the mound for the Misfits. Schmit was in even higher spirits than usual after his domination of the Phillies on August 1. Tom Burns countered with righthander Bill Phyle, whose season record was so bad, he was "working on probation." (*CPD*, Aug 7). With this kind of matchup, the paying customers expected slugging and that is what they got.

There was no run producing in the first frame but in the second Cleveland went to work. Rightfielder Sport McAllister singled. Phyle became wild and walked first baseman Tommy Tucker and shortstop Harry Lochhead. The bases were loaded for overworked catcher Joe Sugden. Joe placed a Phyle pitch along the left field line for a double and two runs scored. Phyle hit mound opponent Schmit and the grinning German took his base. Leftfielder Harley poked a double and two more scored. It was 4-0 for the Misfits. Quinn singled in Harley for number five. In the third, Cleveland tallied three more times on scratch hits. It was 8-0 for the Wanderers. In the Chicago half, a solo run was made but after three it was 8-1 against Chicago. Irate Cubs' fans fussed and fumed and marveled over the pitching of the 31-year old Schmit.

But the Cubs didn't just surrender to the curveballing Schmit. They pecked away with one score in the fifth and three in the sixth inning. More runs would have scored save for two key Cleveland fielding gems. Outfielder Danny Green was caught at home on a double steal. Tucker made a brilliant stop and pretty toss to Schmit covering first to get shortstop Topsy Magoon. At the end of six innings, Phyle had settled down. The score was 8-5 Cleveland.

Phyle got sloppy again, and the Misfits added one in the seventh. In the Cleveland eighth, Harry Lochhead and Sugden singled. Lithe Harry then swiped third base. Another Harry, third baseman Wolverton of Chicago, pushed Lochhead in the dirt in a roughhouse tactic, but umpire Smith ruled Lochhead safe. Crazy Schmit bounced into a double play but an alert Lochhead scored the tenth run.

It was 10-6 Cleveland as the Cubs came to bat in the dramatic ninth inning. First baseman Bill Everitt singled. When lusty outfielder Sam Mertes did likewise, "cheers of the crowd began to break in waves over the West Side." (*CT*, Aug 7). Magoon then lined out to Lochhead, who threw to first base in an attempt to double off Mertes. Tucker had apparently beaten Mertes to the bag, but umpire Smith saw differently and ruled safe. Smith was standing near third base when he made the call. Not quite in agreement with Smith, "Tucker strode across the diamond, grabbed the umpire, and crazily shoved him about while all the Cleveland players flocked around and joined in the kick." (*Chicago Record*, Aug 7). All the while, Tucker was using his famous foghorn and screamed at Smith like a spoiled baby. Perhaps Smith couldn't hear Tucker amidst the din but he politely told the rambunctious first baseman to watch the rest of the game from the bench. McAllister came in from right field to man first base and newcomer Hemphill was inserted into the outfield. Schmit threw three wide ones to second baseman Jim Conner but Conner awkwardly interfered with catcher Sugden's movements behind home plate and was declared out by umpire

Hank O'Day. Fans at the Chicago ball yard seethed at O'Day's unusual call. Two men were out and Schmit needed one more for the victory. In his excitement, Schmit walked catcher Tim Donahue. With the bases loaded, Cubs' manager Tom Burns called on hard-hitting pitcher Jack Taylor to bat for Phyle. Taylor singled in two runs and the score was 10-8. Unnerved, Schmit pitched a bit too delicately to Jimmy Ryan and walked him. The bases were loaded again for the next hitter, Danny Green. With the anxious mob now circling about the field, Green walked to force in another run (*CT*, Aug 7). It was 10-9. Third baseman Wolverton was next. One inning earlier, Wolverton had pushed Lochhead off third base. On May 3rd in Cleveland, Wolverton physically held Joe Quinn on base to prevent him from scoring. Now, Wolverton could be a hero, "but in the supreme moment, Wolverton swung at a curve ball, poked a weakling bounder to Schmit, and amid the sorrow and silence Chicago fell." (*CT*, Aug 7). Schmit held on for the strange victory, his second of the week. Lochhead's baserunning had produced the winner.

The second game could offer no where near the raucous, unbridled excitement of the opener, but it produced a revenge-minded Chicago win. For that the fans were happy, for to lose two games in one day to the Misfits would be akin to your mother telling you to clean your room...after you just did. Fourteen thousand mothers.

Skinny righthander Ned Garvin took the assignment for the Cubs while Harry Colliflower went for Cleveland. Again, Joe Sugden was behind the plate despite the Hemphill acquisition and the plan to use McAllister as backstop. From the beginning, Garvin posed an "altogether too complicated delivery" and eluded the Cleveland lads (*CPD*, Aug 7). Colliflower, "whose odd name was a perpetual delight to some strong-lunged rooters," was hit early and often (*CPD*, Aug 7). Chicago tallied two in the first and third innings, one in the fourth, and batted everyone in the lineup in the eighth. Four singles and errors by Lochhead and Dick Harley were "sufficient inducement to send four runs across the plate." (*CPD*, Aug 7). The Cubs had a 9-1 lead when Garvin decided to let up in the ninth and give the Misfits some false hopes. In actuality though, the *Chicago Tribune* was so bored with the game that they could only make fun of the Cleveland pitcher's name. Taking a tip from several Chicago fans, the *Tribune* wrote that the "Cowboys pickled Colliflower" and "Colliflower vegetated on the rubber." (Aug 7). It ended 9-5. The woeful Misfits had won 17 of 97 games and were 18 games behind 11th place Washington.

Mon Aug 7 In their nostalgic book on American railroads, Lucius Beebe and Charles Clegg described: "Railroad travel exercised a charm upon the human spirit. The rails running to the horizon were indeed a royal road to romance. The cars were places in a microcosm and a whole people rode them to far places and happy destinations in fact and fancy, both literally and metaphorically. Manifest destiny lay around the curves and down the tangents."

But, the Misfits' rail journey to Boston from Chicago was like many of the others, hardly a "royal road to romance" but a trip where more defeats likely lay ahead. There were no "happy destinations" for the Clevelands and "manifest destiny" meant last place.

The *Plain Dealer* stirred up more trouble for the Cleveland franchise by reporting that President M. Stanley Robison was proposing to play some Cleveland home games in Columbus, Ohio. The idea was noble, but considering Cleveland had played thirty-six consecutive games on the road, what could make Robison believe that Columbus would support this team (*CPD*, Aug 8)?

While M. S. Robison was thinking Columbus, St. Louis manager Pat Tebeau was criticizing his players. He said that the play of shortstop Ed McKean had lost the Browns "twenty games this season. I never saw a man go to pieces like he did. He was a grand player. There was no reason to think that he would be anything else this season. He could neither field nor bat. He got a bad start and muffed and fumbled a lot of balls. Then, the crowd got to roasting him. They would blame him for not getting base hits." Perhaps, Tebeau was hinting at a swap: McKean for Lochhead or Sullivan or Quinn or Tucker. With Frank Robison controlling both the fortunes of the St. Louis team and the farm team in Cleveland, why wasn't a deal consummated earlier? Tebeau also railed about Wee Willie Sudhoff for pitching so poorly. Willie was "in a fair way to get a railroad ticket to the next hangout of the Cleveland club." (*SL*, Aug 12).

Meanwhile, back in Cleveland, a group was forming to try to buy out Robison's Misfits "bag and baggage." (*SL*, Aug 19). The men had as little as $500 to as much as $10,000 to invest. Their belief was that a break-even team would make a profit. (*CP*, Aug 7). However, the Misfits were a bit removed from that kind of ball playing.

Tues Aug 8   In front of less than 2000 fans, the Wanderers met the Boston Beaneaters at the South End Grounds. Boston's Harvey Bailey opposed Jim Hughey. In late June, the same two hurlers locked horns in a pitcher's duel. Bailey won that game 3-1. However, pitching domination went out the window on this day as "both clubs had their batting clothes with them." (*CPD*, Aug 9).

The Bostons began the scoring in the first inning. Centerfielder "Sliding Billy" Hamilton drew a base on balls. Fred Tenney singled and shortstop Bob Stafford drove one over the left field fence for a home run. This set the tone for the rest of the game for Hughey, who must have had a sore neck watching balls fall in safe in front of his fielders. The home boys piled up five more in the fourth on two singles, a double, a walk, and a Hugh Duffy home run to right field. After four frames, it was 10-1 Boston. In the fifth, the Misfits did some

116

whacking of their own. Hughey, Quinn, Harley, and Sullivan all hit safely and Tommy Dowd responded with a home run. The score was 10-5. Seeing enough, Boston manager Frank Selee removed Bailey in favor of Piano Legs Hickman. Not having confidence in Hickman's control, the *Boston Globe* said he would "be a more valuable man if he worked with a target a few minutes a day." (Aug 9). Misfits manager Quinn stayed with his pitcher Hughey, proof positive that there were no other fresh arms in the arsenal. In the seventh, Boston scored three more times to make it 13-5. Duffy doubled and catcher Marty Bergen walked. Hickman smashed a pretty triple and Hamilton dumped one safely. To add to the Cleveland misery, Sugden was hit by a "foul fly to the knee that sent him groaning to the ground." (*BG*, Aug 9). He had to be carried to the bench and examined by a kindly Dr. Sullivan who "set right a floating cartilage." (*BG*, Aug 9). The game was halted briefly for the bench operation to be completed and Sugden re-entered the game. Perhaps the kindly doctor was also the Misfits' third baseman. In the eighth, Cleveland found Hickman for three runs and closed 13-8. But, Boston bashed Hughey for five more scores in their half, sending ten men to the plate. The *Boston Globe* commented that "when the champions got through with Mr. Hughey he felt like a tarantula." (Aug 9). That reference was probably lost on everyone in Boston who read the sporting page. The final was 18-8.

Hughey's battering was, if nothing else, a testament to his courage. He gave up 20 hits, five bases on balls, a wild pitch, and 32 total bases in all. Three errors were made behind him and he committed one himself. Every Boston player except pitcher Bailey gathered at least two hits. Hughey's effort was so wretched that the *Cleveland Plain Dealer* left him out of the box score entirely and substituted the name of Frank Bates. The confusion to the newspaper probably resulted from the plethora of runs normally reserved for a pitcher of Bates caliber. Then again, perhaps the typing error was deliberate.

Wed Aug 9   Before two thousand fans, Joe Quinn's Misfits put up a "spunky game of ball" for game two of the Boston series (*BG*, Aug 10). The game promised to be interesting based on the pitching matchups. Frank Selee started his sensational righthander Charles Augustus "Kid" Nichols. Nichols had been defeated by the Misfits 6-3 in Boston. Charlie Knepper was summoned to the mound for Cleveland pitching honors having already defeated the Bostons 7-2 on June 29 at League Park.

The Exiles went with a revamped lineup. To give Sugden a much-deserved rest, Sport McAllister went behind the plate to catch. Manager Quinn was relying on McAllister's four games of league experience at the position. But, considering that in his young career, McAllister had played everywhere on the field, it was not a bad decision. New man Charlie Hemphill started in the right field garden.

In the very first inning, Cleveland jumped on Nichols in a "savage manner." (*BG*, Aug 10). Buttermilk Tommy Dowd popped to first baseman Fred Tenney but Quinn doubled to center and Dick Harley singled home his manager. Suter Sullivan, Tommy Tucker, and Harry Lochhead produced safe blows and it was 3-0. Then, Tucker tried an aggressive baserunning tactic, not his forte. "Bergen whipped the ball to Collins, and the latter sent it back again in time to get Tucker who thought he had a chance to go home when Lochhead cut out for second." (*BG*, Aug 10). The *Plain Dealer* thought a sliding Tommy had beaten the throw home easily, but umpire Lynch called Tucker out. Tommy howled, but was allowed to stay in the game.

In the second inning, Knepper singled and Dowd hit a "hot shot that Collins took close to third and sent it to Lowe at second, from where it went to first for a fast double play." (*BG*, Aug 10). Boston crept back into the game when Knepper walked Hugh Duffy and saw Chick Stahl hit a "lucky drive" over the left field fence (*CPD*, Aug 10). Cleveland's lead was 3-2. With Cleveland batting in the third and one out, Harley singled and was caught stealing. Sullivan grounded to his rival third baseman Collins, who robbed him of a hit. Knepper allowed the Beaneaters to tie in the third on Billy Hamilton's walk, Herman Long's double and Collins' grounder. While chasing down Long's hit, Hemphill injured his hand. Hemphill was to be out of action for a week (*CP*, Aug 11). Manager Quinn put Colliflower in the garden.

The Bostons took a 4-3 lead in the fourth as pitcher Nichols helped his game by driving in Stahl. The fifth inning saw Collins make two more spectacular plays on Quinn and Harley. In the sixth, Cleveland mounted a threat. Sullivan and McAllister singled. Then, "Nichols put on steam and fanned Tucker." (*BG*, Aug 10). Lochhead bounced a hot grounder but Nichols speared it and threw out the Cleveland shortstop. Colliflower was an easy groundout to second baseman Bobby Lowe.

With Nichols firm in command, the Misfits went down with nary a whimper. In the eighth, however, the Bostons tricked the inexperienced catcher McAllister with three runs the result. "With one out, Duffy singled and went for second. The ball passed a few feet back of the catcher, who lost sight of it. Chick Stahl ran back towards the backstop, pointing the bat, and the catcher, thinking the ball was where the Boston the Boston man was pointing, ran away from the plate. Duffy came around to third and scored on Stahl's single that Quinn made a fine try for played wide to Tucker. Lowe was an easy out. Bergen drove Stahl home with a sharp single. Nichols and Hamilton hit safely, but Tenney forced the latter." (*BG*, Aug 10). Cleveland went out meekly in the ninth and the Bostons were winners 7-3.

Thurs Aug 10   A heavy rain fell on the Boston ball yard preventing the finale of the series.   The *Cleveland Plain Dealer* sought out a soggy Joe Quinn, who commented on his charges (Apr 11):

"Tell the public that the Insurgents are all right.   We haven't any home now. They call us 'tramps,' 'exiles,' 'wanderers,' 'misfits,' Aren't there a few more Mac?" he added turning toward McAllister.

"'Forsakens,' 'cast offs,' 'excursionists,'- that's all I can remember just now, except 'caudal appendages,' 'tail-enders,' and 'Clevelanders,'" replied the player.

"We have a good team," said Quinn, "and we can make the best of them work for all they get.   We might have had a much better team if St. Louis hadn't taken away so many of our good men.   Cross, Sudhoff, and Schreckengost were transferred to St. Louis when they were doing their best work for us.   I don't say that we could have made a pennant winner.   We were and are strong enough to make a good try for all the games we play, but can't stay it out with good teams that are filled with perfect and trained men, who have held their positions a long time.

"I've no hesitation in saying that I think that syndicating is a very bad thing.   It not only hurts the strength of a team, but the game as well.   I don't approve of it at all. At the same time I don't have a word to say against the Robison's.   They have treated me splendidly, the players are paid regularly and are treated as well as any team in the league.   I should probably have been in St. Louis myself by this time if the men who employ me had not some reason for keeping me in Cleveland.

"The men who were transferred from Cleveland to St. Louis did not want to go. Sudhoff would a good deal rather have stayed with us.   McKean would have preferred to remain in Cleveland and made a protest against going to St. Louis when the season opened.   He had all his friends and his business in Cleveland, the same as I did in St. Louis.   We would have preferred to play in the cities where we were settled and had our homes, but the Cleveland people have treated us very nicely, and the fact that we have not had a high position has nothing to do with there being no crowds at the games.   Cleveland would not support the old club that was transferred to St. Louis, and they will not support us.

"Over in Cleveland the crowds always root for us to win.   But talk about two teams working for the same people not playing ball against each other- why, we and the St. Louis club are continually at each other's throats all the time we are playing.   I never saw harder games and I have played a lot of fast teams in my time."

The *Cleveland Press* took time to write that the Misfits had lost 21 games by one run.   "Therefore, it might be said, that 42 runs, properly distributed, would have put the Barnstormers in 9th place." (Aug 9).   Actually though, the *Press'* mathematics seemed to be as poor as the Clevelands play on the field.   The Misfits had lost only twelve games by the minimal margin.   With twenty-four extra tallies, scored at crucial times, the Misfits would be only six games out of 11th place.

Meanwhile, in Baltimore, the Perfectos met the Orioles in a showdown of rowdy ball teams. It was Patsy Tebeau versus John McGraw. Neither man would ever be accused of being sissified. The *St. Louis Globe-Democrat* describes the confrontation (Aug 11):

There was a clash of nations at Oysterville yesterday, and the outcome of it was that Patsy Tebeau, after a wordy war with Monsieur LaChance, "Muggsy" McGraw and "Hank" O'Day on the playing field, was guyed by the "fans" upon leaving the park, and after getting back at them verbally, was arrested on the insistence of an enthusiast and marched to the Central police station, where he deposited $2.45 in cash, presumably all he had, and then was allowed his liberty. The trouble all arose over a decision of Umpire Hunt in calling a Baltimore player safe at first, the official ruling that Donlin's foot was not on the bag when he made the catch. Tebeau and Burkett went at Hunt in a threatening way, Burkett being benched for his gaiety. Gentle Patsy was hooted at for the rest of the afternoon, and after the game was over was the target of abuse from a party of "fans" in the grand stand. Tebeau got back the best he could, and his "Kerry Patch" lingo resulted in one of the enthusiasts calling a policeman and having Patsy arrested. As to the game, St. Louis lost, 7 to 4.

Sat Aug 12   On Friday, the Misfits spent the day on the road, moving from Boston to the bright lights and glamour of New York. There, the Misfits faced the Giants at the Polo Grounds for a familiar doubleheader. The Giants were in the middle of a miserable season themselves, with a 38-52 record. They had fired their manager John Day and replaced him with Fred Hoey.

For the opener the Giants named lefty Ed Doheny as starter. Doheny had already beaten the Misfits twice, 9-6 in Cleveland's first game after the loss of Lave Cross, and 8-2 over Frank Bates at League Park. Joe Quinn sent Frank Bates to the rubber. Bates had lost both of his decisions to the Giants.

Tommy Dowd began the game by grounding to third baseman Mike Grady, who parlayed the easy chance into a triple with a wild throw. Grady's toss eluded first baseman Jack Doyle, the coach, and a peanut vendor. Manager Quinn hit to Grady too, but was thrown out. Dowd scored. From then on the Misfits could not tally on Doheny, who pitched a four-hitter and struck out five.

Bates, who confused a *Plain Dealer* typist on Tuesday, was pathetic. The Giants "did not have to exert themselves," on their way to 18 hits, 7 bases on balls, a stolen base, a wild pitch, and Bates' own error that allowed two runners to score (*NYT*, Aug 13). Grady solved young Bates for four hits, including two doubles, while rightfielder Pop Foster and Doheny had three apiece. Said the *Plain Dealer*, "Bates doesn't even seem to be a second rater. He has only average speed, very poor command of the ball, and relies almost entirely on the outcurve." (Aug 13). The *Cleveland Press* offered their criticism, "The games which Bates pitches should be thrown out of the count. It can be conclusively shown that he is ineligible- from lack of ability and refusal to accept advice- to pitch in the same league with Young, Nichols, Griffith, et al." (Aug 17). It ended 13-1. The only bright spot for the visitors was a 7th inning running catch by Dick Harley. The contest actually "became so tiresome for the spectators toward the close that they asked to have it called and the second game began." (*NYT*, Aug 13). It was the Misfits' 100th game of the season and their 83rd loss. Perhaps, the Misfits could take up polo.

By the beginning of the next affair the crowd had swelled to almost four thousand, several of them looking on from trees or from Coogan's Bluff behind home plate. Perhaps word was getting out that the illustrious twirler Frederick M. Schmit was the attraction. The Giants pitched Cleveland native Bill Carrick, who had bested the Misfits twice. Neither club could push across a run in the initial frame. In the second, the New Yorkers imitated jackrabbits. Giant shortstop George Davis scratched out a hit and stole second. First baseman Dirty Jack Doyle singled when his grounder bounced up and bopped Harry Lochhead in the shoulder. Veteran Kid Gleason sacrificed to Dowd in center and the Giants led 1-0. Taking advantage of Schmit's carelessness, Doyle stole second base, though the *Plain Dealer* called him "out by ten feet" on a strong Sugden throw (Aug 13). Doyle then swiped third. Right Fielder Foster hit to Quinn at second base, who elected to throw home to get Doyle. Dirty Jack was ruled safe on the controversial, close call at home. It was 2-0. In the fourth, the Giants scored two more with the help of a walk, a bunt, and a couple of hits. In the sixth, the Giants tallied two more, though their totals would have been bigger if not for some baserunning blunders. The New Yorkers tried quite hard to prey on Schmit's weaknesses. Centerfielder George Van Haltren beat out an infield bunt but when leftfielder Tommy O'Brien flied to McAllister, Van Haltren lost his head and ended up on third base. He was an easy double play victim. Doyle received his comeuppance when he was caught between third and home in the inning.

Against Doughnut Bill Carrick, the Misfit bats stayed silent, scoring only twice. It was "the daily downfall," according to the *Plain Dealer*, 13-1 and 6-2 defeats. The traveling baseball barnstormers were playing with "a marked loss of ginger in the last few weeks." (*CPD*, Aug 13).

The *Plain Dealer*, used to Crazy Schmit's antics, made no cracks about the Cleveland pitcher. The *New York Times* could not resist (Aug 13).

Schmit, the only bona fide German in the league, and at present known as the Cleveland's winning pitcher- whatever that may mean- was in the box for the visitors. His appearance in the game kept the crowd, which now numbered nearly 4000, from going to sleep. He was guyed and tormented by the local players, but he could not see where there was any joke, and pitched throughout with such earnestness that the crowd became amused and cheered him, whether he fooled a batsman or was hit. He had several arguments with the umpires. He probably escaped a fine because Umpire

McGarr could not understand his mixture of English and German. Schmit is the man who told a catcher in Baltimore that he was the deceiver, and the catcher the received.

Sun Aug 13   There was no Sunday baseball in New York.   The *Cleveland Plain Dealer* took the time to print the won-lost records of pitchers in the National League.   Several of the figures were inaccurate.   Crazy Schmit was credited with one victory instead of two.   That fact might have prompted the German to raise a ruckus.   Jim Hughey, on the other hand, was cited for a few victories more than his record indicated.   Jim might have smiled at the error of the newspaper's ways.

Mon Aug 14   The large New York gathering of 4000 on Saturday dwindled to an almost imperceptible intimacy.   Wrote the *New York Times*, a "few hundred spectators who could work up enough interest to watch Cleveland try to play ball seemed to be in a trance.   This lasted until the Clevelands took it into their heads to make a bluff at least.   The bluff woke up the crowd and set the local players to playing real baseball." (Aug 15).   The *Plain Dealer* remarked, Baseball is about as dead in New York as it is in Cleveland." (Aug 15).

Charlie Gettig pitched for the home team while Jim Hughey took his rotation turn for the visitors.   In the first inning, Cleveland could not muster a run.   In the Giants half with one out, leftfielder Tom O'Brien drew a base on balls. Hughey, sensing the speedy O'Brien was trying for a steal, threw over to first on a pick off play.   Tommy Tucker muffed the toss and O'Brien went to second. Shortstop George Davis singled to give the Giants a 1-0 lead.   Hughey braced himself with an "abundance of speed," and there was no further scoring until the fourth (*NYT*, Aug 14).   In that inning, two men were out when Pop Foster's bounder went over Quinn's head.   Foster then stole second and scored on catcher John Warner's single to left field.   Gettig shut the Misfits down until the fifth, but errors by Davis and O'Brien, and some crazy bounces, led to four runs.   The Exiles led 4-2.   In New York's fifth, "Hughey was too prodigal with his gifts and sent O'Brien to first on four balls." (*CPD*, Aug 14).   Davis' single eventually scored O'Brien and it was 4-3 Cleveland.   The Giants tied the game and went ahead in the 7th on Tucker's muff of a Suter Sullivan throw, a passed ball by Joe Sugden, another stolen base, and a sacrifice fly.   The lead went to 7-4 in the 8th.   Second baseman Kid Gleason dashed for a triple and scored when Dick Harley and Tommy Dowd collided on Foster's fly.   Pitcher Gettig's single scored Foster.   "Cleveland made things interesting in the ninth inning, probably due to a little overconfidence by Gettig." (*NYT*, Aug 14).   Misfit singles by Hughey, Dowd, and Quinn filled the bases with no one out.   Harley hit a sacrifice fly to George Van Haltren in center field.   Sullivan followed with the same to O'Brien before Sport McAllister flied to Foster to end it 7-6 for the

Giants. Once again, the Misfits had rallied, only to fall short. When a big hit was lacking, the Misfits were also.

Umpire Emslie's partner McDonald failed to show for the contest. Emslie was assisted by New York catcher Parke Wilson.

Tue Aug 15 From the Polo Grounds, the Clevelanders made a short ride to Brooklyn's Washington Park. There they were greeted by the front-running Brooklyn Superbas, managed by Ned Hanlon. The game was short, punctual, and a neat pitcher's struggle. Doc McJames went for Brooklyn while the Misfits used Charlie Knepper.

"Knepper showed fair control of the ball and showed more speed than any pitcher Joe Quinn has turned loose on the metropolis since he has been here. The Wanderers appeared to play with some confidence behind him, and it was all that Hanlon wanted to tackle to squeeze out a victory." (*CPD*, Aug 16). The *Brooklyn Daily Eagle* described Knepper as "an oddity in the league ranks. He is a tremendous specimen of manhood, probably the biggest player in the league." (Aug 16).

"Dr. McJames was trotted out to oppose them. The doctor isn't in the best favor on the Brooklyn side of the river and had he lost the game if would have been the last straw that would have broken the Brooklyn camel. Luckily for him he had fair control of the ball and the visitors couldn't solve the drops he sent floating up to the plate." (*CPD*, Aug 16).

The 6-2 Brooklyn victory was expected by every one of the 1300 souls in attendance. The Trolley Dodgers used clever baserunning and timely hitting to sink Knepper. The Misfits' only two runs came in the sixth inning and were greatly assisted by errors. Again, the lack of clutch hitting hurt the Misfits and they secured only five safeties off McJames.

Wed Aug 16 Baseball, it is said, is "a game calling for unusual quick reactions intellectually and prompt and easy cooperation muscularly." (Sullivan 41). Game two of the Misfits in Brooklyn matched the league's most intellectual and muscularly cooperative squad versus the league's worst. The pitching matchups also featured the same. Jim Hughes went for Hanlon's Superbas while Quinn tossed in his lad, Frank Bates. The result was predictable:

Of course, the Clevelands did not win the game, and it is hard to see when they will win a game so long as they persist in playing Bates. The young man demonstrated long ago that he is not fast enough even for the tail-enders of the big organization. He had little speed today, was quite as wild as usual, and the Brooklyns had little or no trouble in making runs and plenty of them. (*CPD*, Aug 17).

Bates best pitches were beat around Washington Park; otherwise he proceeded to walk nine men, one with the bases loaded. The lackadaisical Misfits made matters worse by committing five fielding muffs. Suter Sullivan was injured in the sixth inning and his replacement, Charlie Hemphill, wasted no time in dropping a fly ball. Brooklyn rightfielder Wee Willie Keeler bopped a triple. First baseman Honest John Anderson "came to the plate with a bat heavy enough to be used as a battering ram," and doubled, as did shortstop Bill Dahlen and pitcher Hughes (*CPD*, Aug 17). Second baseman Tom Daly scored from first on a single and the home town heroes even stole three bases.

After tossing balls easy, Hughes retired in the sixth inning with an 11-0 lead. His replacement, Wild Bill Donovan coasted into the Misfits final inning with a 13-0 advantage. "The Brooklyns evidently did not relish the idea of having a double hoodoo 13 to 0, so they allowed the Clevelands to make a couple of runs in the ninth inning." (*BDE*, Aug 17). The final was 13-2.

Thur Aug 17   On Thursday, the Misfits turned baseball into mathematical progression. Game one of the series went to Brooklyn by 6-2. The second game added seven more runs to the Superbas score and the final was 13-2. So, to continue the pattern, the front runners added seven more runs in game three and crushed the tail-enders by 20-2. It was the worst loss of the season. Wrote the *Brooklyn Daily Eagle*, "It would be an injustice to the Cleveland team to consider the game at Washington Park from a serious point of view." (Aug 18).

Manager Ned Hanlon started his fine righthander Jack Dunn while Quinn chose Crazy Schmit. For the Misfits it was a queer pitching choice. In practice, the mercurial German walked up to home plate where Joe Sugden was catching the tosses of Charlie Knepper. Sugden spied Schmit and asked him to join in the workout. Schmit responded enigmatically, "I guess not to-day. I can't pitch because I have a sore back, and if I was going to pitch I wouldn't be warming up." (*BDE*, Aug 18).

The pattern for the game was set from the beginning. Dunn easily fooled the Cleveland batters with slow curves and took the rest of the day off in the sixth inning. Dunn's team led 15-2 at the time. He was replaced by ex-Spider lefty Bill Hill, who was up to some fooling of his own. Schmit, meanwhile, took to hitting batters, when they weren't hitting him. Cleveland fielders bumbled their way to six errors for the game. Sport McAllister was "all off at third base and couldn't get to the ball to save his life." (*CPD*, Aug 18). He booted three balls by himself. The Brooklyns scored three in the first, one in the third, eight in the fourth, one in the fifth, two in the sixth, four in the seventh, and one in the eighth. Because of errors, fourteen of the runs were unearned. After hitting a batter in the third inning, the sore-backed Schmit was removed. The performance reminded some fans of a game Schmit once lost in the minor leagues by the close shave score of 22-4. With the crowd jeering and showering bottles of glass in his direction, Schmit walked calmly to the grandstand to address his critics. "Ladies and gentleman. Listen to me. What can you expect of eight amateurs and one professional!" Upon the utterance of the last word, he struck out his chest dramatically and strode back to the place of his work.

Schmit's replacement, Harry Colliflower, gave up so many scores that in the seventh inning the "crowd grew tired and fairly begged the Brooklyns to allow themselves to be retired." (*BDE*, Aug 18). In all, 19 hits were secured off Cleveland pitching. Third baseman Doc Casey and catcher Deacon McGuire doubled. Daly encored his baserunning performance of the day before by going from first to third on a bunt to the pitcher. After shortstop Bad Bill Dahlen homered over the brick right field fence, a spherical object came from behind the Brooklyn dressing room towards outfielder Dick Harley. He picked it up, examined it, and tossed it to Lochhead who flung it to Colliflower. The pitcher let it go to the grandstand, in plain view of the spectators. It was a melon, rather indicative of the Misfits performance, and everyone laughed.

As the Cleveland series with Brooklyn continued, the *Cleveland Press* wrote: "The efforts of Quinn's Barnstormers at Brooklyn are likened by one writer to those bunch of colonial dames playing bean bag in the weedy back lot of an asylum for the feeble-minded." (Aug 18).

Fri Aug 18   After their demolition of the day before, the Misfits may have expected "to be beaten in a walk." (*BDE*, Aug 19). However, in baseball's uncertain world, that was not the case. The end result was the same, though, as Cleveland was shaded once again in Brooklyn by 4-2. Of the inevitability of another Cleveland loss, the *Plain Dealer* commented, "Today's games were like unto the other funeral ceremonies." (Aug 19).

Ned Hanlon sent out Doc McJames for his charges. Joe Quinn called Frank Bates. Like Thursday's curious pitching choice of Schmit, Quinn gambled with Bates, pitching on one days rest. The move almost paid off. Bates pitched his best game and although he walked six men, he exhibited a "little high class form." (*CPD*, Aug 19). The scoring began in the Brooklyn third inning. Catcher Duke Farrell walked and McJames singled. Fielder Jones' bunt hit loaded the bases. Wee Willie Keeler hit one where they weren't and it was 1-0. Hughie Jennings forced Jones at third base and McJames scored. Joe Kelley flied to Dick Harley but then Bates walked Tom Daly and Bill Dahlen to force in the third run. In the Brooklyn fourth, "Bates pitched a wild one into Farrell's ribs." (*CPD*, Aug 19). McJames grounded into a double play but Fielder Jones lashed out a home run. It was 4-0 for the Superbas. The Exiles scored a couple in the 7th to pull close at 4-2. The game was called in the eighth so the Misfits could catch the proverbial train to Steeltown. The most notable feature of the contest was Cleveland's stunning triple play. With runners on first and second, "Quinn took Casey's liner; Tucker and Lochhead doing the rest." (*CPD*, Aug 19).

Hanlon's front-runners had demolished the tail-enders 43-8 in the four games.

Sat Aug 19   Before a sizable weekend gathering of four thousand ball cranks in Pittsburg, the Misfits had "two arguments with the Pirates at Exposition Park in the way of ball playing." (*CPD*, Aug 20).   It was to be an abbreviated one-day series before the Wanderers moved on to Chicago.

In the opener Jim Hughey faced Jesse Tannehill, who was making a living beating the Misfits. So far, Tannehill had allowed only 15 hits to the Clevelands in three complete games, winning 6-0, 10-1, and 7-1. There was no reason to think that this affair would be any different. It wasn't. Tannehill again dominated, "keeping the tail-enders from hitting the ball no more than the board of health allowed." (*PP*, Aug 20). Hughey gave up eight hits to the Pittsburg outfield alone, four by player-manager Patsy Donovan. The Buccaneers also made it a point to jaunt merrily around the bases by way of steals, doubles, triples, hit batters, passed balls, and a wild pitch. The game was "too one sided to be even worth looking at," but the fans that did saw an 11-1 Pirate victory.

As the *Pittsburg Post* related for the second game, "the worm will turn, as the most ancient citizen will relate." (Aug 20). The worm certainly did, and the Misfits, led by the playful coaching banter of Tommy Tucker and sharp pitching by Charlie Knepper, defeated the Pirates 8-3. It was the first Cleveland win in 11 games.

Knepper pitched "gilt-edged ball," wrote the *New York Times* (Aug 20). It was a rare effort by the blond twirler whose "work was attracting attention all over the country. If Tebeau does not demand his transfer to St. Louis, some other team will probably snap him up by making 'Brother Stan' a liberal cash offer." (*CP*, Aug 7). Sam Leever was the unfortunate Pittsburg hurler to take the loss. He was knocked off the rubber in the seventh. Leever was replaced by Tully Sparks, whom the Exiles also hit freely. Misfits' hitting stars included Sport McAllister, Joe Quinn, Charlie Hemphill, and Suter Sullivan. McAllister hit a ball to center field in the fifth inning. "Beaumont ran for it, missed it, and then turned tail and chased it to the fence." (*PP*, Aug 20). The result was a home run. The Clevelands further stunned the Bucs by slugging three consecutive triples in the seventh inning. The partisan Pittsburg crowd, "never dreaming they (Cleveland) would win out," took to cheering the Misfits on, as they continued to surprise the gathering with their fine play. (*PP*, Aug 20).

Sun Aug 20   The 1899 Cleveland Misfits, who pre-dated the travel craze around the world, chugged their way to the Windy City. Their Chicago stay was brief, but the single game they played there was as wild and wacky as any. The West Side Grounds was swarming with cranks, anxious to have a good time. They were not disappointed.

Chicago manager Tom Burns called on righthander Dick Cogan, whose league resume showed one solitary game. Said the *Plain Dealer*, "Alderman Cogan made his first appearance before his Chicago constituency." (Aug 21). Joe Quinn sent in homegrown lefthander Germany Schmit, who was certainly no stranger to politics himself, especially the way he cajoled his audiences. Every contest seemed more of a rally than a ball game to the eccentric Schmit.

In the early stanzas, the game was too close to call. Both pitchers survived numerous fielding miscues. It stood 2-1 for the Chicagoans after seven innings. Schmit was pitching well, two weeks removed from his strange victory over the Cubs. Then, with Chicago batting in the eighth, the Misfits found ways to kick the ball instead of catch it. The damages gave the home boys three more scores and a 5-1 lead. Down by four runs, the dispirited Clevelands took their whacks in the last inning. Sport McAllister, who was trying his hand at catcher, went out. Then, "hits, scratches, and clean drives rained around the fields." (*CT*, Aug 21). Schmit singled to left field after two previous strikeouts. Swift Tommy Dowd singled to center and Quinn walked to first. With the bases loaded and Cogan reeling, third baseman Suter Sullivan's scratch scored Schmit, who was perched on third. The bases remained loaded at 5-2. Shortstop Lochhead went out on a force, but Dowd tallied. Charlie Hemphill's little puncher to left field plated Quinn and it was 5-4. With the "huge crowd yelling in disgust," Tommy Tucker squibbed one in front of the mound (*CT*, Aug 21). An easy catch and toss by Cogan should have ended the game, but "Cogan himself, took a policeman by the rightfield bleachers for the trusty Everitt on the initial bag." (*CPD*, Aug 21).   The Chicago pitcher's error tied the contest at five. McAllister, the tenth batter of the inning, solved young Cogan for a ringing triple and the Misfits led 7-5. Schmit, trying to secure more votes, was next. He huffed and puffed, but again fanned the breeze. The Misfits' amazing inning was over with six runs to the good.

Schmit now believed he had the election and grinned from ear to ear. The Misfit fielders along the perimeter of the diamond must have felt otherwise. Ex-Oriole shortstop George Magoon popped a fair fly to McAllister. Inexperience won out and the ball was dropped. Catcher Frank Chance singled to left, helped by Dick Harley's muff. Pitcher Cogan sacrificed both runners a base but Schmit walked outfielder Jimmy Ryan. Continuing his wildness, Schmit threw two balls wide of home plate. The *Plain Dealer* picks up the description (Aug 21).

There appeared on the scene the familiar 'Sandow' Mertes- not an alderman but one of the common herd of men, with a good batting eye and an arm of brawn as his stock in trade. Three of his associates anchored on the bags around the diamond turned to him for triumphant release, and not in vain. Common muscle proved more effective than deceptive aldermanic arguments. Comedian Schmit sneeringly tossed him the sphere and the last seen of it thereafter it was pocketed by a small boy out at the club house, while Mertes stopped at the three quarter post and doffed his cap at the cheers of 5000 spectators over a victory snatched from defeat.

Mertes scathing three base hit won the ball game. The Misfits were customary losers again, as their record went to 18-91. Only fifty-three games separated them from front-running Brooklyn.

Tues Aug 22 To chronicle the rail journeys of the Cleveland Misfits since their last home appearance would take an extensive log book. But, team secretary George W. Muir was keeping careful track. On July 1st Cleveland played Boston at League Park. Then they found their way to Pittsburg, St. Louis, Philadelphia, Baltimore, Washington, Atlantic City, Baltimore, Louisville, Philadelphia, Chicago, Boston, New York, Brooklyn, Pittsburg, Chicago, and now Louisville. The Wanderers had traveled untold thousands of rickety rail miles, piling up losses and laughs. They were men playing a boys game like boys.

Once in the bluegrass country of Louisville, Kentucky, the Misfits met Fred Clarke's Colonels. Charlie Knepper got the assignment for Cleveland. The Colonels went with Deacon Phillippe, who after losing 4-3 to the Exiles on May 21, no-hit the New York Giants.

Just ten days before, a fire had destroyed the grandstand of the ball park in Louisville. The fire was said to have come from an electric light wire during a massive thunderstorm. Accommodations for the temporary grandstand were not good, but workers were frantically trying to restore what was lost.

The game itself was a joke, played before twelve hundred. "The aggregation from Cleveland stumbled all over the diamond and even failed to do that well." (*CPD*, Aug 23). The *Louisville Courier-Journal*'s description was no kinder saying that Cleveland "sustained fully the reputation it has hitherto enjoyed worst aggregation of ball tossers ever in the National League." (Aug 23). The Colonel's Phillippe was knocked out of the box by the fourth inning but his successor Walt Woods held the Exiles at bay. Knepper, meanwhile, was hammered to the tune of 14 singles, three doubles, and a home run. Outfielder Dummy Hoy bashed out four hits of his own. And if that wasn't enough, "Ritchey hit an ordinary double along the right field foul line. It rolled into the crowd seated on the grass near the fence, and some big fat man sat down on it.

128

He refused to get up until Ritchey made a circuit of the bases. It was certainly a peculiar home run." (*LCJ*, Aug 23). In support of Knepper, the Misfits comically averaged an error an inning; nine in all, kicking the ball about the yard with astonishing regularity. Three of the folly came from Tommy Tucker and two were by manager Quinn. Louisville might have scored in triple figures had they not managed to leave eight men stranded on base. It ended 15-6.

There was another amusing sidelight to the game, which exposed the era as an age of prudery. "In the first inning Wagner, in sliding into third base, tore a large rent in his pants, where they were widest. He was compelled to sit on the sack until Clingman carried a coat with which to hide the tear. Hans walked to the club-house and changed trousers with Willis." (*LCJ*, Aug 23).

Manager Quinn could take no solace that a local Cleveland amateur baseball club from Painesville had beat Warren by 50-2. Painesville hit fourteen home runs in the contest. It was doubtful that Quinn was aware of a Brooklyn physician's rules for the prevention of "glass arms" in pitchers.

1. Pitch only one day in four. That is, if you pitch on Monday, do not pitch again until Friday, and again on the following Wednesday.

2. Do not practice pitching the day after a game. Give the arm a rest that day. Most pitchers practice
too much.

3. Massage the pitching arm every day with warm olive oil. This supplies waste and removes soreness from the muscles. Twenty minutes is long enough.

4. Keep the general health good by walking, bicycling and bathing. Exercise, but avoid dumbbells.

5. The diet for a pitcher should be the same as for a boxer in training.

These rules, observed, a pitcher will be in good form throughout the year, and will never have a "glass arm."

Wed Aug 23 The short, terse series with Louisville concluded on Wednesday with another downer for the Misfits. In keeping with the horse-racing motif, the *Plain Dealer* explained that the Misfits "again demonstrated today that they need slower company for pacers." (Aug 24) The pitching matchup offered a battle of Harry's. Rookie Harry Wilhelm took to the rubber for the Colonels. Joe Quinn sent out Harry Colliflower, he of the perpetual "glass arm."

Once again, the Misfits played miserably. New recruit Wilhelm easily handled the Clevelanders and bashed out a triple and a home run. Bowlegged Honus Wagner, the first player to endorse a bat, laced out three more two-baggers for a total of five (Einstein 131). On two other occasions, Wagner hit balls near the fence, but Dowd and McAllister played Wagner deep and tracked down his long flies. Chief Zimmer cracked a home run against his ex-mates in the 6th. Colliflower wasn't much, starting the game by walking the first three Colonels. "In between innings the crowd of 500 took a nap." (*CPD*, Aug 24). The lone Misfits' highlight was a Charlie Hemphill hit that wormed its way under the fence for a home run. It added up to another loss for the Misfits, 13-3.

Not exactly helping matters, the *Cleveland Press* reported that Cleveland would probably reach 100 defeats during their upcoming homestand. "Not since the days of J. Palmer O'Neill's famous aggregation of ancient and honorable has-beens has any team been able to score 100 defeats by September 15. Plans are already well under way to celebrate this achievement, by the Homeless Ones, in appropriate style. The program will be ready for announcement by next Saturday." (Aug 23). The team referenced was the 1890 Pittsburg Pirates team. One of their pitchers was a rookie named Frederick W. Schmit.

Ossee Schreckengost, in the safety of the St. Louis team since July 31, spoke of two of his former mates. "I told Tommy Tucker and Wheels Schmit of the Wanderers, that a rodent was loose in their garret when they got on their hobby horse and chinned about their popularity as coaches. Schmitty and Tom were as jealous as a pair of rivals about their coaching talents and Joe Quinn eggs 'em on." (*CP*, Aug 23).

Thur Aug 24 During the Misfits seven week travail away from home, they had participated in fifty games and won exactly six. All of their victories had come as part of doubleheader splits; something the weary Misfits had grown quite accustomed to. The embarrassed home town losers were Baltimore, Washington twice, Philadelphia, Chicago, and Pittsburg. The Misfits somehow managed to drag their bones to fifteen two-game affairs in that stretch, thinning their pitching and catchers threadbare. Thirteen times in the fifty games at least ten runs were scored by the opposition. Now, because New York Giants' President Andrew Freedman insisted on playing games as they were scheduled, the Misfits returned home to League Park. It was certainly strange to be back in Cleveland, a town where once the "soot-covered Antebellum stone monstrosity" known as Union Depot once boasted in a sign, "Don't Judge This Town by This Depot." (Condon 189). It could well have said, "Don't Judge This Town By Its Ball Club." Joe Quinn spoke of the elongated road trip in a heartless whisper: "No we haven't won many games on the trip, but we drew pretty fair crowds and are

130

ahead on the season. I think we did as well as you could expect when you remember how crippled up we have been, how many doubleheaders we have been forced to play, and, considering the fact that we play all our games on foreign diamonds, where we never get a friendly word of encouragement. If I may be permitted to paraphrase Gilbert, I might add, 'A ballplayer's lot is not a happy one,' especially if you happen to be on a cast-adrift team." (*CP*, Aug 25).

With Quinn's remarks in mind, the reception afforded the players was less than rousing. There were no parades, nor balloons, nor marching bands. Instead, the Exiles took up their places in the field in their usual way; complete anonymity. The *Plain Dealer* picks up the description: (Aug 25)

Evidently the interest in baseball in this city has revived in just about the same proportion that the team that is supposed to represent Cleveland in the National League has improved. There were at least 100 at League Park yesterday when the wandering aggregation of barnstormers called the Clevelands reappeared on what used to be their home grounds. Such a welcome was about what the players expected. They have long since become accustomed to walk up and take their daily beating without hope of sympathy, and they looked for no support at home.

Individually, the players still seem to be full of life and anxious to play ball. Collectively, the team is worth just about what it would pay if the team remained here all the time. The players seem to realize that they cannot win and are not expected to, so they take their medicine in as palatable form as possible.

Frank Bates took to the mound for Joe Quinn's boys while Bill Carrick hurled for New York. "As to the game itself, it reminded one a good deal of two dimes and ten pennies, for compared with ordinary National League baseball it certainly looked like thirty cents." (*CPD*, Aug 25). Thirty cents wasn't a lot, but it could get a fan a bleacher seat in Cleveland with a nickel to spare (Suehsdorf 36).

The Exiles jumped ahead 2-0 in the first but Carrick settled. Bates seemed satisfied to offer up a litany of walks and long hits; in short, his normal outing. Giants catcher Parke Wilson doubled. Third baseman Mike Grady tripled. Leftfielder Tom O'Brien "lost a ball in the seats" for a home run. For the Misfits, Sport McAllister split his hand on a foul tip (*CP*, Aug 25). Six to two and loss 94.

The *New York Times* wrote "President Robison hoped the New Yorks would prove a drawing attraction, but he was mistaken." (Aug 25). What Robison based his assumption on was unknown, for the Giants were buried in 10th place with a 45-58 record. His Misfits were simply buried. After all, the manager was an undertaker.

Fri Aug 25   Two dignitaries of note turned up at League Park for the second game of the homestand.   For perhaps the first time all season, Messrs. Frank Robison and his brother witnessed a ball game.   What they saw from their box seat perch was a pleasant surprise. Again, the *Plain Dealer* describes (Aug 26):

An eighth wonder has come into the world and the Colossus of Rhodes, the Pyramids, the Statue of Zeus and the rest of the seven wonders better look to their laurels. Cleveland won another game.

How it happened is beyond explanation. Something must have inspired the Exiles. They really played baseball after a fashion that is supposed to be played in the National League. They put up such a sharp, fast game that the 200 people who had gone out to League Park to get a little clean air and take a quite siesta were given something very close to enthusiasm.

Cleveland started out so well that there were evidences of a contest from the first. Of course, everybody expected that the New Yorks would turn in at some time in the game and wipe the earth with Quinn's men; but even with such an outlook well established by precedent the locals, or ex-locals, or whatever they are, played so well that it was quite interesting.

When the game was over and New York had struggled in vain to overcome the Quinnites lead, the astonishment was so great that it is fortunate there were no serious results. No one who witnessed the game need have the least fear of heart disease. All who survived that surprise can survive almost anything.

It was the second time on the season that the *Plain Dealer* referred to a Transfers victory as the eighth wonder of the world. Charlie Knepper started for the home team, pitching in fine and rare form. He was backed up nicely by shortstop Harry Lochhead's fielding, catcher Joe Sugden's throwing which "cut big hunks of ice," and Buttermilk Tommy Dowd's batting heroics (*CPD*, Aug 26). Big lefthander James Bentley "Cy" Seymour went for New York, with a nickname that reminded no one of the other Cy in the National League. However, Knepper was a tad better and thanks to third baseman Mike Grady, who spent the day throwing wildly, the Misfits were 4-2 victors. It had taken the Spiders 13 games to beat the Giants.

Sat Aug 26   After his heartbreaking Monday loss to the Cubs in Chicago, Crazy Schmit took the mound for Cleveland. His opposition was New York lefthander Ed Doheny. But, for rather obvious reasons, Schmit was not his usual self.

On an overcast day before a typical Cleveland crowd, which is to say very few, the game began. The Misfits batted first to no result. In New York's half, shortstop Harry Lochhead ended the inning with a beautiful catch. "He ran close to the foul line and far out into left field to pull down Doyle's drive that looked as safe as a man in jail." (*CPD*, Aug 27). In inning two, rightfielder Pop Foster, shortstop Scott Hardesty, and third baseman Charlie Gettig singled.

Gettig was playing in place of Mike Grady, called home to visit his sick mother. The singles, coupled with a passed ball and a wild pitch, led to two runs. Doheny checked the Misfits until the fifth. Amid darkening skies, Lochhead tripled and Tommy Tucker drove home the shortstop with a sacrifice fly. It was 2-1 New York. The side was retired. Then, Mother Nature let loose with a cannonading barrage. Thunder cracked and rain came pelting onto the field. While the players scrambled, umpire Manassau quickly called the game. The Wanderers, who if they didn't have any bad luck, wouldn't have any at all, watched raindrops to their 95th loss.

Sun Aug 27 No Sunday baseball was played in Cleveland, but *Sporting Life* was spending recent issues desperately trying to find ways to complement the downtrodden Mudville nine. On their pitching, the weekly observed, "Cleveland has two fine pitchers in Hughey and Knepper. With a strong team they would be talked about." But, this was the same team that the *Cleveland Press* had compared to inmates at an asylum. On infield play: "Tom Tucker is playing just about as good as ever and the way he is stretching himself to save wild throws is something that must be seen to be appreciated." But, what did that say about Sullivan at 3b and Lochhead at shortstop? Finally, on outfield defense, "Both Harley and Dowd ought to be on a big team."

Mon Aug 28 On Monday, the second place Beaneaters from Boston arrived. Almost two hundred gawkers showed up to watch.

Frank Selee sent in the strapping righthander Vic Willis to oppose the Misfits while Joe Quinn handed the ball to reliable Jimmy Hughey. Willis, one of the league's best, had the misfortune of pitching in the July 1st debacle, won by the Misfits 10-9 at League Park. Hughey simply had the misfortune of hurling the entire season for the Misfits.

In the first, some sloppy fielding by Cleveland gave Boston two runs. The Misfits cut the margin in half in the second with the help of Tommy Tucker's wondrous triple. In the Boston third, Tommy Dowd made two eye-opening catches to the delight of the crowd. It stayed 2-1 until the Beaneaters fourth inning. Hard hitting Stahl singled to left and advanced when Dick Harley muffed. Stahl went to third on an out and scored when new hire catcher Jim Duncan dropped Harry Lochhead's fielder's choice grounder. The flyweight Duncan had come over from the 11th place Washington team and immediately began contributing. Boston had scored three runs and the Misfits had three errors. Then Cleveland came up with a baserunning rally in their half that bedeviled Willis and his catcher, Boileryard Clarke.

Charlie Hemphill began with a single before being forced by Quinn. Suter Sullivan drove one far to the fence and before the crowd stopped yelling, the

Misfit stood on third. The blow scored Quinn to make it 3-2 Boston. A perturbed Willis walked Lochhead. Then, the Misfits attempted something right out of a Frank Merriwell dime novel. Right under the noses of Willis and Clarke, Sullivan bolted for home and Lochhead for second in a double steal. The game was tied. Catcher Duncan dumped a weak grounder in front of the mound between pitcher and first base. Fred Tenney knocked the ball down, but Willis recovered and ran to the base unassisted to get Duncan. Meanwhile, an alert Lochhead sped around and scored when Willis' throw was wide to Boileryard Clarke. An egg could have been fried on the forehead of manager Selee, not to mention Willis and Clarke. Shortstop Herman Long snatched a Hughey drive to end the inning. The Misfits led 4-3.

The Bostons stayed mad until the seventh when their focus shifted to winning the game. Sliding Billy Hamilton, Tenney, and Long all hit in succession to even matters at 4-4. Hughey retired the next two hitters, but Duncan's passed ball and third baseman Jimmy Collins' double plated two more. After that the teams traded outs, the boys from Boston were winners 6-4. Like the little girl in the fairy tale, Cleveland had played an erratic contest, sometimes good, as their daring baserunning would attest, and sometimes horrid. Six errors were made before the home faithful. The loss dropped the Clevelands to 19-96, 21 and a half games behind Washington. Commenting on the humanity of the Bostons traveling to Cleveland to play, Beaneater President Soden smugly proclaimed, "Every win for the Boston club is a victory for the best in the national game." (*BG*, Aug 29).

Tues Aug 29   Due to an earlier rainout in Boston, the home boys and Beantowners played two for the price of one at League Park. Relatively speaking, the crowd size was good but later it ballooned to an "almost record breaking attendance." (*CPD*, Aug 30). In a city of 370,000 just what that figure was is unknown, but at least the peanut vendors were busy.

Game one featured Boston's ten-year veteran Charles Augustus "Kid" Nichols versus Charlie Knepper. The kind of pitching heroics that righthander Nichols had already been part of, Knepper could only fantasize about. The contest required "no deep analysis;" the Boston hurler was untouchable and the Misfits "had as much chance of going against Nichols to any purpose as they would going head first against a well constructed brick wall." (*CPD*, Aug 30). The scoring and hollering began in the first inning. Umpire McGarr called Herman Long safe on a Lochhead throw when Long was "apparently out beyond question." (*CPD*, Aug 30). The crowd howled and while late arrivals took their seats, they joined right in the screaming session. The Boston shortstop then stole second. Knepper walked Chick Stahl and Jimmy Collins doubled Long and Stahl in. It was 2-0 Boston. No further tallies were made until the Boston fourth. In that stanza, "more wrath expended upon McGarr." (*CPD*, Aug 30). Hughey Duffy started with a ground out. Bobby Lowe bounced to Lochhead but the latter's fumble put Lowe on first. Catcher Marty Bergen lifted one to the sun field in left for a hit. Pitcher Nichols then dribbled to Knepper who threw to second baseman Joe Quinn to start a double play. Quinn relayed the ball down to first baseman Sport McAllister but McGarr ruled Quinn did not touch the second base bag and all hands were safe. Lowe scored for 3-0. The ensuing kicks raised enough dust to have some players think they were in the Mohave desert. Fan reaction towards McGarr was scathing. Knepper wilted. Billy Hamilton and Long drew free passes to force in another run. There was no further scoring until the Boston seventh. Five tallies came in due to sharp stick work and strategic bunting. Knepper and catcher Duncan were rendered helpless, a feeling similar to the Misfits batting against Nichols. The final was 9-1.

After the first debacle, the second game made even less sense. Cleveland decided to change things by batting first against Jouett Meekin, late of the New York Giants. The Misfits could only send Harry Colliflower in to pitch. Umpire McGarr "gave decisions on the bases so inconsiderate of Clevelands rights that Snyder was implored to change places with him." (*CPD*, Aug 30). Boston opened the scoring in the initial inning. With one out, Fred Tenney and Herman Long singled, the former moving to third. Stahl popped to Harry Lochhead at short. With two out, Boston fooled young Colliflower into a delayed double steal. Long broke for second while the throw came from Colliflower to Quinn. Tenney raced home while Quinn held the ball; standing and staring as if contemplating space travel. Perhaps, Quinn was wondering how on earth did he ever become involved in the undertaking of managing. In the second inning, Bobby Lowe hit safely, stole twice and came in on a Quinn error. The Misfits stirred against Meekin in the third. Colliflower led off with a single but met an untimely end in a Tommy Dowd double play. Dick Harley drove safely to left and Quinn doubled. Harley was "going like a racehorse," and scored (*CPD*, Aug 30). Charlie Hemphill popped to centerfielder Duffy who promptly dropped the ball. "The crowd went into fits and Duffy probably fined himself 30 cents." (*CPD*, Aug 30). Quinn came in to tie at 2-2. Boston went ahead by two in their half with a Long hit, a Collins triple, and a sacrifice fly. In the next frame, Colliflower gave up a barrage and the game was lost. Seven Bostonians crossed the home rubber on an assortment of singles, doubles, and stolen bases. By the seventh inning, the umpires called the game. "Darkness was the pretext, but it was really because everybody had become tired of the one-sided contest." (*CPD*, Aug 30). It ended 11-3.

Cleveland's lone highlight for the double loss was Crazy Schmit, who surfaced from his Chicago and New York Giants doldrums to coach first base in his unique and lively way. The Clevelands again sank into the abyss of defeat, losing games 97 and 98.

Wed Aug 30   As the month of August drew to a close, the Misfits played one last game at home against Frank Selee's Beaneaters. Before a smattering of sun worshippers, casual observers, and picnic goers, the Misfits again were losers; this time by 8-5. Loss number 99 was in the books.

"Once again, it was simply a battle between a fox terrier and a rat at League Park yesterday and Cleveland again appeared in the role of the rodent." (*CPD*, Aug 31). Mr. Bates took the mound for the Misfits. His opponent was righthander Parson Lewis. To Bates, all hitters must have looked like Cap Anson. He seemed to make no discernible difference between a .200 hitter and a .400 hitter. Of course, neither did the hitters with Bates' delivery. But, unlike most his previous efforts, only one Boston sticker walked. That was probably due to the fact that they seldom let Bates pitch long enough to any given batter (*CPD*, Aug 31). Among the 16 hits Bates surrendered, five went for extra bases, including three doubles, a triple, and a homer by Chick Stahl. Lewis wasn't much better. His slants were also hammered about the park freely. But, the pattern was for the Misfits to let the other team mount a big lead and the Clevelands to fall short in the final tally.

Joe Quinn provided most of the Misfits highlights. In the third inning with two out and Stahl on first, the Bostonians were on offense. Hugh Duffy grounded to Quinn at second base. Umpire McGarr, in an attempt to get close and call the play correctly, toppled over Quinn, and knocked the manager out temporarily. McGarr got up, dusted himself off, and then had the gall to rule Duffy out on "interference" of all things. Needles to say, the Boston team raised quite a fuss, hurling not a few four-letter invectives on the base umpire. The *Plain Dealer* box score notated mockingly, "*Duffy out for McGarr's interference." (Aug 31). Later, in inning eight, Quinn chose a most opportune moment to scald a triple as the bases were loaded at the time. Quinn was thrown out trying to score on the play.

After the conclusion of the series sweep by Boston, Elmer E. Bates of *Sporting Life* commented that several Beaneaters had been loafing on the field. But, even a team of loafers could defeat the Clevelands. Bates singled out Hamilton's play in center field as "lamentably poor" and said that shortstop Herman Long once refused to run home from third. When Spider pitcher Hughey yelled at him, "Why don't you come home?" Long's reply was "Oh, what's the matter with you? Do you want me to kill myself? I'm near dead now." (Sep 9).

The Misfits woeful lack of fan support brought to mind a commentary in a Milwaukee newspaper penned 20 years earlier: "Base ball, it will be remembered by old settlers, is a game played by eighteen persons wearing shirts and drawers. They scatter around the field to try to catch a cannon-ball covered with rawhide. The game is to get people to pay two shillings to come inside the fence." (Leitner 10).

Cleveland's season series with tough Boston ended with a commendable three victories in 14 tries.

Thur Aug 31   "Good bye: see you in a month," said Tommy Dowd, as he boarded a train a Union Depot for Brooklyn, after the final game with Boston last week.

"Coming back, then, are you?" somebody asked.

"Oh, yes," said Tom. "You know we must make a good finish. So we'll come here about Sept. 28 for a few days rest in order to get in shape for the fast clip up the stretch." (*SL*, Sep 9).

From Cleveland, the Misfits moved on to the big city. In New York, the Misfits could have taken the $8.00 train excursion to Niagara Falls to drown their sorrows. Or they could have rode a parlour car via Lake Placid, Loon Lake, or Fire Island to catch bluefish. Instead, as per National League rules, the Misfits played in Brooklyn to absorb loss number 100.

A sparse crowd of just over one thousand souls saw Brooklyn's high-flying Superbas send Jim Hughes in to easily beat the low-flying Misfits' Crazy Schmit. The score was 9-3. The Cleveland loss came despite the fact that they scored the first three runs and Brooklyn committed five errors. The big hit was a bases loaded double by Suter Sullivan, who "seems to be out of place on such a poor team as the Clevelands." (*NYT*, Sep 1). The question begged, who exactly was in place on a team that needed a telescope to see Brooklyn in the standings?   Harry Colliflower played first base for Tom Tucker.   Sport McAllister moved to second for Joe Quinn. Perhaps neither Tucker nor Quinn wanted to be on the field for the historic defeat.

Loss #100 was especially profitable for a St. Louis "joker" who wagered between $250-$500 that the Clevelands would lose 100 games before they won twenty. "He had nervous prostration after the Nomads victory over the Giants last Friday. He soon recovered, however, and Thursday night, walked triumphantly up to the stakeholder's office and dragged down his money." (*CP*, Sep 1).

September

"The Inevitable Met Once More."

Fri Sep 1

Mournfully the Clevelands departed for the west this afternoon with nothing to show for their pilgrimage east but three games lost and a few dollars that barely compensated for making the trip. The Clevelands are so utterly bad that they can't draw even in a city where the prospective champions are playing. And, too, Brooklyn cranks are so much disgusted with the fast and loose methods in use by the league magnates that they are not patronizing the games as they did early in the season.

The Clevelands go their parts as bravely as any team in the National League. The mere fact that they can't win seems not to have the slightest effect upon them. They are out every day playing as hard as they can for what is in sight. Were the team furnished with a pitcher or two that amounted to something, it might be possible now and then to mark other than defeat on the ledger. But, there isn't a pitcher in the lot, except Knepper, who appears to be worth much as a winner. Hughey started out well in the first game today and for a while there were fears expressed that Brooklyn might lose the game. Just at the critical point, Hughey slipped a cable and away he went, soaring into the air, while the Brooklyns hammered out seven runs and with them the game. (*CPD*, Sep 2).

The Spiders jumped out first off Brooklyn hurler Jack Dunn. Buttermilk Tommy Dowd doubled into the left garden. Gentleman Dick Harley grounded out and Dowd took third. Undertaker Quinn smacked a ball to the outfield on a line. With the resulting sacrifice, Dowd tallied. In the sixth, Charlie Hemphill drove a deep one to center fielder while Fielder Jones chased. With the fence being some five hundred feet away, the sphere rolled and rolled like a billiard ball. Hemphill ran in for a home run (Lowry 40). Then Hughey cracked in the seventh. Five runs scored; the big blow being a Hughie Jennings three bagger with two on. Two more came in for the home towners in the eighth thanks in part to Bill Dahlen's triple to left and veteran Deacon McGuire's double. No sweat for the Superbas; 7-2.

The *Cleveland Press* called Hughey a "great six-inning pitcher. If he could only get over his habit of weakening in the seventh, he could fix his own price for his services." (Sep 3).

For the second affair the crowd ballooned to 2500, though many of them must have wondered where the sport was in the Brooklyns playing the Clevelands. Ned Hanlon's Superbas could probably win these games blindfolded and with their hands tied behind their backs. They resorted instead

138

to crafty baserunning and solid pitching. "Hanlon decided on McJames to puzzle the tailenders." (*CPD*, Sep 2). The baserunning laurels went to Hughie Jennings and Willie Keeler, who between them both weighed 300 pounds, soaking wet. Big Charlie Knepper was scheduled to work for the Spiders but his arm came up sore. Instead, Quinn relied on Harry Colliflower. Five crossed the plate for the Brooklyns. Suter Sullivan was the only score for Cleveland. After the Misfits took their somber hitting drill in the seventh, the game was called so they could catch a train to Johnstown, Pennsylvania. The double loss meant eight straight and zero for fourteen against Brooklyn.

Sat Sep 2   In a city that had been devastated by a flood just ten years before, the Misfits barnstormed into Johnstown. It was to be a diversion for Cleveland, a time for fun, and a chance to play a local amateur bunch. The bunch beat the National Leaguers by 7-5. Frank Bates pitched.

Sun Sep 3   The hot and stuffy journey from Johnstown to Cincinnati allowed the players on the Exiles to play cards in their underwear to relieve some of the boredom of the trip.

A crowd of 7316 witnessed the "triangular doubleheader" at Redland Park (*TEC*, Sep 4). Louisville defeated the Reds in the opener. Then the Misfits took on the Cincinnatis in the second contest. Ten Thousand Dollar Ted Breitenstein went for the Reds. His monetary appellation was a tribute to his two no-hitters. His opponent was Charlie Knepper, fully recuperated from his lame arm. From the get-go, the game was a tight, pitching dominated affair. Breitenstein was "in elegant style," quelling the Misfits all day (*TEC*, Sep 4). The Misfits only run was scored on an outfield mixup 'twixt Algie McBride and Kip Selbach. It allowed Sport McAllister a triple. Knepper, with his deliberate motions between pitches, unnerved the Cincinnati spectators who taunted him and called him 'Ice,' on account of the slowness of an ice wagon (*TEC*, Sep 4). Unfortunately, Dick Harley killed the big Cleveland lefthander's chances when he muffed a fly ball in the fifth inning. The error, dropped after Harley's valiant chase, let in the two runs that won the game. In the eighth frame, after the Clevelands had put away their bats, the game was called on account of darkness. A 3-1 loss meant 103 for the season.

As a sidelight to the game, Cincinnati rookie outfielder Socks Seybold received 32 packages of tobacco after his fly ball plunked a spot in the left field fence. He freely distributed the tobacco to his teammates (*TEC*, Sep 4).

Mon Sep 4   A doubleheader occurred between the two Ohio teams on Monday. Both contests, attended by just over three thousand, were devoid of any real drama. Like previous affairs, the *Cincinnati Enquirer* sports page printed its curious one-word headline followed by several other short remarks. "Two" as in "two more for the Reds." Other headlines for Cleveland-Cincinnati games read "Showed," "Eighteen," and "Ear Muffs." They referred to (in order) a lack of early season training by the Misfits, the number of innings the Clevelands were held scoreless in a doubleheader, and a particularly cold day in Cincinnati.

Game one pitted bulky righthander Emerson P. "Pink" Hawley for the Reds against one James Ulysses Hughey, winless in six weeks. Two symbolic fielding plays told the story. With Cleveland batting in the first, a short fly was punched to left field in foul territory. "Selbach took it on a dead run. He was pitched over as he reached the ball. He could not regain his equilibrium and fell over on his face. He pluckily held onto the ball." (*TEC*, Sep 5). In the third, Harry Colliflower, patrolling centerfield for the cramped-up Tommy Dowd, muffed a fly. Colliflower's mishap led to a run. The Reds made the plays and the Spiders did not. Hawley was hit hard but kept the Cleveland blows scattered. Hughey was again beset by terrible luck, and his mates' best scoring rally consisted of a hit batsman, a stolen base, and two outs. At least Cleveland was having some fun losing. With Hughey batting and the bases loaded, the Misfits pitcher yelled instructions of manager Quinn. Before Quinn could reply, Crazy Schmit hollered, "Touch all the bases as you go around, Hughey." The Misfits bench erupted in laughter (*TEC*, Sep 4). The Reds won 6-3.

The second exhibition was less a game than it was a stage for the pitcher. Crazy Schmit went for Cleveland against the Reds' Brewery Jack Taylor. The Reds' pitcher brewed up a froth of good tosses and the Misfits were hitless into the seventh. Schmit, meanwhile, reverted back to his inscrutable self after a brief personality slump. Realizing he could control the ball and the attentions of fans and players alike, Schmit pitched and clowned. To be downcast on the Misfits seemed a lost cause in itself. The Wanderers made six errors behind Schmit; two by Harry Lochhead and one each by center field novice Colliflower and the newly-bespectacled Hemphill. The German wasn't sure whether to laugh or cry. Soon enough, though, he decided, to the delight of the derisive Cincinnati fans. The final was 8-1 for the home team.

A piqued Dick Harley responded to a Cincinnati sportswriter who said life couldn't be so bad for the perpetually road-weary Clevelands because they could save a lot of money. Harley's comment: "We don't save any money by having our board paid. Anybody knows that you will spend just double the money traveling than you do at home. Getting the board money is only a snap. We count that much as gained, and then spend just twice as much because it is velvet." (*TEC*, Sep 5). "Velvet" was a term for extra cash.

Tue Sep 5 The Ladies Day doubleheader in Cincinnati was blistering hot with temperatures near 100 degrees. The stands were filled with the fair sex and their escort. The ladies perspired daintily. The male rooters pointed out all the rules of the game to their dates, but the action on the field was not exactly conducive to explanation or excitement.

In the first tilt, righthander Whoa Bill Phillips was Buck Ewing's pitching choice for the Reds. Phillips had been a teammate of Crazy Schmit's nine years previous with the horrendous 1890 Pittsburg Pirates. Joe Quinn went with dark, handsome Frank Bates. If the amount of newspaper ink devoted to each pitcher was a direct correlation of ability, Bates would have won easily. Both, the *Cleveland Plain Dealer* and the Cincinnati paper spent most of their column trying to explain Bates, and for that matter, why he was in the league.

Phillips faltered only in the Cleveland seventh when three Spiders touched home plate. Bates, on the other hand, was butchered to the tune of 22 hits, 37 total bases, eight walks, two hit batsman, and 180 pitches (*TEC*, Sep 6). "After the third inning it fairly rained singles and triples, and Jake Beckley sandwiched a homer in between all of this." (*CPD*, Sep 6). The *Plain Dealer* also wrote, "To go into the details of how the runs were made would take up too much space." (Sep 6). The *Enquirer* was more descriptive, calling Bates' pitches "tapioca," and saying that it was a "hit and run game with the Reds doing the hitting and the tail-end Wanderers doing the running." (*TEC*, Sep 6). The mustachioed Jake Beckley, "jolted one of Bates curves on the jugular. It went like a streak to right field. It took a bound, jumped over Hemphill's head and rolled to the fence embankment." (*TEC*, Sep 6). Six triples overall were hit off Bates, including two by his rival Phillips. Right hand batting Kip Selbach embarrassed Bates further by moving to the left hand batters box. Selbach took his usual minute and a half to fidget with his cap, belt, and shirt. Then, he took about one and half seconds to whack a triple. Several ladies must have innocently asked their men what the Misfits could possibly be doing. That same question had puzzled baseball experts around the country. When the basepath dust had finally cleared and the scoreboard could be seen, it read 19-3.

A Sydney, Ohio man presented the Reds with two dozen new bats before the doubleheader and judging by the results, Buck Ewing decided to order more (*TEC*, Sep 6).

The second game offered much more in the way of sport. Because the Misfits took an early lead, partisan Reds fans rooted for the visitors for a time. Then, it was feared that the home towners could actually lose a "cinch" game, they switched their loyalties back again (*TEC*, Sep 6).

A new recruit from Detroit, big righthander Emil Frisk started for the Reds. The pitching vegetable, Harry Colliflower, planted himself in the Misfits' box. The scoring began in inning two for Cleveland. Tommy Tucker and Sport McAllister got base hits and when pitcher Colliflower did the same, the Misfits led 2-0. The Reds cut the advantage in their half when third baseman The

Tabasco Kid Elberfeld drew a walk. Eighteen year veteran 2b Bid McPhee and pitcher Frisk singled to make it 2-1. In the third, Cleveland's Charlie Hemphill drew a base from Frisk and Suter Sullivan doubled to make it 3-1. The same pair combined for another tally in the fifth. Hemphill hit and stole second and Sullivan again batted him in for 4-1. The Spiders advantage was short-lived. Ancient Jake Beckley bunted safely. Elberfeld walked. McPhee and catcher Heinie Peitz conspired to tie the game at 4-4. The Reds moved ahead easily in the 6th when Ted Breitenstein, playing center field for an injured Algie McBride, doubled. Kip Selbach hit and Beckley tripled. An Elberfeld hit and Crazy Schmit's error in center field made it 8-4. Schmit was getting a chance to use that glove he carried along. But, Tommy Dowd he wasn't. The Misfits managed to draw a tad closer against rookie Frisk but the late inning comeback fell short again. Near the end of the second affair, the Cincinnati players were exhausted from running around the bases. The Spiders outfielders "looked as though they would like to have ponies or bicycles to chase the ball." (*TEC*, Sep 6). It ended 9-7. Losses 106 and 107 were secure.

This brief article appeared in the Cincinnati paper. It chronicled the pharmaceutical career of Dr. Frederick Schmit and his patient, the charley-horsed Tommy Dowd.

Tommie Dowd, the sick centerfielder of the Clevelands, who has been sick for several days, was able to be around yesterday. "Tackie Schmit nearly put me away." said Tommie last night. "Tackie looked in my room last night and inquired how I was getting along. He looked at my tongue and said, 'I know what's the matter with you. Your stomach needs to be revolutionized. I'll fix you.' He did fix me. He went to a drugstore and returned with a dose of medicine. For ten minutes afterward I nearly died vomiting. I vomited for over an hour. He certainly revolutionized my stomach. There was nothing left in it. It did me good, however. I was a great deal better this morning."

After the activities of the day had commenced, Cleveland team Secretary George Muir was given instructions from President Robison to inform two players of their release. Silently, Muir slipped notices into the player's boxes at the Cincinnati hotel. The two men being let go were pitcher Frank Bates and well-liked Tommy Tucker. Both were given the "usual ten days notice of release." (*SL*, Sep 9).

The twenty-two year old Bates' release certainly came as no surprise, especially after his performance on the day and on the season. He held no hard feelings and said he would like to go back to the Interstate League (*TEC*, Sep 6). Bates came to Cleveland from the St. Louis team with Ossee Schreckengost in exchange for Lave Cross and Willie Sudhoff, Bates' wildness was a constant negative. He was always adverse to the advice of his veteran teammates and his looks reminded one of an angry, young man. There was constant speculation that Bates was the worst pitcher in the league. Once his name was errantly placed in a boxscore after a particularly bad effort by Jim Hughey. The typist must have saw all the hits and assumed it could only be Frank Bates. Perhaps though, Bates was born a little late. He might have done much better in 1884 when 9 balls constituted a walk. At the time of his release, the *Plain Dealer* speculated: "Why he was kept on the payroll so long is a mystery, but it was probably to help the Clevelands make a new record." (Sep 6). The *Cincinnati Enquirer* said of Bates' record with Cleveland that he was "still a maiden, that he has not pitched a winning game in fast company." (Sep 6). Interesting how newspapers could compare winning a single baseball game to a loss of virginity. But, had the newspaper done better research they would have known that Bates' lone 1899 Cleveland victory came as the result of the miracle batting rally versus the Bostons at League Park, July 1, 1899.

In defense of Bates, Cleveland batting support behind him was miserable. Six times in his starts the Spiders scored but one run. Four times they made only two and two times they managed but three tallies. But, even if the Cleveland hitters sprayed balls all over the yard against the opposition, it is doubtful that Bates record would have improved. New York baseball teams were not kind to Frank Bates. Five times he lost to the lowly Giants and thrice to Brooklyn. Twice John McGraw's Baltimore's beat him by lopsided scores. What would McGraw have done to Bates after watching him pitch considering he was a man who fired his hurler Jeremiah Nops for losing a game to the Misfits? Bates record at the time of his release was 1-17. He had lost his last twelve games in a row.

Letting go long-time National League veteran Tommy Tucker was a much sadder proposition. Oft-times, Tucker's vivacious, rambunctious, and aggressive behavior on the field and on the coaching lines was the only thing the Misfits had. But, Tommy, who had been an integral factor on the 1891-1893 championship Boston teams, had several failings late in his career. His one-time sensational hitting had dipped drastically, an extra base hit being somewhat of a shock. When he wasn't getting thrown out on base, he was getting thrown out of games. In May Tucker said that the Spiders President Stanley Robison would pay all umpire-inflicted fines as an inducement for aggressive play. But, Robison denied Tucker's comment (*SL*, May 20). Tucker also pilloried umpires who in turn punished him by barring him from coaching. Tommy's vicious tongue went at it with Messrs. Burns, O'Day, McGarr, and Lynch, among others in Nick Young's umpiring stable. But, Tucker could hold his head up. He was always the first man to stand up for his team despite his quick temper that annoyed many. An early description of Tucker said he was "a hot-tempered and tough talking lad about as big as a doorway, who was still looking for a man or group of men that could lick him." (Smith 62).

Poor company, that being the Misfits' team, probably had a lot to do with Tommy's suspect playing and he vowed to continue his career. Tucker desired to be picked up by Pittsburg or Philadelphia (*CPD*, Sep 6). Sport McAllister or Jim Duncan were likely candidates to fill Tommy's vacancy at first base for the remainder of the season.

Wed Sep 6   The Spiders latest losing skein had now reached thirteen games, but theirs wasn't the only team in the league in turmoil. The *Cleveland Plain Dealer* printed this sensational tale on the fortunes of the St. Louis team. The article was entitled, "Ball Players and Detectives." (Sep 7).

A story that will cause considerable amusement in baseball circles leaked out here yesterday, after the facts had been carefully guarded for months. Evidently the magnates are trying to outdo each other in absurdity, and doing their best to establish a reputation for unique management. Freedman held the record for smallness in his management of players until the St. Louis magnates cut loose, and now they have the New Yorker beaten so far he is unlikely to see the flag.

Nearly all sorts of abuses have been heaped upon the players, but it remained for the owners of the Old Cleveland club to establish a record for belittling the men that make baseball.

There is no news about the story of the latest outrage of the magnates. It occurred way back in July, when the season was young. Of course everyone will remember the Old Cleveland team was sent to St. Louis to win the pennant for that city. The start the team made was good, but after a while the transplanted players began to lose games rather rapidly. Then it was that somebody wrote a letter to one of the alleged owners of the team and stated therein that the club was losing because of the behavior of the players "after hours."

This letter caused the most unique move that has ever been made in baseball.

Instead of investigating the charge the magnate in question went to a detective agency and employed men to shadow each player not even neglecting Manager Tebeau, who owns more stock in the club than the man who employed the St. Louis manager. For several days the players were subjected to the indignity of being followed from dawn to midnight, and then to dawn again, and in the meantime, it is said, that as everything was not running smoothly, they were requested not to push their claims for salaries. But, the detectives were all paid no doubt.

This state of affairs went on until every man on the team learned of it. Finally an indignation meeting was held. There was much talk of resentment, and had the new league been sufficiently far advanced to warrant a revolt the St. Louis club would have been without players.

It was finally decided that the best way to break up the shadowing was to break up the shadowers. This was done most effectively on the night of July 2. The players were about to start for Chicago and they learned that their shadowers were to follow them. The management cared nothing for expenses.

On the date mentioned, however, there was a little mix up that the detectives and the management did not anticipate.

The detectives were employed to follow the men; so when two of them, namely Harry Blake and John Powell- two very husky lads by the way- left their hotel they were followed. Now, it chanced that the following process required a walk into a dark and unfrequented neighborhood. The detectives followed, but they soon wished they hadn't. After Powell and Blake got through with them they had just enough strength to carry a message to the rest of their clan, and that message was to the effect that it would not be safe to shadow ball players. The detective agency threw up its contract immediately after this little incident.

The lengths that Frank Robison would go to. It can be safely assumed that the Cleveland Spiders had no undercover escorts following them around. But, had the Misfits gotten into the same situation, one Thomas Joseph Tucker or one Frederick W. Schmit would have probably been happy to play the parts of Powell and Blake.

Thur Sep 7 From Cincinnati, the Misfits' Express chugged its way northwest to Chicago, Illinois. There they were met by the leftfield bleacherites who had recently taken up the practice of lobbing pop bottles into visiting outfielder's territory (*SL*, Sep 2).

Before a crowd of only 400, Chicago started workhorse righthander John W. Taylor. The Spiders countered with long-haired Charlie Knepper. Up until the seventh inning, the "Orphans had been gathering their runs one at a time, in a listless fashion, that betokened confidence of winning without much effort." (*CPD*, Sep 8). The key blows were provided by leftfield veteran Jimmy Ryan, centerfielder Bill "Little Eva" Lange, and sturdy third baseman Bill Bradley. Thanks to a typographical error, Bradley is listed in the *Macmillan Baseball Encyclopedia*'s second edition as being 12 years old in 1899. But, the way the Misfits played, a ballplayer of that age had better than an even chance against the Clevelands.

Taylor, meanwhile, was sailing along in the seventh inning with a three-hit shutout. The *Chicago Tribune* reported that at the stage the game was "as tame as a french duel." (Sep 8). Trailing 4-0, the Spiders took their swings in the eighth and "the way they straightened out Taylor's slants was a caution. McAllister and Knepper started the fusillade, each making a hit. Dowd bunted, but was thrown out. Harley singled, but passed to second when Lange made a useless throw to the plate. Quinn followed with a double, and to add to the misery, two bounders by Hemphill and Sullivan took nasty directions, and succeeding in eluding Conner.

The case was beginning to get serious, but Tucker went out. A minute later Lochhead singled, sending home the tallies that put Cleveland ahead. McAllister, not content with having started the trouble, made another hit, but Chance made a quick throw and nipped Lochhead off third, putting an end to the slaughter." (*CT*, Sep 8). The Misfits had miraculously moved ahead with a six run inning. It was 6-4. The Misfits took this two-run advantage into the bottom of the ninth inning. The Cubs had "only a vague idea of winning out the game," as several hundred Chicago spectators grabbed their hats and headed for the exits. Knepper was ready to close out the 7th place Cubbies then and there. Taylor began by being hit by a pitch and Ryan forced him out. Bill Lange sent a parabola to centerfielder Buttermilk Tommy Dowd, fresh from his stomach revolution on Tuesday. Dowd caught the ball and two men were out. "Nothing seemed surer for a victory for the Clevelands." (*CPD*, Sep 8). First baseman Everett singled and up stepped Sam Mertes to the bat. Mertes, whose swing vanquished Crazy Schmit on August 20, singled home Ryan. It was 6-5 and the "crowd began to hope again." (*CT*, Sep 8). Bradley hit a grasscutter to Suter Sullivan at third. The toss was clean to Tommy Tucker, but the first baseman, possibly suffering the strain of his release, muffed it. The ball rolled 15 feet back to the bleachers. "Tucker made no effort whatsoever to recover the ball, but stood still, and to offset Tucker's brainless action, Everett stopped at third and had to be pushed and dragged before he would start for the plate. Mertes, who kept moving all the time, scored with Everett while Tucker was still standing motionless, and Chicago won by a score of 7-6." (*CT*, Sep 8). As the remaining cranks left the West Side Grounds, some were heard murmuring that a frustrated Tucker may have deliberately thrown the game (*CT*, Sep 8). Tucker would later deny throwing the game saying, "If I was fired, fined, and blacklisted, I would still play to win; that is more than some players can say." (*CP*, Sep 11). A sarcastic *Plain Dealer* said that the "Clevelands narrowly escape a victory." (Sep 8). The loss was the 14th in a row for the Misfits.

Fri Sep 8   Upon a soggy, muddy field, game two of the Misfits series in Chicago was played before half a thousand fanatics. Manager Tom Burns of the Cubs pitched minuscule righthander Clark Griffith while Joe Quinn called on affable Jim Hughey. On paper, the matchup did not appear to be competitive. Griffith was a proven veteran while Hughey was still trying to find some victories in his arm. What Griffith lacked in size, he more than made up for in tenacity and intimidation. He threw the sandpaper ball and the licorice ball and was the originator of the "cut-ball," a pitch finely honed from his spikes. When batters complained of illegality, Griffith would reply that he was just knocking the mud off his shoes (Thorn 179). Hughey, on the other hand, was not the originator of anything, save for the perpetual grin he carried on his face even after losing. Hughey grinned quite a bit.

For two innings, Hughey matched pitches with Griffith. "Lange was first in the third inning, when Hughey pitched low. The ball struck catcher McAllister on his bare hand and hurt him. McAllister chased the ball to the stand and threw back, whereupon Hughey slipped and sat down in the mud. The catcher and pitcher were both mad as hornets, and McAllister walked straight to the bench and quit the game. Duncan, who was once with Washington, caught the rest of the game." (*CT*, Sep 9). Despite Hughey's mudbath, no runs scored until the Chicago fourth. Rightfielder Sam Mertes lashed one toward the rightfield bleacher barrier. He clogged around to third base and spent all of the next batter taking mud off his spikes before Jim Conner hit a sacrifice fly to Tommy Dowd. In the fifth inning, Chicago's Frank Chance roped one down the left field line but missed first base, possibly to avoid an ugly puddle. Umpire McDonald called Chance out and no one complained. Griffith, meanwhile, just "toyed with the tail-enders and bowled slow twisters, which kept the junior trust from banging away without result." (*CT*, Sep 9). Leading by only 1-0 in the seventh, the Orphans scored two more off Hughey, making a double steal work to perfection. Shortstop George Magoon was on third and Griffith was on first. Duncan made a beautiful on-line throw to get Griffith but "Quinn became bewildered and forgot to use the ball. Magoon raced home and Griffith second without an attempt being made to put them out." (*CPD*, Sep 9). Perhaps, Joe Quinn figured that by trying to brace himself in the mud for a throw home, he would slip to the earth and waddle in the mud like unto a pig. Down 3-0 in the eighth, the Spiders' smallish shortstop Harry Lochhead helped manufacture a run on an error, a passed ball, and a Dowd single. The Cubs added two more to the score and it ended 5-1. The Misfits loss string had reached fifteen. A *Plain Dealer* headline: "Cleveland Lost Because They Could Not Win." (Sep 9).

Sat Sep 9 Saturday's edition of the *Sporting Life* printed a queer ditty about what a pitcher feels like when being hit hard (Sep 9).

How the Pitcher Feels

A League pitcher was recently asked to describe the emotion incidental to that condition known as "being up in the air." He replied: "Well, the pitcher's box seems to be on a hill. The opposing batsman looks to be in a hollow. Their bats look as big as telephone poles. The home plate look to be about the size of a postage stamp and over a mile away, your catcher looks like a dwarf, and the whole thing is like a nightmare. That is the way I feel when I am on a ballooning expedition."

Though the pitcher describing that nightmare was unnamed, there was a good chance that he belonged to the Cleveland contingent. That honorary group; comprised of Messrs. Hughey, Knepper, Schmit, Bates, Colliflower, Sudhoff, Hill, Carsey, Stivetts, and Maupin had been ballooning all year. They had traveled to exotic locales like St. Louis, Chicago, Baltimore, Brooklyn, Louisville, and Cincinnati.

The Saturday doubleheader between the Misfits and the Cubs had about as much interest as a Spanish bullfight. Yes, it was a bit entertaining and bloody gory to the fans cheering on the bull, but the end result was almost always the same. On this day, the Clevelands played the animal without the sword. The *Chicago Tribune* took time to add the queer comment that the games were about as exciting as "heavy, heavy hangs your head." (Sep 10).

Before a sizable weekend audience of about three thousand, game one began. Nixey Callahan was the choice for Tom Burns' Cubs, having easily beaten the Misfits 11-2 in May and 4-0 in August. In the latter affair, Callahan added insult to injury when he stole second and third in the game. For the Clevelands, "Chicago prairie product" Crazy Schmit took his turn in the box (*CPD*, Sep 10). Schmit was well aware of his last outing in Chicago, when Mertes stopped him with a bases loaded triple. But, the Misfits simply rolled over and died in the first game. Schmit was bashed for 15 hits, and continually wiggled out of jams, but in the end Chicago had five runs. Against Callahan, the lowly Clevelanders "poked away feebly" to secure only five safeties and two runs (*CT*, Sep 10). The Misfits' runs came only as the result of errors by the home side. In a small bit of revenge, Schmit swiped two bases, but it really didn't matter. Tommy Tucker, playing with the noose of release around his neck, "made a funny move in the eighth inning. Magoon outraced a throw and slid to the base. He got the decision and Tucker made a kick. He ran towards the umpire, then turned suddenly and picked Magoon up, swinging him clear of the ground, after which performance he stood the shortstop on his feet and brushed the dust off his uniform." (*CT*, Sep 10). Perhaps, Tucker realized just at the moment when he was about to argue with the umpire that he was on his way out, so any disagreements would be senseless. So, turning good Samaritan, he helped Magoon to his feet. It ended 5-2. National League President Nick Young could pencil in loss number 16 in a row in his record book.

Game two of the doubleheader was another easy Chicago romp. Behind chubby righthander Ned Garvin, The Orphans shutout the Misfits by 11-0. Cleveland's other man with his walking papers, Frank Bates, went for the Spiders. The Cubs played a strong glove game as if they were conducting a fielding clinic. However, so atrocious was the play of the Misfits afield that "errors were thicker than hits among the visitors." (*CPD*, Sep 10). Two miscues apiece were made by 3b Suter Sullivan, catcher Joe Sugden, and 1b Jim Duncan. The latter was subbing for Tucker and trying to learn a new position. Duncan's play was called "laughable" by the *Tribune* (Sep 10). Rightfielder Charlie Hemphill and shortstop Harry Lochhead also booted balls to make a grand total of eight. For these goofs, the Chicago crowd was "howling with pure enjoyment." (*CT*, Sep 10). The batting wasn't much better for Cleveland. Garvin "served the ball over the plate at eccentric angles" and gave the Misfits only six hits. The only decent blow was a shot by Joe Quinn off the right field fence for a triple. As for Bates, so innocuous was his performance that his name was not even mentioned in the *Chicago Tribune*'s 340-word summation of the contest. It was the Spiders' 17th consecutive defeat. Chicago ended their season against Cleveland with 14 wins in 15 games.

So... the Spiders boarded yet another train prepared to get coal soot in their faces and hair. They were headed back to Cincinnati, a city from whence they just came, to play a single game against the Reds.

Sun Sep 10   Before 7200 ball fans in the Queen City of Cincinnati, "Quinn's Queer's" played the Reds. The new moniker was the latest of the Cleveland name handles (*SL*, Sep 16). The crowd certainly didn't show in those numbers to see the Misfits. Instead, it was a doubleheader picnic between the Reds and Cleveland and the Reds and Louisville. It would have been about as easy to make another mark in the loss column as to play what would become the Misfits' 18th consecutive loss.

Actually, all one had to do was read several choice words in each cities newspapers and a mental picture of the game could be drawn. The *Cleveland Plain Dealer* triple headlined, "The Inevitable Met Once More," and "Another Case of Where the Wanderers Had No Hope," and "A Listless Contest Intended Only to Fatten Averages." (Sep 11). The forlorn *Plain Dealer* sportswriter dispensed few words about the contest saying only, "To go into detail of how the Reds made their runs would be a tiresome story, in which singles, doubles, and triples played the principal part." (Sep 11). In contrast, the *Cincinnati Enquirer* matter-of-factly reported, "Taking the first game from the poor, despised, downtrodden Clevelands was as easy as that proverbial easy job of falling off a log." (Sep 11).

Before the game, the respective managers met and decided that the affair would be called at the end of seven innings. An eastbound locomotive for Philadelphia awaited the Misfits.

Muscular righthander Emil Frisk, who sported all of two unimpressive league games, started for the Reds. Harry Colliflower went for the Clevelands. In an era when naive rookie pitchers were told by veterans that the green netting slung in Pullman berths to hold incidentals were to "rest their valuable throwing arms"- Colliflower must have listened (Suehsdorf 34).

Frisk's prescription for a good outing was a game against Cleveland. His speedy, yet sometimes wild deliveries allowed only five visiting hits, three by Dick Harley and two by Charlie Hemphill. Colliflower, as per usual, gave up a spate of safeties (17) from his "dinky curves." Rightfielder Socks Seybold collected four on a double, triple, and two singles (*CPD*, Sep 11). Young Sam Crawford made a splashy 2-hit debut in Cincinnati garb while Tucker was playing one of his final games. Oh, ten crossed the plate for the Reds, two for the Spiders.

Mon Sep 11   The Misfits' tour of Philadelphia began with a rain postponement. The *Plain Dealer* focused their baseball attentions on the machinations of the new league being proposed. Other brief articles appeared on one of the scourges of the game: rowdyism. The first is opined by Joe Quinn and the second is by NL Pres. Nick Young speaking about a proponent of violent behavior on the field, John J. McGraw (Sep 12). Young's statement was printed from the *Washington Post* (Sep 12).

Quinn- "I have been playing professional ball for twelve years, nine of which were with championship teams, and in all that time I have seen no necessity for all the senseless kicking and abuse of umpires that is so common, and for which the magnates provide no effective remedy. An umpire who does his whole duty has every magnate in the league after his scalp, and for that reason they tolerate much abuse. A little more sportsmanship and less throat cutting on the part of the magnates would make baseball a real sport again."

Young- "Mr. McGraw of the Baltimore club may be a trifle unkind to my umpires at times, and greet their decisions with conversation that Chesterfield would never endorse. But, after all, he pays for the privilege. Every other day- perhaps not quite so often, but pretty near it- I receive a $5 note wrapped up in a businesslike letter, reading: 'Dear Mr. Young-enclosed please find $5, which I pay for the privilege of calling Umpire So-and-So a stiff. I think he was a stiff on this particular occasion, but we all have our faults, heaven knows. Please acknowledge receipt and oblige, sincerely your, J. J. McGraw. P.S.- Kindly offer my regards to Umpire So-and-So, who compelled me to separate with the enclosed five spot.'"

Tues Sep 12   To make up for the rainout of the day before, the Misfits and 2nd place Phillies crossed bats for two games at venerable Baker Bowl. The Bowl was a smallish stadium surrounded by tin fences. It was also called the Cigar Box and Huntingdon Grounds because of its proximity to the street of the same name. Just over six thousand were on hand to witness the action.

Quaker righthander Al Orth took the pitching slab for the home team. Charlie Knepper twirled for the visitors. In the very first inning, centerfielder Roy Thomas was hit by a pitched ball. Shortstop Monte Cross and leftfielder Ed Delahanty measured Knepper for doubles. Later, hard-hitting Cleveland native and Phillie catcher Ed McFarland tripled. The Phils led 3-0. In the third, the Phils hammered in five more scores with the big hits being a Delahanty double and a Pearce "What's the Use" Chiles home run. Chiles' blast cleared the 40-foot high right field fence and bounced on some railroad tracks across Broad Street (*PE*, Sep 13). It was 8-0. One inning later, Joe Quinn made two marvelous catches. He went far to his right to spear a liner near second base off the bat of Cross. Then he gathered in Delahanty's bruising drive. As the inning ended, Quinn was forced to oblige the Philadelphia ball cranks by doffing his cap as he walked off the field (*PE*, Sep 13). In the fifth, even pitcher Orth got into the offense by bopping a home run over the tall right field wall. For the Misfits, the bats again remained rather silent against Orth, his name sounding similar to the grunts of Cleveland batters trying to hit him cleanly. The shutout was 13-0.

In the second tilt, Wiley Piatt took the mound for the Phillies. His opponent was Crazy Schmit. On August 1, Schmit had beaten the Philadelphians by 6-2, when he "gave unmistakable evidence of being shy a few buttons." (*PE*, Sep 13). The Phillies were shy a few gloves that day, making five errors in one inning. Two days later, Piatt beat the Spiders 6-1.

On this day, the Spiders started well. Buttermilk Tommy Dowd, he of the quick feet, singled and stole second. Catcher Ed McFarland, who was miffed he was playing both games of the doubleheader, threw wild to second base (*PE*, Sep 13). Dowd was called out at third on McAllister'sgrounder. Quinn topped one in front of the mound, but Piatt's failure to cover first base, a subsequent passed ball and an out led to the first run. The Clevelands ended better. In the eighth inning, Joe Sugden got aboard on a single, Schmit walked, Dowd got a base hit for a run, and McAllister went out. Joe Quinn drove a Piatt pitch to short right field for two more runs. In between those four runs, the Spiders were awful, stumbling their way to their 20th consecutive loss. "Schmit started out to make trouble for the Phillies but soon he was beyond all hope of winning the game after he came to realize how wretched was the support being given." (*CPD*, Sep 13). Tommy Tucker, Quinn, and Dowd played well in the field, but Harry Lochhead was less fortunate. The Misfits' shortstop committed four errors, all seemingly in the middle of Philadelphia rallies. Pearce Chiles tripled and doubled at key moments and Sugden and Suter Sullivan added their own blunders, six in all. The Spiders were losers again by 8-4. Said the *Philadelphia Enquirer*, "Phillies Take Two Falls Out of the Clevelands Without the Recourse of a Net." (Sep 13). The woeful Misfits were now 19-114, 30 games out of 11th place, and had beaten the losing record of 113 games established the 1890 Pittsburg club.

Wed Sep 13   After the game of Wednesday, Sigmund Freud, or any of his psychoanalytic buddies would be hard pressed to figure out the Misfits. With the new science of psychiatry on the scene, the 1899 Cleveland baseball team would have made an excellent test case. This game, in particular, could be picked apart, detail by detail, perhaps Joe Quinn retelling the story. In the end, though, even modern scientific method would probably be dumbfounded. How could a team which made six errors in a single game and which was outhit, lose? The answer was very simple. The Misfits played badly the day before, and lost by 8-4. The sport of baseball offered few graces. But, now, take the game of Wednesday. How could a team which committed seven errors, "being of the simple kind that make both the players and spectators laugh," win (*CPD*, Sep 14)?   A perplexing question, indeed, especially when one considered the opposition fielded brilliantly.   But, for amateur psychiatrists, or anyone associated with Cleveland in 1899, the answer was all to apparent. The Phillies made seven errors to Cleveland's none, and won 8-2.

Red-haired righthander Francis Rostell Donahue started for the Phils. Newcomer Howard P. "Highball" Wilson went for the Spiders.   Wilson, Philadelphia-born, was making his league debut. In the first inning, the Quakers jumped in front. Highball nervously walked Roy Thomas and Monte Cross. Ed Delahanty bunted.   Bill Lauder singled and then catcher Klondike Douglass blasted a ball near the flagpole in right center field (*PE*, Sep 14). It went for a triple and a 5-0 lead. Then, Billy Shettsline's boys began making errors. Over the course of the game, second baseman Joe Dolan booted two ground balls. Shortstop Monte Cross and third baseman Lauder kicked one each. Outfielder Ed Delahanty dropped a fly as did Pearce Chiles, but Chiles chance was on a hard liner from Charlie Hemphill. Douglass made a wild throw. But, despite all the Philadelphia goofs, two thousand five hundred baseball gawkers shook their heads. Donahue, "not in the least annoyed by the misplays behind him," was as good as he was on August 3 when he blanked the Clevelands 4-0. By the third, Donahue was enjoying the comedy so much that after he struck out Tom Dowd, he laughed heartily (*PE*, Sep 14). The only two Misfits runs scored on a balk and errors.   Wilson settled and scored high marks for his future from the commentary of the *Philadelphia Enquirer* (Sep 14). For the traveling baseball bedouins from Cleveland, it was loss number 21 in sucession.

Thur Sep 14 Loss number 22 in a row was the same as many of the others. A rather neighborly group of 2057 smug Philadelphians dared to show their face at such a game. Bill Bernhard versus Jim Hughey. Of Bernhard, the *Plain Dealer* said, "The big, husky young twirler of the home team shot the ball across the plate with such bends and twists to it, and with such speed, that the opposing batsman could not see it, and once Tommy Dowd almost forgot to run after hitting safely over second base, he seemingly not aware at first that his bat had come in contact with the ball." (Sep 15). Bernhard then picked the confused Tommy off first base. Unlike the day before, the Quakers fielded sharply and smartly. On the Cleveland ledger, only five hits were secured. No one ventured past second base. As for Hughey, was again done in by the proverbial "bunched hits." (*CPD*, Sep 15). Bad ball hitting Ed Delahanty bruised two singles and a home run. Delahanty's slugging was such that he prompted Patsy Tebeau to say once, "If you let that bat-mad galoot step into the ball, he'll knock its cover off." (Grayson 59). Shortstop Monte Cross doubled and singled and centerfielder Roy Thomas had a hit and three walks. Had public address systems been available in ballparks, the all too familiar phrase, "Losing pitcher, Jim Hughey," would have been voiced. It was 8-0.

But, not only were the Spiders beaten by the Quakers, but by the *Philadelphia Enquirer* as well. They said that their team. "disposed of the wandering Clevelands without turning a hair," and that it was the "visitors last appearance in this city this season, and possibly forever. At least it is hoped so." (Sep 15). The Spiders had been outscored in Philadelphia by 37-6. Years later, the imminent comedian W.C. Fields would make famous the phrase, "On the whole, I'd rather be in Philadelphia." Mr. Fields never met these Misfits. On this September day in 1899, the *Enquirer* uttered, "On the whole, it was a rather wearisome occasion." (Sep 15).

Fri Sep 15 From Philadelphia the Misfits headed to the Nation's Capital, Washington, D.C. to take on Arthur Irwin's Senators. There, the Cleveland game with Washington was just as ludicrous from a sporting standpoint as many others during the losing streak. The Senators trotted out a rookie from the Eastern League, righthander LeRoy Evans to pitch. The Spiders countered with the kooky Crazy Schmit. The *Washington Post* described the Misfits hurler and the game this way. "Comedian Schmit, philosopher, connoisseur of the festive wiener wurst, and manipulator of the roundhouse scroll that wafts up to the plate with the nonchalance of a dapper youth flaunting through Burlington Arcade, was the dispenser of an inviting, appetizing toss off which the Senators fattened their batting averages at National Park yesterday." (Sep 16). Schmit, who had been so angry at John McGraw's team in Baltimore for bunting against him on July 28, was no match for the filibustering Senators. Again the *Post* described, "The Senators established a record that will probably hold on the season in the matter of bunts for a limited number of innings. During Schmitty's brief reign on the rubber- three innings- the Senators tickled the barrel-hoop flourishes for six bunts. Slagle worked the Teuton for two safe taps in front of the plate. Mercer and O'Brien got in their work for one, safe tap apiece. McGann also applied a gentle tickle to one of the philosopher's high bowlers, and Roy Evans applied a half hook to Germany's delivery for a bunt." (Sep 16). After the third inning, the score was 11-0 with the visitors in arrears. The Washingtonians also took advantage of Schmit's diamond mates, Suter Sullivan at 3b and Jim Duncan at 1b whose fielding liabilities were easily exposed. All pitcher Evans had to do was just toss a few balls and go home a winner.

After Schmit's three comedic innings, Colliflower, stationed in centerfield for an ailing Tommy Dowd, came in to pitch. Since radio play-by-play was yet to come on the baseball scene, had Dowd been listening in to the game, he probably would have been in hiding, fearing Schmit would return to his hotel room and recommend another stomach revolution. Sport McAllister replaced Colliflower in the garden. Colliflower, the local Washington youngster, afforded himself well for the duration of the game, holding the Senators to three runs and banging out three hits off Evans. In the eighth inning, Buck Freeman waltzed up to one of Colliflower's tosses and knocked it into the rightfield bleacher seats. The debacle ended 14-3. Afterwards, the *Post* spoke of the Exiles as "a pathetic galaxy to look upon." It was their 23rd straight loss.

Sat Sep 16   A blurb in the day's *Washington Post* just about described the Misfits losing streak and season to a t- "Cleveland will soon arrive at that stage where a defeat will not lower the club's percentage a point." (Sep 17). With that in mind, Secretary Muir of the Cleveland team announced the signing of two new players to replace castoff Bates and Tucker. One was righthanded pitcher Jack Harper of the Springfield, Ohio ball club. Harper was reputed to have great speed and was expected to debut in Washington on Monday. The other ballplayer acquired was a bulky third baseman named Otto Krueger from the Fort Wayne team.

The following is a partial description of the *Cleveland Plain Dealer*'s view of the Saturday ball game. What the paper didn't point out, as no one was keeping track, was that the loss was the twenty-fourth in a row.

HARD WORK TO LOSE

The Wanderers Nearly
Made a Mistake at
Washington

They Took a Big Lead
but Pulled Up in
Time

A Good Exhibition of Town Ball

Washington 15-Cleveland 10.

Special to the *Plain Dealer*.

WASHINGTON, Sept. 16.--The Senators and Quinnites were entitled to membership in the order of Sons of the Revolution following the afternoon's game at National Park. They ran the circuit of the bases during the nine innings like a lot of toy soldiers fixed to a merry-go-round. Fifteen Senators and ten Quinnittes circumnavigated the paths and registered at the home plate. It was more like a game of country town ball than an exhibition between two National League clubs.

The visitors got away in the second inning and looked as if they never would be headed. In this inning they ran as under whip, spur and electrical devices and the race looked hopeless for the home entry. But they proved quarter horses and slowly, but surely, the Senators beat down the lead. Fifield was pounded all over the lot in the second, though errors of omission and commission by his support were largely responsible for the big bunch of runs. After the second, Fifield got down to business and allowed very little trifling to his delivery. The Senators, especially McGann, Barry, Freeman and Stafford, came to his assistance, and by swatting the Spalding hard and often, pulled the ex-Philadelphian out of a deep, dark and dangerous hole.

Knepper pitcher steady ball, but the home folks had an appetite for speed and murdered it. The record for the afternoon both clubs was thirty-three hits for a total of fort-five bases. This does not happen often in National League circles.

Capt. Quinn tried out his new man, Cruger (sic) at third base. The Grand Rapids recruit looks a bit like Bobby Wallace in the field and he is a ringer for Lave Cross in moving about on the field. He seems rather slow and has got to learn to get a hustle on himself in handling bunts. Pitcher Harper, also late of Grand Rapids, reported to Capt. Quinn today and will be worked next week.

The fielding feature of the game was Lockhead's (sic) work at short. His throwing was sometimes marvelous. He cracked a half dozen hard chances over to first like bullets out of a Krag-Jorgenson. Dowd is still sick at the hotel, but will probably be able to play in Monday's game. By arrangement between Messrs. Wagner and Robison a doubleheader for one admission will be played Monday afternoon. It is the idea that a double game will draw better at the gate, and besides give the teams a chance to rest up on Tuesday.

Sun Sep 17   A few items of interest occurred on the Misfits and Senators relaxing Sunday. First was the *Washington Evening Star* note that "Manager Torreyson has sold pitcher Harper of the Springfield, Ohio team to St. Louis." (Sep 18). This was strange since the *Plain Dealer* had only the day before reported the selling of the same pitcher to the Cleveland team. But, since St. Louis and Cleveland were one and the same for owners Robison to shuffle players as they pleased, Harper was sold to St. Louis and Cleveland at the same time. As fate would have it, he was selected to pitch for the Misfits for the remainder of the 1899 season.

Frank DeHaas Robison, whose Clevelands had lost 24 straight games, said, "Cleveland and Louisville could go to the Western League, making that organization a top-notcher. Places for Brooklyn and Baltimore could be found in the Eastern League." But, the *Cleveland Press* was quick to point out that the Brooklyn-Baltimore syndicate had been a $100,000 success, so why would they quit the big leagues (Sep 17)?

Mon Sep 18   The *Cleveland Press* reported that "Quinn's Exiles seem determined not to win another game this season." (Sep 18). The *Cleveland Plain Dealer* was too busy reporting horse racing, bicycling, golf, and yachting. Or perhaps, they had forgotten quite how to comment on that rarity of rarities. Nonetheless, it was true.   The 1899 Cleveland Spiders, a.k.a. Misfits, Wanderers, Exiles, Tourists and a host of other disparaging names, won a baseball game. It was their 20th victory, against 118 defeats. The *Washington Post* said that "Cleveland played with a snap and vim quite in contrast with their usual apologetic work, and very few of the thousand odd spectators begrudge them the game they won." (Sep 19). It was their first victory in 25 games and it came in the first of a dipsy doodle doubleheader.

In game one, newcomer Jack Harper pitched his debut for Cleveland, though by now, the city appellation had long since become a misnomer. Bill Magee hurled for Washington; a man with the unlikely distinction of losing to the Misfits as a member of the Louisville Colonels and the Philadelphia Phillies. Now, donning the Washington flannels, Magee went at the Misfits again. For seven innings, the Senators sailed along, building a 4-1 lead. Harper, who "worked diligently and at all times effectively," was on his way to scattering twelve hits (*WES*, Sep 19). Magee, though, was brilliant after seven innings of work, allowing only one scratch single. In the Cleveland eighth, the miracle commenced. Pitcher Harper drew a walk. Dick Harley singled and Charlie Hemphill's triple sent home two runs to make it 4-3. The Misfits tied the game in the ninth when ex-Senator Jim Duncan drove a Magee pitch to left. The ball hopped over the fence for a home run. Harper held down the Senators and the game went into extra innings. In the tenth, the returning Tommy Dowd doubled,

156

Harley singled, and Hemphill punched one past a drawn-in Washington infield for the winner. The Misfits were 5-4 winners. It can only be surmised what manager Quinn, who missed the contest, and the rest of the Misfits thought. A few smiles and sighs of relief were probably in order. Washington hurler Bill Magee now had the misfortune of losing to the Misfits three times with three different teams.

Game two began at precisely 4:30 much as the first game ended. Cleveland was content to hammer the ball all over National Park against the deliveries of righthander Bill Dinneen. Cleveland pitched Jim Hughey. In the first two innings, the Misfits scored five times with little Harry Lochhead belting a home run. Hughey gave up three tallies to the Senators in that same span. "Right here is where the Clevelands stopped dead, as Billy Dinneen, who was twirling for the home club, doubtless concluded it was time to go to work, and ciphers (zeros) were placed up against the Clevelands with enjoyable regularity." (*WES*, Sep 19). In the sixth, the smallish built Buck Freeman "thought he was due for another homer" and deposited a high Hughey pitch far out into right center field. Before Cleveland outfielder Charlie Hemphill could track it down, Freeman had run the bases. Rookie Shad Barry ran out a bunt and 2b Stafford's sacrifice eluded Otto Krueger, whose wild throw put Barry on third base. Catcher Frank McManus hit a sacrifice fly to tie the score at 5-5. In the seventh, the Senators Freeman singled and soon found himself on third base. With Barry batting with two out and two strikes, Freeman broke for home. Senators manager Irwin was no doubt capitalizing on another Exiles' weakness. Hughey delivered. Barry swung and missed but Sport McAllister, "playing" catcher, dropped the third strike. At first, Barry refused to budge from the home plate area with Freeman coming down the line and McAllister trying to get to the ball and tag Freeman. There was the obligatory cloud of dust. Freeman was safe and Barry, incredibly, ran all the way to second. With Hughey and McAllister terribly confused or frustrated or both, Hughey "threw the ball on the ground," wild pitching Barry to third (*WP*, Sep 19). McAllister then allowed a short passed ball and Barry slid in safe. McAllister then left the game with a dislocated finger from all his scrambling around home plate. Barry had circuited the bases after striking out without the benefit of a ball being hit. After the Misfits went out in the eighth, umpire Frank Dwyer, working alone, called the game at precisely 6:17 p.m. (*WES*, Sep 19). The umpire's reason for the games abbreviated ending was darkness, but perhaps he was blinded by the lingering cloud of dust around home plate. It ended 8-5.

Players from both teams walked off the field, exchanging farewells, and knowing that the season series had come to an end.

Tues Sep 19   The Misfits went all aboard for their short ride to Bal'mer. The game on Tuesday was rained out. Tommy Dowd was heard to remark, "There is no moss on us even if we are tail-enders. We are the fastest team in the league. At least we cover more ground." Swift Tommy wasn't talking about the Cleveland outfield, that had spent the season scampering after pitcher's mistakes. Tommy clarified: "Who's talking about the field? I said more ground. Don't we spend half our time skipping over the earth in sleeper cars?" (*SL*, Sep 8).

Wed Sep 20   The next day, Mother Nature co-operated with the weatherman. The sun shone. John McGraw's feisty Orioles came to play.   Joe Quinn's Misfits, well...they just came.

The Cleveland manager named Crazy Schmit as his starting pitcher. The Baltimore boss chose Frank Kitson. From the beginning, Kitson held the "Harley-Quinn's" powerless, their only two runs scoring as the result of Baltimore fielding miscues (*BTS*, Sep 20). The other Cleveland batting threat was smothered in the fifth when Schmit struck out on three pitches. On the mound, Schmit's outing was far better than his performance in Washington, but the ever-wily Orioles again used bunts as a chief weapon. Described the *Plain Dealer*; Schmit was in a "very conversational mood and in his tiffs with the umpire had the crowd behind him, although he came out second best, as umpire Snyder plastered him with a fine at $5." (Sep 20). The Misfits' woeful fielding accounted for most of the Orioles runs. Leftfielder Dick Harley, third baseman Otto Krueger, and shortstop Harry Lochhead all made bad throws to figure in the scoring. Baltimore 2b Gene DeMontreville had a safe bunt because "no one covered the bag." (*CPD*, Sep 20). For this failure Schmit blamed 1b Jim Duncan and shook his fist at the new first baseman while using a few choice German words. The Union Park crowd doubled up in laughter. So silly was this baseball exhibition and its principal comedian that when Kitson batted in the eighth inning, he was guffawing so hard he had to retire to the bench (Sep 20). McGinnity took his place. The Orioles were easy winners, 6-2.

For his efforts, Frederick W. Schmit was given his ten days notice of release and fined for insubordination by Cleveland management (Sep 21).

Contrary to his record and his clowning, Schmit was quite serious about his pitching. He was the first to tell you so. But, the prideful Schmit bristled over his nicknames, "I have stood for this thing long enough. I am neither tacky nor crazy, and without wanting to throw flowers at myself, I will make the statement that there is not a better left-handed pitcher in the business who uses as good judgement in pitching as I do." (*SL*, Sep 16). Unfortunately, even good judgement would not win games on this team.

The Spiders did afford Schmit horrible support (as they did all their pitchers), and he often took the mound with everything going against him. The newspapers that reported sports always referred to him as somewhat of a buffoon, chronicling his adventure with his little notebook on the weaknesses of hitters, his German ancestry, and his every move. Once, in Philadelphia, Schmit fanned Ed Delahanty. Immediately, he "swelled out his chest, walked right up to the grandstand, waved his arms and yelled, 'Me! I am the only professional on this team. I am the ball player." (*TSN*, date unkn). But, Schmit's beer mug was empty on his claim that he was the most popular man in the league. Surely, players that imbued a sense of winning were far more admired. A re-cap of his season follows.

In Schmit's very first game on June 27 against the Giants in Cleveland, the *Plain Dealer* said it was too soon to win after the Spiders' victory in St. Louis. Schmit lost 6-1. The next time out he was hammered 14-0 in only six innings against Boston. The Cleveland crowd was almost nonexistent for those two contests. Then, he lost by a single run in Pittsburg as the game winner scored while he stood on the mound oblivious to the catcher's relay. That was on July 4th. Two days later, his catcher Joe Sugden called him a winner. The next time out, Schmit was beaten badly in St. Louis as Lave Cross homered with the bases loaded and St. Louis discovered Schmit's horrible weakness- fielding bunts. Eleven thousand crowded into Sportsman's Park for that affair. In Baltimore, a 10-0 loss followed, largely attributable to a Ducky Holmes home run and poor Misfits fielding. Schmit was livid at his teammates for their poor play behind him. Dick Harley was injured on July 17 and Schmit took over in left field in Baltimore and Washington for a few games. There he found time to confer with John McGraw and boasted that in 1900, he would be one of the top batters in the National League. Schmit also worked his "science" on the coaching lines and philosophized on his checkered pitching career. Checkered it continued as he was defeated 6-2 in Washington, the local papers having a field day describing his "grotesque antics."

When Schmit began tossing full-time again, he lost in an exhibition game to Atlantic City 12-8 and 8-2 in Baltimore when his personal batting mentor John McGraw and the Orioles practiced "too much bunteration." Six stolen bases were also swiped by the opportunistic Orioles. On the 1st of August he won a game in Philadelphia, fooling the Phillies with a "tantalizing slow curve ball." The fumbling Philadelphians helped out his effort with five errors in one inning. On a Sunday in his hometown of Chicago, fourteen thousand came to see one of the better games of the season. In a whirlwind finish, Schmit held off a fearsome Cubs batting rally to preserve a 10-9 win. He would never gain another victory.

With the Misfits deep in their barnstorming phase, he lost 6-2 to the Giants, giving up several steals to the New Yorkers. Schmit was angry at a lot of things that day and when he yelled at umpire McGarr, the newspapers said he probably escaped a fine because the umpire couldn't understand his mixture of English and German. Five days later in Brooklyn, the Trolley Dodgers bumped him 20-2. The Misfits fielding behind him was almost laughable. His next game in Chicago was also a disaster. After leading most of the way, Sam Mertes late-inning triple with the bases loaded sunk Schmit and the Spiders 8-7. The next lost 2-1 to the Giants in Cleveland in a rain-shortened game, 9-3 to Brooklyn again and 8-1 to Cincinnati while six errors were committed behind him. Briefly, Schmit took off his pitching flannels and became a doctor to ailing Tommy Dowd on September 6th, inducing a stomach revolution in his patient.

On the 9th, he was beaten 5-2 in Chicago. The next day, Schmit claimed, lightning struck the trolley he was riding in with his Gibson girl and he missed the team train. Imagine that scene: "The grinding clash of steel wheels over steel streetcar tracks, the pop-pop noise of the circuit breaker when a motorman accelerated too fast, and the electric clang-clang" with lightning thrown in. Occasionally, the motorman would have to get out of his streetcar to reposition the trolley wheel back onto the overhead wire power source. The occurrence was so common that "to be off one's trolley" was an expression relating to craziness (Flexner 186). Well, they didn't call him "Crazy" Schmit for nothing.

In Philadelphia with Harry Lochhead's four errors, Schmit's foes gave him more woes, 8-4. Next was Washington, where the Senators bunted both Schmit and his teammates silly. Finally, the string ran out. The mercurial German, always quick with a quip, lost 6-2 to Baltimore on September 20. He was fined $50, for missing the train in Chicago, and released.

Thur Sep 21 On a wet and slippery field, the Orioles and Misfits concluded their season series at Baltimore's Union Park. Two games were played...sort of, but the *Cleveland Plain Dealer* could only report, "Of course it would not do for the Forsakens to win." (Sep 22). With that in mind, Cleveland went right out and lost them both.

In game one Handsome Harry Howell started for the Birds against Charlie Knepper of the Spiders. With John McGraw returning to the lineup after a brief absence, the Orioles simply bunted their way to victory. McGraw "braced the Orioles infield wonderfully," and dumped the ball three of his five times up (Sep 22). The first time, the *Baltimore Sun* reported that McGraw was safe by a yard but umpire Snyder called him out. Strangely enough, no great row was raised over the incident. But, the Clevelands "played in their usual halfhearted way" and despite catching up against Howell in the late innings, they succumbed 5-4 (*CPD*, Sep 22). Joe McGinnity relieved. In the 10th inning, Jim Duncan blasted one past Jimmy Sheckerd in right field but the latter made a remarkable throw to erase Duncan at second base. Sheckerd's play was rather incredible considering that the field sloped downhill to the fence and "stream water from Brady's run created a perpetual swamp oozing underneath the right field fence." (Lowry 35). The next batter, Joe Sugden singled, but a run was already lost. The Orioles eventually won the game in the 11th inning on manager McGraw's shrewd bunting tactics.

In the second affair, Joe McGinnity simply kept the ball and pitched against wild rookie Jack Harper. It was a pitcher's duel, but one of those kind of affairs that was about as exciting as watching grass grow. The *Plain Dealer* said that both clubs played as if in a hurry (Sep 22). Umpire Snyder thought so. After the Misfits had batted in the sixth, Snyder threw up his hands and announced the game was over. The sun was still shining and several more innings could have been played. Both teams agreed on the excitement level and scampered off the field, satisfied at the day's work. The Orioles won 4-1, winning twelve of the fourteen season games from the Clevelands.

Fri Sep 22   The Spiders took the day off to make their way to Pittsburg. For a nickel, the players could have picked up the recent issue of *Sporting Life* and read an article by a Scottish yachting expert describing baseball (Sep 23).

I have now sampled base ball. Base ball is great, and the greatest thing about it is the spectators. The great American language, classic as it is on the tongue of an expert, is a medium all too mild to render the feelings of a base ball enthusiast. There are sports at which the spectators play a passive part, but base ball is not one of these. Every man who joins a base ball crowd feels that it lies upon him to contribute his share to the entertainment. Every motion on the part of the player brings a response from the crowd, and the response is couched in language such as Professor Gardner never met in his exploration of monkey land. Yeh! Yeh! Yeh! Wow! Wow! Hoo! are the words of cheer and encouragement, but no stenographer has ever yet been trained to wrestle with the sounds of adverse criticism and the only attempt to record it by phonograph ended in disaster to the cylinder. The superlative degrees of this adverse criticism are reserved for the umpire, who seems to be used principally as a dumping-ground for abuse. The treatment of the umpire by a base ball crowd is palpitating proof of the evidence of free speech in America. Therefore, long live base ball, and more power to the lungs of the base ball crowd.

For the first time since late August, professional ball was returning to Cleveland. The Western League's Minneapolis club, under the directorship of Mgr. Charles Comiskey, was coming to the warmer climes of the Forest City to play out their season (*CP*, Sep 21).

161

Sat Sep 23   In Exposition Park, the Pirates entertained the Clevelands in another doubleheader. But, this was a different Spiders team. Gone were almost all the personalities that one could consider lively- the enormous potential of outfielder Louis Sockalexis was lost to alcohol. Loyal Lave Cross had provided a steady bat and glove at third base. Ossee Schreckengost was a rising catching talent. But, both Cross and Schreck had been summoned to St. Louis. Thomas Tucker could always be counted on to stand up for his team. He was back in native Holyoke, Mass., vowing "I'll be in the game next season if I have to organize a new league." (*SL*, Sep 23). Finally, Crazy Schmit was gone, and with him the last vestiges of how much fun it was to be a ballplayer.

Even the *Plain Dealer* showed a marked loss of interest in the team, filling the sports page with music and society news. They reported on "the Normal Result" and that the "Wanderer's succeeded in losing the usual amount of games." (Sep 24). Game one began in front of 2000 ambulance chasers with Jim Hughey opposing the Western League righthander Chummy Gray. The Pirates, like other teams, could afford to send raw-boned recruits right into the breach as long as they pitched against Cleveland. Gray "performed in a manner quite satisfactory to local fandom," while Hughey was done in by a three-run sixth inning (*CPD*, Sep 24). Player-manager Joe Quinn sat out and was replaced by Charlie Ziegler. The new man, a Canton, Ohio native and veteran of the Interstate League, "did not burn any grass in the vicinity of second base." (*CPD*, Sep 24). Lithe Pirate centerfielder Ginger Beaumont collected three his and the Bucs were easy winners 4-1.

Game two was no better, at least for Cleveland. The invincible Spider killer Jesse Tannehill went against Harry Colliflower. Said the *Pittsburg Post*, the game was "uninteresting" but "some bits of brilliant fielding saved both sides from utter decay." (Sep 24). Pirate shortstop Bones Ely made an excellent one handed stop and Ginger Beaumont made a solid running catch in the outfield. For the Cleveland team, Otto Krueger wowed the crowd with his fine third base play. Tannehill and the Buccaneers breezed 6-2. The *Cleveland Plain Dealer* had almost nothing to say about the litany of losses. The Misfits had now lost 30 of their last 31 games. Next stop: St. Louis.

Sun Sep 24   The long journey from Pittsburg to St. Louis took the Misfits train through the heart of Ohio, Indiana, and Illinois, before finally arriving at its destination. There they met the Louisville Colonels who had taken to the road for the rest of the season due to a ballpark fire. The Colonels beat the Browns in game one behind rookie hurler Rube Waddell. So excited was Waddell over his victory that he turned a handspring as he left the field (*GD*, Sep 25).

The finale of the Louisville-Misfits series was played under cloudy skies. Eight thousands cranks stayed for the second affair. The St. Louis partisans were squarely behind Joe Quinn's boys. The Misfits were cheered loudly with "good honest applause" as they took their positions to practice (*GD*, Sep 25). The Misfits batted first and got off to a roaring start against Louisville pitcher Bert Cunningham. Tommy Dowd led off and scored. Later in the inning, speedy rightfielder Honus Wagner took an extra base hit away from Charlie Hemphill, snaring the latter's drive on the dead run. But, after that, "he (Cunningham) had 'em (Cleveland) guessing and they guessed about as good as a man playing the lottery." (*GD*, Sep 25). In Louisville's first with young Harper pitching, Joe Quinn managed the game in civilian clothes and watched as his replacement, Otto Krueger made an error that led to three runs. Business as usual. The clubs struggled in the sixth as the skies began to darken. But, before the sun could recede on another St. Louis day, Wagner came to bat for Louisville. The free swinger stepped into a pitch and lined it to left field for a home run. More bat endorsements. Louisville led 5-1. Umpires Arlie Latham and Tom Connolly had seen enough. They called the game due to darkness. It took exactly one hour to play. The best thing that the *St. Louis Globe-Democrat* could say was that Harper pitched good ball and "the cheers that Dowd, Harley, and Hemphill received covered up a multitude of sins, as applause and enthusiasm always does." (Sep 25).

Tues Sep 26   The Cleveland series in St. Louis resumed in chilly conditions; this time the Spiders playing St. Louis' entry in the National League. The result was predictable but the manner of reportage by the *Plain Dealer* was simply absurd.

Cy Young pitched for St. Louis with Mrs. Cyrus Young looking on from the grandstands (*GD*, Sep 27). The Spiders pitched Charlie Knepper. No loved ones were present for Charlie. Perhaps, this bit of inspiration spurred Young on to victory, but if truth be known, he was a slightly better hurler than Knepper. The *Plain Dealer*'s headline read: "Youngish Not Cyish Were the Tactics Displayed by Cy Young No. 2." (Sep 27). The reference was for Knepper, always seemingly billed as a potential great. It meant that Knepper pitched as if he were young enough to be an amateur, or at least pitch like that but that he was hardly cyclonic, or the least bit effective. Knepper "obligingly kept the leather over the plate most of the time and long hit after long hit followed." (*GD*, Sep 27). The Perfectos managed a "terrific ash-wielding" at Sportsman's Park with 22 hits and 42 total bases, scoring in every inning (*GD*, Sep 27). So numerous were the hits that the *Plain Dealer* and *Globe-Democrat* disagreed on the number and type. Everybody on St. Louis got into the act of making life miserable for poor Knepper and the Cleveland fielders, who at games end "were a weary looking lot." (*GD*, Sep 27). Even Cy Young hit two triples; in the sixth inning the "ball went past Duncan with the speed of a catapult." (*GD*, Sep 27).

There was a scary moment late in the contest. Ex-Misfit Ossee Schreckengost was beaned on the head by a pitch in the eighth. "He fell to the ground like a log, and it looked as if Ossee was clean out. The members of both teams rushed to him, but, before they could give him any assistance, he was on his feet and trotted to first." (*GD*, Sep 27). When the scorer could finally put away his pencil, it was 15-3.

Thur Sep 28   The Cleveland ball club needed a couple of days of recuperation to recover from their thrashing by Pat Tebeau's Perfectos. Nick Young and the National League schedulers obliged. But, if the Misfits were getting copies of the *Plain Dealer* delivered to their hotel, they could have read these two fantastic stories.

Earlier in the month, a suit was being brought against the Cincinnati baseball club by St. Louis Circuit Attorney Theodore Eggers. Eggers charged that the Reds had failed to file and report properly their business in St. Louis. Now, the anti-trust suit was widened to include the Louisville and Cleveland National League clubs, dallying in St. Louis for the offensive crime of playing baseball. So, the Misfits now even had lawyers go against them. Eggers was asking for $1000 in damages.

Or, perhaps, Joe Quinn's boys could fantasize about a crack Ohio Interstate baseball squad from Ashtabula, whose season had just ended with 53 wins and 12 defeats. Their championship victory was 5-4 over the Greenville, Pennsylvania nine. Ashtabula was the independent champions of northern Ohio, western Pennsylvania, and western New York.

Sat Sep 31   After taking another day off, the wandering Clevelands decided to try their hand again with the No. 1 syndicate team, the St. Louis Perfectos. It was a frigid afternoon in St. Louis on the last day of the last full month of the season. Why the game was contested at all in the conditions was unknown. Maybe it was to add to the Spiders record of futility.

Patsy Tebeau started righthanded rookie hurler Savage Thomas Thomas, a tallish chap from Detroit of the Western League. Thomas was making his big league debut. Tebeau was keeping with the National League tradition of pitching rookie hurlers against Cleveland to build up their confidence. Quinn's Misfits went with Jim Hughey. As the weather was not conducive to ball playing or fan viewing, the teams went through the motions of sport while the paying customers simply shivered, bundled, and moved closer to each other. Neither club really exerted itself but the St. Louis lack of effort proved more successful. As the *Globe-Democrat* stated, "St. Louis, of course, won." (Oct 1). Hughey was banged away at for twenty safeties and ten runs. St. Louis' slugging outfielder Jesse Burkett secured four "frozen rope" drives and took dead aim at league batting honors. Burkett was dueling Ed Delahanty of Philadelphia, McGraw of Baltimore, and Willie Keeler of Brooklyn. First baseman Ossee Schreck recovered sufficiently from his Knepper beaning to collect four hits of his own. Outfielder Turkey Mike Donlin and Fritz Buelow added three apiece. For the Clevelands, Jim Duncan, who split time at catcher and first base, blasted a home run, a double, and a single. St. Louis' rookie Thomas was a bit shaky afield, with two wild throws, but gave up only three tallies. In the eighth, umpire Brennan declared the game over due to darkness, cold, score, and lack of interest. Ten to three. As the month ended, the Misfits could count their victory totals not on one hand, but on one finger.

Perhaps, there was a new reason for the Misfits' depressive play. This brief, telling article appeared in the *Plain Dealer* (Oct 1).

There is trouble in the Cleveland baseball club. The men want their salaries. They claim six weeks back pay, and they want to know when they will get it.

The men are at the Southern hotel (in St. Louis). Today, there were almost ripe for a strike, but the test of the Sunday game and the probability that it would attract such a crowd that the management would divide the profits with the players restrained them.

Joe Sugden said: "There is dissatisfaction among the players, but I don't want to talk about it. It is about money. The management is behind with salaries. I haven't gotten anything to say about it. See Dick Harley."

Harley said frankly that the men had not received their salaries, but he refused to discuss the matter.

"See Quinn," said Harley, and Quinn said: "See Lochhead, or Schmit, or Knepper, or anybody." And there you are. But as all agree to a grievance something must be wrong.

In answer, the aloof syndicate owner Frank Robison commented that the delay was due to the fact that it was unusual to pay players on the road and that his players could draw money as needed from the club treasury. Their contracts stipulated that they "be paid on the 1st and 15th of the each month except when they were away on a trip, and in that event on the first weekday after they return home." (*TSN*, Oct 7). But, the Spiders hadn't been "home" since August.

Imagine the situation. Members of the homeless Cleveland baseball club wearily tour the United States by rail so as to be trounced in another game of baseball in another city. The losses pile up and the players are not paid. What man on the team would dare ask for a salary advance, especially as most of the players were marginal at best and fighting for their very baseball existence? The *Plain Dealer* was not lost on the situation. The newspaper headline tied horseracing events in Louisville, Springfield, and Gravesend to the plight of the Cleveland baseball team (Oct 1). "Money Makes the Mare Go and When the

Money is Not in Sight, she Quits. Cleveland players follow the mare's example. Pay days are rather scarce." (Oct 1).

Another article appeared in the *Plain Dealer*, buried amidst the news of baseball, running and trotting, pugilism, bicycling, golf, and yachting. It was entitled "Homing. A 300-Mile Fly." and it concerned 70 homing pigeons that were to be liberated in Green Castle, Indiana and fly to Cleveland. The destination was the base for the Cleveland Association Homing Pigeon Club. One of the members in good standing was Cleveland native Lave Cross. Lave had six birds in the event. It was curious that the pigeons could fly home to Cleveland on their innate, biological sense, but the Misfits were doomed to wander hapless, hopeless, and without pay.

"The End is at Hand."

Sun Oct 1 Judging by the amount of ink and space devoted to the Misfits at St. Louis, one could wonder if the reporters from the *Plain Dealer* and the *Globe-Democrat* saw the same game. Cleveland's scribes reported a crowd of 3000 and chilly weather. The St. Louis writers said that the "day was ideal for baseball," and that "2000 holiday seekers" were present (Oct 2). But, aside from the inaccuracies of the description- both dailies agreed on the final score, and therein lies the tale.

It was the finale of the St. Louis/Cleveland syndicate series. Pat Tebeau and his underachievers versus undertaker Joe Quinn's Misfits. Fifth place versus last place, and fading. A team nineteen games over .500 opposing a aggregation 107 games under .500. So bad were the Clevelands that the *Globe-Democrat* made the intentioned snipe, "the contest was closely waged throughout, and was only settled after the third." (Oct 2). Clearly a mismatch...but, it didn't turn out that way.

Ex-Misfit righthander Willie Sudhoff pitched for St. Louis. Tough luck Jack Harper tossed for Cleveland. From the beginning, it was a pitcher's duel par excellence. The Misfits managed a run in the second inning when Sudhoff walked two men and Ossee Schreckengost made an error at first base. It stayed 1-0 in favor of the visitors for five full innings, despite novice Cleveland first baseman Harry Colliflower, who dropped a thrown ball. No scoring resulted, though. Sudhoff's control was a bit shaky but Cleveland had yet to secure a hit. Harper, pitching heady and steady, "dished up puzzling shots to the heavy hitters of the home team," and St. Louis was also without a safe hit (*CPD*, Oct 2). The *Plain Dealer* also took time to say of Harper, "The boy is more than promising." (Oct 2). In Cleveland's sixth, Sudhoff again held down the visitors but Harper was not so fortunate. St. Louis centerfielder Turkey Mike Donlin led off. "He caught one where he wanted it, and drove a sizzling bounder over second. It had passed Lochhead and Sullivan before they were out of their racks (Pullman sleeping car berths) and had sufficient speed to beat Dowd to the club house." (*GD*, Oct 2). Donlin scampered home with a home run to tie the score at 1-1. Harry Blake tried the same but speedy Charlie Hemphill tracked down his long drive in right field. Jesse Burkett tripled to right. Schreck was the next hitter. He hit to third baseman Otto Krueger, who erred. Burkett scored for a St. Louis lead. Next up was pigeon master Lave Cross. "Cross fouled to Colliflower near the local player's bench. Cleveland's vegetarian pitcher and utility man stood still, holding the ball and congratulating himself on his catch.

167

Schreck took advantage of Colliflower's tardiness, and by a great run gained second. He was left, however, as Wallace pop flied to Sullivan." (*GD*, Oct 2). Despite Colliflower's and Krueger's bonehead maneuvering, the Misfits made it into the seventh trailing by only one run. The *Globe-Democrat* picks up the description: (Oct 2).

The "Exiles" were again blanked without a hit in the seventh, and the "fans" were pulling hard for Sudhoff to let the Wanderers down without a "bingle." Burke opened the locals half with a single, was sacrificed to second by Buelow, but never got any further, and Sudhoff, and Donlin were easy outs. The tail-enders first safe drive came in the eighth. Colliflower began with a pretty drive to right for two sacks. He was caught at third on Duncan's sharp hit to Wallace, Cross getting the put-out. Harper flied to Lave, but Dowd was on hand with a clean drive to left. Harley, too, hit into the same garden. Duncan tried to score from second, but Burkett's great throw to Buelow beat him, though he made an effort to slide into the plate. Thus did the visitors waste a double and two long singles, the dumb baserunning of Colliflower costing them at least one tally. The Braves tallied twice in the eighth. Blake walked for a starter. Burkett bunted safely. Blake tried for third on the "dump," Colliflower had Harry caught easily but his throw went far over Krueger's head and Blake trotted home while Burkett gained second. Schreck's out, Colliflower unassisted, advanced Jesse to third, from where he counted on Cross' fly to Hemphill.

It looked all off for the Wanderers when they came in for their final time at the bat. Sullivan drew a free pass. Hemphill hit savagely to Schreck. Ossee knocked the ball down, and by a head-first slide beat the batter to the bag. Krueger also walked, and on his fourth ball Sullivan made a neat steal of third. Lochhead followed with a long double to right, and Sullivan and Krueger sprinted home. One run meant a tied score, and the Wanderers tried hard for it. Colliflower, who had been batting well, gave Cross a pop fly. Duncan came next with a hard grounder. It struck Sudhoff on the side and bounced far over to the third base line. "Wee Willie" recovered it quickly and his fast throw to Schreck just did beat Duncan, bringing the highly exciting game to a close.

Once again, the Misfits were losers 4-3, their patented ninth inning rally falling short. Cleveland's 10th straight loss took only 86 minutes to play. But, that was too long for goat first baseman Harry Colliflower. His fielding, baserunning, and hitting, or lack thereof, conspired to lose the game for Cleveland.

Mon Oct 2   The season series between Tebeau's Perfectos and Quinn's Homeless Wonders finally concluded. The Spiders could count but one triumph. For the *St. Louis Republic*, that lone moment of Misfit glory was proof enough that baseball was an honest game (June 27).

Tues Oct 3   The Misfits reward for their showing in St. Louis was a few days off and a one-way ticket to Pittsburg. The *Cleveland Plain Dealer* editions reported, "The Cleveland baseball team, known to the game as the Wanderers, blew into town last night evening. They will leave for Pittsburg Saturday. While here, by diligent practice at League Park, they will endeavor to fathom some of the mysteries of the National Game." (Oct 3).

Fri Oct 6   With the Misfits idle, the *Cleveland Plain Dealer* found space to print this article about their not so beloved Misfits (Oct 6).

TO BE VICTIMIZED AGAIN

The few scattered remnants of the Cleveland team left for Pittsburg yesterday, and will accept the usual pounding this afternoon. The players realize that nothing but the rarest of accidents can cause them to win, and there is really no reason to expect them to exert themselves. Their games are played merely as a matter of form, and if there had been a disposition to hurry them though and get supper soon as possible there is no wonder.

Sat Oct 7   As predicted, the Cleveland team walked onto the field at Pittsburg's Exhibition Park, "expecting the usual pounding" and then hurried off to supper, a 16-3 loser to the Buccaneers. The *Pittsburg Post* treated the Misfits team as the butt of jokes, showing a cartoon of a symbolic judge (Pgh team) sentencing a handcuffed youth (Misfits). It was the Cleveland Wanderers last game in Pittsburg "and it may be many years before they are seen here again. They will not be missed, at least not the crowd that pretended to play ball here yesterday." (*PP*, Oct 8). Again, according to the *Post*, the Cleveland team "can neither bat nor field and do not care who knows it" and the best play of the Clevelands "was not the worst of some class F minor league aggregation." (Oct 8). The *Plain Dealer* was no kinder, devoting a small space to harp on negatives. No mention was made of Pittsburg pitcher Hoffer, since all opposition hurlers probably looked like Cy Young to the Misfits (Oct 8).

PITTSBURG, Oct 7.- It was the same old story today. Cleveland's Wandering Willies were biffed and beaten with ease by the Pirates. Young Mr. Harper essayed to do the twirling for the Clevelands, and for the first time since donning National League toggery he was hit hard. The Pirates liked his style real well and sent the ball, to divers and sundry sections of the broad field. Dillon enjoyed a regular feast at the expense of Harper, but the latter took his medicine like a little man, and to his credit, be it said, he did not pout or suck his thumb when his companions failed to afford him proper support.

Errors of commission were numerous enough, but the errors of omission were fully as numerous and decidedly more exasperating. The two Joes, Quinn and Sugden, were absent and they were sadly missed. About the only redeeming feature of the woeful work of the Wanderers was a most remarkable one-hand catch by Lochhead of a high liner, resulting in a double play.

To tell in detail the story of the slaughter would be painful. Suffice to say that not for a minute were the Clevelands in it. They put up an amateurish exhibition and the spectators would have interposed no objections had the umpire called the game long before the completion of the ninth round. Harry Colgan of this year's interstate staff umpired the game and gave excellent satisfaction.

Sun Oct 8   After Pittsburg, the Spiders packed their bags, bats, gloves, and crying towels and headed westward to Chicago. Their experience before a "big festival crowd" of 7000 at the West End Grounds was typical of recent contests. Typical in the sense the Spiders lost, lost big, and had to travel a long way to do it.

Righthander Jack Taylor started for Tom Burns' Chicagos while Jim Hughey was slated to take his lumps for Cleveland. Quickly, the "Orphans moved to shut out the hard working team from Cleveland." (*CPD*, Oct 9). "Hard working" being an adjective of virtue for if the Spiders were anything, they were game. Their baseball playing ability, or facsimile thereof, had long since been taken for granted.

In the first inning, up stepped muscular Chicago centerfielder Bill Lange, who like late hours, practical jokes, and women (Porter). Lange immediately "started the panic in the Cleveland team by a desperate steal of third. He came up the line at a terrific clip, dived head first, slid along the dirt on his chest bone, and caromed against the legs of Krueger. For one instant Krueger occupied Lange's neck, but the crisis soon passed and Connolly called Lange safe." (*CT*, Oct 9). In the same inning, Spider shortstop "Lochhead made a record by making three consecutive fumbles and each cost a run." (*CPD*, Oct 9). Three runs scored in that inning and the fifth. The sixth inning for Chicago was a "slaughter of the innocents," with four runs scoring after two were out. Sam Mertes reversed a Hughey pitch into the right field bleacher seats and Cleveland native Bill Bradley also homered to left. Six errors in all were committed by the Wanderers. Loss number 130 ended 13-0. The Spiders had captured one of fourteen games from the Chicagos.

In the line score tradition of the day, the *Plain Dealer* printed this, as if Cleveland hadn't been there at all.

Chicago 3 0 0 0 3 4 0 3 *-13

Mon Oct 9   With the season winding down, the *Plain Dealer* printed a list of the top batters in the league; Delahanty of Philadelphia, Burkett of St. Louis,

Lajoie of Philadelphia, Keeler of Brooklyn, and McGraw of Baltimore. The Spiders top hitter was pitcher Colliflower.

Thur Oct 12   After a few more days off, the Clevelands played the Cincinnatis to begin their last series of the season. The crowd at Redland Park was extremely small. Fewer than 100 showed for the "struggle that was completely devoid of interest." (*CPD*, Oct 14). "The wag who remarked that the entire audience came downtown on the front platform of a Clark streetcar car fractured the truth slightly, but at that there were not many over two good car loads to witness the contest." (*TEC*, Oct 14).

Cincinnati's Emil Frisk opposed Harry Colliflower. The latter was brilliant for Cleveland...after the first inning, giving up only one hit. But in the first, "the Reds got a whack at Harry Colliflower's benders," and scored six times (*TEC*, Oct 14). Frisk gave up two mere runs to the Misfits in the second and that was all the scoring. In the seventh frame, umpire McDonald called the came to darkness, at least that was the "alleged reason. It was plenty light to go on with play at the time the game was stopped but both players and the crowd were willing it should end." (*TEC*, Oct 14). So bored were the respective newspaper's accounts of the day's activities that no descriptions of the run scoring was given. Instead, the *Plain Dealer* simply put together a 150 word narrative while the *Enquirer* remarked on the Reds' squabbles with umpire Hank O'Day (not present at the game due to "cowardice" and Reds' first baseman Jake Beckley renting a winter cottage at New Orleans with his wife near a race horse track. For the Cleveland players, Sport McAllister talked about hunting in Texas, Tommy Dowd spoke of the new league, and Harry Lochhead was anxious to go home to California.

Sat Oct 14   The next game wasn't exactly a nail-biting affair. Realizing that it probably wouldn't be, the Cincinnati fans went to the game as "small but select as they say in the society column" and with "just about enough people in the bleachers to start a game of marbles." (*TEC*, Oct 15). The *Plain Dealer* also picked up the theme saying the crowd "took just about as much interest as John L. Sullivan (boxer) would in a golf tournament." (Oct 15).

Despite the minuscule gathering of souls, a baseball contest did take place on the field. Righthander Pink Hawley hurled for the Reds against Jim Hughey. The latter gave up four runs in each of the first two innings and the Spiders were in arrears 8-0. It was a familiar position. "The Exiles were so anxious to get through the season that several of them displayed nervous attacks at times, and fielding blunders were almost as plentiful as base hits." (*CPD*, Oct 15). Harry Lochhead "made a mess" at shortstop with three errors. Six were made in all by Cleveland (*CPD*, Oct 15). By the time it was over, the Cincinnati outfield trio of Jimmy Barrett, Sam Crawford, and Kip Selbach had battered Hughey's pitches for ten of the team's seventeen hits. First baseman Jake Beckley and third baseman Bid McPhee had three safe drives each. Cincinnati won in a cantor 12-4. It was the Misfits 14th consecutive loss.

As if retelling the last moments of life before a condemned man's execution, doomsayers at the *Plain Dealer* remarked, "the end is at hand" and that there would be "only one more tale of woe from the Exiles." (Oct 15). Actually, a doubleheader finale was scheduled for the next day. When finished, the 1899 Cleveland season would be over.

Sun Oct 15 About 2000 cranks afforded themselves an afternoon of Sunday baseball at Redland Park for the double finale. Buck Ewing's Reds were battling the St. Louis Perfectos for fifth place honors. Joe Quinn's Misfits were battling to go home. The 1899 National League season was ending.

Tommy Dowd spoke for many of the Cleveland players when he said: "At least fifty times the past season we have got together at the hotel before going to the grounds and said 'We'll win that game to-day or break our necks.' We would mean it too, but the other teams would jump up at the start and skin us so bad that we'd all come off the field with our heads hanging down and our good intentions all shattered."

During the two ball games, the crowd enjoyed the good-natured, rib-poking "kidding matches" among the players (*TEC*, Oct 16). There was a lot to kid about since the games were "about as exciting as a Coroner's inquest or a chapter of a state geological survey." (*TEC*, Oct 16). But, for the Cleveland players, the merriment was most likely to hide their anger and bewilderment over club ownership.

In the first affair, sore-handed Sport McAllister pitched against the Red's John Cronin. The Misfits went through the motions while the Cincinnatians ran rings around the bases. Sixteen to one. The second game and season finale was predictable. The Misfits disintegrated again, and lost for the last time. Dick Harley in left, Suter Sullivan at third, and Harry Lochhead at short fielded bravely for the visitors, probably out of self-defense. The Cincinnati outfield was responsible for eleven safe hits out of the total of eighteen. When the dust finally settled on the field, it was a "hard days labor for the tired-out, smiling aggregation of players." (*TEC*, Oct 16). Noodles Hahn twirled for Cincinnati but the real story was the Cleveland pitcher. It was not grinning Hughey, nor Adonis Knepper, nor Colliflower vegetable, nor young Harper. This was a pitcher who had his catcher Joe Sugden so befuddled that the backstop made three errors. This was a 19-year-old pitcher appearing in his first game. The *Cincinnati Enquirer* explains (Oct 16):

Eddie Kolb, who pitched for the Clevelands in the second game, runs the cigar stand at the Gibson House. He became acquainted with Captain Quinn during the team's visits to the hotel Saturday night when he heard that pitcher Harper was sick, he volunteered to pitch yesterday. He pitched a very fair game, all things considered. True, he was hit hard at the outset, but after he got the 'hang of the shop' he did fairly well. Some of the drives that went for hits would have been outs had the Cleveland fielders tried very hard. They did a little loafing behind the youngster in the latter part of the game.

The Reds scored a run for each of Kolb's nineteen years of age. After the affair ended 19-3, "Manager Quinn and his players gave three mighty cheers and hustled off the grounds." (*CPD*, Oct 16). The Misfits were on their way to Cleveland to receive six weeks of back pay from club management. "If these salaries are not forthcoming tomorrow President Frank Robison will have a pleasant time of it, for the players do not hesitate to make open threats against the St. Louis-Cleveland syndicate. The players expect another standoff tomorrow, but if the Robisons attempt that game they will be besieged with lawsuits, for the players insist they be payed in full, and argue that they have conceded enough in waiting as long as they have." (*CPD*, Oct 16).

The Wanderers not only lost all fourteen of their contests with the Reds, but also were outscored 53-10 in the last four meetings. For the campaign, the Reds outscored the Exiles by a 4-1 margin and averaged ten runs a game.

1899 final standings:

TEAM	W-L	PCT	GB
Brooklyn	101-47	.682	--
Boston	95-57	.625	8
Philadelphia	94-58	.618	9
Baltimore	86-62	.581	15
St. Louis	84-67	.556	18.5
Cincinnati	83-67	.552	19
Pittsburg	76-73	.510	25.5
Chicago	75-73	.507	26
Louisville	75-77	.495	28
New York	60-90	.400	42
Washington	54-98	.356	49
Cleveland	20-134	.129	84

The 1899 Misfits lost 40 of their last 41. In a bit of an understatement, the *Plain Dealer* uttered philosophically, "It has been a bad season for Cleveland fans." (Oct 16). Harry Lochhead, speaking for Dick Harley and Charlie

Hemphill said of the Cleveland faithful: "I have never seen an audience so loyal to its home team. During the games we played here, there was never a hiss or a call down for a Cleveland player." Only six thousand saw them play in Cleveland.

But, perhaps, the story of the Spiders remarkable propensity for losing can be explained this way. In those early days of baseball, teams were driven from their hotels to the ballpark in horse drawn carriages. Visiting teams who had defeated the home town club had a very real chance of being "pelted with fruits and vegetables on their return hotel trip." (Suehsdorf 36). Were not these Misfits, who played almost every one of their games on the road, fearful of flying rutabagas and lemons? More incredible was the Misfits' road attendance. Despite the non-support at home, Cleveland played to a total of 264,000 fans on the road- second in the league to Brooklyn. Of course, they also played a few more road games than the Superbas. In fact, the 1899 Cleveland Spiders hold the major league record for the two longest road trips, a 50 game in 52 days swing marathon in which they won six games and a 36 game trip that included a solitary victory.

The Cleveland team was retaining fifteen players for the next year. Following is the Cleveland team reserve list for 1900 as printed in the *Plain Dealer*. No one honestly believed there would be a team in Cleveland in 1900. Thomas J. Dowd, James Hughey, James Sugden, H.R. Lochhead, Suter Sullivan, L.W. McAllister, R.J. Harley, Henry Colliflower, C.J. Hemphill, Charles Knepper, J.J. Quinn, James Duncan, Harper, Krueger, Ziegler.

Mon Oct 16 The day after the close of the season, the *Plain Dealer* printed this article about the confusion surrounding the financial reparations among Messrs. Robison and Messrs. Quinn, Dowd, Harley, et al. Once again, the newspaper wasted no time in attacking players and management. It was headlined, "Not Worried About Their Pay." (Oct 17).

The members of the baseball aggregation that (mis)represented this city during the season just closed arrived in Cleveland yesterday, tired out by the almost superhuman exertion required in winning an even twenty games out of 154, and finishing with a remarkable percentage of .129, feats that stand out almost pre-eminent and alone in the history of baseball in any league or organization.

The players returned here for a settlement with the Cleveland club and while there has been a rumor afloat for some time that they feared to get the small end of the financial straightening up, the men are not in the least worried. In fact, they are indignant because they have been quoted as being fearful of losing their last two months pay. A special from Cincinnati, published in this paper yesterday stated that the players would return here with fire in their eyes and law suits in their minds, ready to force a settlement.

No statement has been more vigorously denied in a long time as the one yesterday. The players besieged the sporting editor's sanctum nearly all day in delegations of from two to five, all prepared to refute the story. Finally, they drew up a signed statement denying that they had ever given occasion for the story sent out from Cincinnati, and declaring neither grievance nor misunderstanding with the club concerning their salaries. They expect to receive their back pay today and the congratulations of their friends will follow.

Tue Oct 17 The sticky financial situation continued on Tuesday with the *Plain Dealer*'s reportage. The daily called it "a novel situation in baseball" and that it was, but the amount of words devoted to the tale could have been a baseball novel in itself (Oct 18).

The settlement that the Cleveland baseball players were expecting yesterday did not materialize, and there are a few angry ball-tossers in this city this morning- all reports to the contrary notwithstanding.

Several weeks ago, when the players discovered they were getting behind in their pay, they received all sorts of promises that they would get their money as soon as the affairs of the St. Louis-Cleveland syndicate could be settled.

Of course, the players stood for this for awhile, but they wanted to see a little money later on and when the season closed they rushed to this city in a bunch and demanded their pay.

Then the stories of the troubles between the players and the management began to crop out. At first it was said that there would be enough lawsuits to disrupt the league, but the players denied all intentions of going into court. They were sure they would get a settlement yesterday. But they didn't. When the few remaining players went to baseball headquarters yesterday to draw their pay for the past two months they got more promises than money.

It is now said that the players have received $50 each to go home and keep quiet and that those who do not accept this may pay their own board bills in this city until they can get a settlement. There are several players who prefer to wait, but there is no doubt that the Cleveland club players will eventually get all that is coming to them.

Finally, the November 4 issue of *Sporting Life* reported that the Cleveland players had been paid the balance of their season salaries.

Shortly after the 1899 season ended, financial considerations and fierce competition from the Western Association and the yet to be realized American Association forced the National League to drop four of its teams. In some strange and desperate money maneuvers, the League bought out the Louisville franchise for $10,000. The Colonels players were pooled with the protected Pirates players, forming the foundation of a strong Pittsburg team. The Baltimore half of the Brooklyn-Baltimore syndicate was given $30,000.

175

Brooklyn remained in the league until 1958. Baltimore fielded an American League franchise for two years, and then moved to NY to become the Highlanders and later the New York Yankees. The Washington Senators ownership was handed $46,500. The Senators resurfaced two years later in the American League to begin a woeful baseball history. And, of course, the Cleveland Spiders vanished from the National League only to return in American League incarnations as the Naps, Blues and then Indians. The syndicate baseball idea was outlawed.

As 1899 drew to a close, a debate centered in America over which was the last year of the century. Historian Mark Sullivan wrote that it was a "human disposition to sum things up, to say who had been the greatest men of the century just closed, what had been the greatest books, the greatest inventions, the greatest advances in science..." (*Our Times*, 12-13). But, there was no debate over who was the worst ball team. The 1899 Cleveland Spiders/Misfits easily held that distinction. Today, over 100 years later, they remain baseball's best losers.

Appendix A
The Participants' Careers

pitchers:

William Cicero Hill b. 08/02/74 Chattanooga, TN   d. 01/28/38 Cincinnati, OH.

Still Bill Hill spent the first seven weeks of the 1899 campaign tossing for Cleveland, winning three of nine decisions. Later, he pitched with Brooklyn and Baltimore. With the Orioles, Hill tallied 14-1 and 9-4 July victories against the Misfits.

But, with a four year 36-69 career slate, nobody signed Hill to a league contract again.

John William Sudhoff b. 9/17/74 St. Louis, MO d. 5/25/17 St. Louis, MO.

After being sent to St. Louis with Lave Cross for Ossee Schreckengost and Frank Bates, Sudhoff pitched to a 13-11 slate with Pat Tebeau's Perfectos. For the next two seasons, Sudhoff worked for the St. Louis National League team. In 1900, Sudhoff fashioned a 6-8 record. The next year, he had begun to realize his potential. But, an August 1901 incident damaged his career. Sudhoff was accused by teammates of having "peached" on their liquor habits and the team spent the rest of the year playing poorly behind him (Phillips). Willie finished the year 16-10.

The Cardinals became disinterested in his contract and for the next four seasons, Sudhoff hurled for the American League franchise in St. Louis; the Browns. Willie pitched so well in '02-'03 that he became a Sunday pitcher; matched up with the other team's best. Willie won 20 games in 1903. Sudhoff was at the height of his career in 1904, but several inexplicable events occurred. Sudhoff lost his fine pitching abilities. His fastball remained but it had no movement. His curves didn't break as they should. Sudhoff became so distraught that he constantly sought out his teammates and manager Jimmy McAleer for an explanation. No one could help him. Then, in early September 1904, a train carrying the Browns team crashed in Huron, Ohio. The accident was a result of the train running into a handcar loaded with rails. No one was reported injured physically, but Sudhoff was so shaken that he never again could sleep during rail travel. His pitching career was never the same again. "Cottontop" ended 1904 with an 8-15 record. In 1905, his downfall continued. Sudhoff lost 19 times and spent a partial season with Washington in 1906.

After his playing career, Sudhoff had a nervous breakdown and was confined to a sanatorium. He stayed ill for several years and died away from his wife and four children in May of 1917. Obituaries say Sudhoff died of the traumatic nervosa resulting from the train mishap and that Willie was forgotten by his family. However, his son Emmett Wallace Sudhoff said that Sudhoff died as a result of injuries sustained by being hit by a batted ball over the left eye in practice.

James Ulysses Hughey b. 3/08/69 Wakashma, MI d. 3/29/45 Coldwater, MI.

Described by contemporaries as lacking in ambition and judgement, "Coldwater Jim" spent most of the 1899 season pitching in hot water. He finished 4-30, defeating only Baltimore twice, Louisville, and the number one syndicate team, St. Louis. He needed luck to secure those. One victory over Baltimore occurred when Baltimore pitcher Jeremiah Nops was hung over; another was bolstered by Harry Lochhead's late inning baserunning heroics. Louisville's Honus Wagner baserunning blunder in the ninth helped Hughey win another. Smiling Jim's hardest earned triumph was a 3-1 nailbiter over St. Louis. In mid-July, Hughey was 4-14. He then lost his last 16 in a row.

Jim Hughey's entire season could be summarized in one damp September day in Chicago. His catcher, Sport McAllister had such a terrible time sloshing after Jim's wild tosses. McAllister threw the ball back to his pitcher and Jim promptly sat down in the mud.

At the end of the 1899 season, Hughey had a career record of 24-73. The Cardinals signed him. Hughey won five of twelve decisions on a mediocre 1900 Cardinals squad. Later he pitched for the Toledo Mud Hens and ended his baseball days with Shreveport of the Southern League. After Jim retired, he bought a country store and ran it with his wife for 40 years.

Wilfred Carsey b. 10/22/70 New York, NY d. 03/29/60 Miami, FL.

In mid-June 1899, Kid Carsey took his junkball floaters and quit baseball for racehorses. Just a short while later, he quit racehorses to pitch for the Washington Senators. In 1901, Carsey surfaced in Brooklyn. Manager Hanlon saw enough after two games and released the righthander. His league talents on the wane, Carsey twirled for a semi-pro outfit in New York called the Metropolitans.

Charles Knepper b. 2/18/71 Anderson, IN d. 2/06/46 Muncie, IN.

He was the tallest player on the team. Newspapers constantly referred to him as a giant of a man with long blond locks. He was compared to the Biblical Samson. But, righthander Charles Knepper's Delilah was that he had the misfortune of pitching on the 1899 Cleveland Misfits. Knepper was often called a pitcher of promise, but was doomed by his employers.

Knepper tossed but one year in league employ, winning 4 of 26 decisions. Yet, he completed every game he started.

178

Frederick M. Schmit b. 2/13/66 Chicago, IL d. 10/5/40 Chicago, IL.

Early baseball had its share of clownish characters. (f.ex. Rube Waddell, Nick Altrock, Arlie Latham, etc.). However, few could surpass the feats of the illustrious lefthander, Frederick W. Schmit. Many of the tales have already been told herein. However, a few more remain.

In 1889, Schmit related on his experiences in pro ball. "Yes, last season was my first in an active professional way. I had played in the Chicago City League, also in a semi-professional team at Oconto, Wis. I started in too well at Kalamazoo last year. In fifteen games they made but seventy-five hits off me. The moment it was discovered I was pitching good ball they worked me four games a week. That was too many. I am certain I never heard of a left-hander getting that dose. I won sixteen of my first twenty games. When Kalamazoo disbanded I went to Saginaw, where I finished the season." (*TSN*, Mar 19, 1890).

The next year, 1890, Schmit was so anxious to play big league ball, that he went out to practice from his Chicago home...in the snow (Mar 19, 1890). After a series of pitching misadventures with a seemingly endless array of ball clubs, Schmit landed in Cleveland. He had been taking notes all the while. Many years later, Schmit's Misfits' catcher, Joe Sugden would talk of the pitcher's less-than-spectacular skills. Sugden explained, "Schmit was a nuisance to a catcher. No matter what you signalled he always shook his head. Never did he fail to do this. He didn't have much stuff anyway and I used to get sore.

"Gwan pitch what you want to without signals. I'll get you."

And Schmit would say, "No, no, Joe. Try me again."

But it never did any good. Schmit had to shake his head once at least every signal." (*TSN*, date unkn).

Sugden also recalled that once when Schmit had quaffed a few too many the night before a game he fielded half a dozen bunts without attempting to toss out the batters. He would just "wobble over, carefully take off his glove and pick up the ball with his right hand." (*TSN*, date unkn). Schmit accused the Orioles John McGraw of "bunteration" but even when Schmit was sober on the field, he didn't have much of a chance in the league.

But, as baseball makes strange bedfellows, Schmit was signed two years later to pitch for McGraw's American League Orioles. Schmit appeared in four games, won zero, lost two, struck out two, and walked sixteen in 22 innings. McGraw released Schmit to scout in the Wisconsin-Illinois League. Here, Schmit also pitched a few contests for Fond du Lac. A local newspaper article headlined "Crazy Schmit Couldn't Pitch Against Boneheads" relates:

"One day the team was playing Rockford, the leaders in the pennant race. Schmit's team were the tail-enders. Along about the seventh inning, with

Rockford leading by 4-0, the first man up got on. Schmit pitched out three times in an attempt to get the runner going down to second base, but the runner made no attempt to purloin the sack. With the count three and nothing on the batter he grooved the next one, only to have the batter lean on it and drive it over the left field fence for a home run.

After the runners had circled the bases the umpire threw up another ball. Schmit took it, shook his head and walked over to Bobby Lynch, who was playing third base and was captain and manager of the team, and said to him: "Say, Bobby, no wonder I can't beat these fellows. I won't pitch against them any longer. I quit right now. They don't know how to play baseball and yet they are leading this league. The runner that was on first base just let me waste three balls and yet he does not attempt to steal. When I put one over for the batter, who has three balls and no strikes, he hits it. Tell me, how can a man of my intelligence and baseball knowledge pitch a game of baseball against such a bonehead and unscientific playing of the game?'" (source unkn).

Creed F. Bates b. Chattanooga, TN. D. unkn.

In just three months with the 1899 Clevelands, Mr. Bates managed to lose 18 times. Holder of one of the most inglorious one-year pitching records, Frank Bates never pitched in fast company again.

James Harry Colliflower b. 3/11/69 Petersville, MD d. 8/14/61 Washington, D.C.

Dick Harley's friend, James Harry Colliflower, must have went through life the butt of constant jokes about his name. Baseball scribes in Cleveland and around the league certainly did their part, using phrases like the opposition "pickled Colliflower" and that Harry "vegetated" on the mound.

In mid-July, Colliflower's pitching debut in Washington was a rousing success. After two innings, he trailed 3-0, but the Spiders shocked the Washingtonians and won out 5-3. Harry even helped himself with a double. But, Colliflower worked that game without a contract. He disagreed with manager Quinn on the money offered and soon was off the team. A week later, Colliflower signed and promptly lost to John McGraw's crafty Baltimores 9-4. His pitching career disintegrated from then on; wildness helped him to eleven straight losses. But, Colliflower did hit well and substituted in the outfield on several occasions. But, Colliflower certainly didn't fondly remember his October 1st game in St. Louis.

His pitching unsuccessful, Colliflower became a minor league umpire in a host of leagues; Eastern, New England, South Atlantic, Southern, Western, Piedmont and Interstate until 1915. In 1903, Colliflower's arbiter skills in the

Eastern League left a lot to be desired in the eyes of sportswriters who were doing "some beautiful roasts of his work." (Phillips). In 1910, Colliflower umpired one year in the American League. Later, Harry worked as a member of the Detroit scouting staff and baseball coach for Georgetown University.

Colliflower became well known in the Washington, D.C. area as a luncheon speaker for athletic gatherings. Like contemporary DeWolf Hopper, Colliflower entertained audiences with his mimed/recital versions of Ernest Lloyd Thayer's "Casey at the Bat" poem (*TSN*, date unkn).

Charles William Harper b. 4/02/78 Galloway, PA. d. 9/30/50 Jamestown, NY.

Righthander Jack Harper's career was marked by controversy and bad luck. Easily the most successful of the Misfits' pitchers following 1899, Harper's professional career began in Montgomery, Alabama in the Southern League in 1898. For most of 1899, Harper twirled for Grand Rapids, Columbus and Springfield. In mid-September, he was reported signed by St. Louis and Cleveland. He ended up with the Misfits.

Harper recalled his first big league game almost half a century later. "We were in one hell of a long losing streak. The day before we finally ended it, I was horsing around with another player and hurt my shoulder. I didn't think I could start, but kept still, and when the game began, I found if I threw more sidearm than usual, it didn't hurt. Along about the third inning, manager Joe Quinn wanted to know what was the matter, but I told him I was all right. Then, about the fifth inning, I worked the kink out of my shoulder and went back to my natural style, more of an overhand." (Jamestown, NY newspaper, date unkn). The Misfits went on to win that game 5-4, snapping a record 24-game losing streak. It was to be his only Cleveland victory.

In 1900, Harper was back in the minors for more seasoning. Late that year, Harper was picked up by the Cardinals and bombed in his only start. In 1901, though, the seasoning had paid off. Harper won 23 games for the 1901 Redbirds. His teammates included ex-Misfits Willie Sudhoff and Otto Krueger. In 1902 Harper jumped to St. Louis of the American League with Sudhoff, Jesse Burkett and Jack Powell. Joe Sugden and mediocre Mike Kehoe were his catchers. Harper won 15 of 26 decisions. But, American League President Ban Johnson suspended Harper for arguing and in 1903 he was back in the National League. Between 1903-1906, Jack pitching winning ball for the Reds, topping out with 23 wins in 1904. But a chipped bone in the elbow forced Harper into a bad 1905 campaign. In 1906, a finger injury curtailed his record. That year, Harper hit Cubs manager Frank Chance with a pitch. Soon afterward, in a curious trade, Harper moved to Chicago. The Cubs, who were busy piling up the best record in major league history, refused to use Harper as punishment for his hitting Chance. He never pitched in the majors again.

So, Harper had the bizarre distinction of pitching on the worst team and finishing up with the best team in the history of big league ball.

Howard Paul Wilson b. 08/09/78 Philadelphia, PA d. 10/16/34 Havre De Grace, MD.

Right hand hurler Howard P. Wilson pitched one game for the Cleveland Spiders. He lost. Three years later, Wilson enjoyed some success on Connie Mack's pennant winning Athletics (7-5). In 1903, he made his way to the Washington Senators, where he pitched poorly for two years. It is not known whether or not the "Highball" cognomen was a pitching or drinking weakness. However, in February of 1899, six months before Wilson's debut, this article appeared in *Sporting Life*. "In an encounter at a road home, on the 4th pst., Frank (Howard) Wilson, pitcher of the Cleveland (Ohio) Base Ball team, was shot in the hip and seriously wounded. During the trouble, Wilson cut several gashes in the side of the face of Joseph Teale. It was about a woman." (Feb 9).

Lewis M. McAllister b. 7/23/74 Austin, Miss d. 7/17/62 Wyandotte, MI.

Sport McAllister's claim to fame was that he played all nine positions for the 1899 Cleveland Spiders. He even umpired.

Wherever McAllister went in baseball after 1899 (Detroit, Baltimore, Buffalo among others), he retained his trademark utility position. In 1901, he was in Detroit to "cavort behind the bat." (*Wash Star*, Sep 1901). During the course of the next two seasons for the Tigers, Sport played all of the infield, all of the outfield, and caught. After his pitching disasters with Cleveland, he never cared to or pitched again. But, McAllister did find time to take tickets, sell peanuts and beer, sweep the stands, and eject rowdy fans.

Career games by position OF-147, C-83, 1B-65, SS-62, 3B-27, P-27, 2B-7

Henry Carr Maupin b. 7/11/72 Wellesville, MO. d. 1952, unkn.

Most talent scouts realized that Harry Maupin was not another Cy Young. After 1899, he never played in the majors again. His career (0-5) showed all of seven games with St. Louis and Cleveland and an earned run average near ten.

Edward William Kolb b. 7/20/80 Cincinnati, OH d. unkn.

As a 19-year old cigar store clerk, Edward William Kolb was Joe Quinn pitching choice to close the Misfits' season in Cincinnati. Quinn chose Kolb because his scheduled starter Jack Harper was ill. The Spiders went up in smoke in the finale, 19-3. The *Cincinnati Enquirer* was not very kind to Eddie saying he had the "underpinning of a Kansas grasshopper and the complexion of a yellow fever convalescent." (Oct 16). It was the newspaper's health assessment since Kolb hadn't been in the league long enough for a physical. It was to be Kolb's solitary league game. He remains one of baseball's most curious pitching footnotes.

Six years later, Kolb managed a Vincennes, Indiana ball club. Details are sketchy, but Kolb made his money in the restaurant business and bought Western Canada League Calgary in the early 1920's. Also included in that league were teams from Moose Jaw, Regina, Edmonton, Saskatoon, and Winnipeg.

John Elmer Stivetts b. 3/31/68 Ashland, PA d. 4/18/30 Ashland, PA.

Thirty one year old "Happy Jack" Stivetts washed out with the 1899 Clevelands. Out of shape, he pitched in but seven games to a winless 0-4 record. His once tremendous batting skills also plummeted. Stivetts never played in the big leagues again.

After his Cleveland release, Stivetts drove beer wagons in his native Ashland, Pennsylvania. The son of a coal miner, Stivetts was a carpenter and aspired to be a preacher.

In 1961, the *Ashland Daily News* printed an article about Stivetts by Martin J. Corcoran that made a case for his inclusion in the Baseball Hall of Fame. Stivetts won almost 200 games in his 11-year career with St. Louis, Boston, and Cleveland. He was 19-7 as a reliever. Stivetts hit .297 with an astonishing 35 home run and 314 runs batted in.

catchers:

Joseph Sugden b. 7/31/70 Philadelphia, PA d. 6/28/59 Philadelphia, PA.

Joe Sugden lasted the entire season at catcher behind probably the worst pitching staff in the history of baseball. For this he should be commended. It could even be said that Sugden was not so much a catcher as he was a watcher; having a clear view of opposing batsman whack baseballs all over National League ball fields. So bad was the Cleveland pitching staff that opponents often resorted to bunting as a main batting strategy. Hurlers such as Hughey, Bates, and Schmit didn't seem to have a clue as to how to field these balls. Sugden had the best seat in the house.

After the Misfits folded, "Peanut Hands" Sugden played a few more campaigns in the newly formed American League with the Chicago White Sox and the St. Louis Browns until 1906. Again, he toiled in a backup role. With his playing days behind him, the Detroit Tigers made Sugden a coach.

In early 1912, AL firebrand Ty Cobb charged into the stands to beat up a heckler. Strangely enough, the loudmouth man Cobb was after had no hands, but Ty pummelled him anyway. American League President Ban Johnson promptly suspended Cobb. Without their leader, the Tigers simply refused to play until Cobb was reinstated. Johnson replied with a warning of forfeit, fine, and possible loss of franchise. Detroit manager Hughie Jennings was left in a lurch. But, three days later, the Tigers traveled to Philadelphia to play a game with the Phillies- sans a team. But, Jennings had signed several Philadelphia sandlotters just in case. They were needed. Jennings summoned ancient coaches Deacon McGuire to catch and Joe Sugden to man first base. Philadelphia manager Connie Mack used a few subs and still beat Detroit by a laughable 24-2. It must have reminded Sugden of his days with the Misfits. Thankfully, the real Tigers ended their strike and Cobb returned.

After his stint with the Tigers, Sugden was made a scout by the St. Louis Cardinals. Perhaps the Cardinals brass thought that a player used to so much mediocrity could judge talent as good as any. Sugden remained a Cardinal scout for decades.

Once Sugden was approached by a collegian who was happy to shake a league catcher's hands. The lad took one look at Sugden's mangled digits and said, "Those hands indicate you've caught a lot of baseballs." Joe's reply: "No son, they indicate I've missed a lot of baseballs." (*TSN*, June 6, 1959).

John J. Clements b. 7/24/64 Philadelphia, PA d. 5/23/41 Norristown, PA.

After catching only four games with Cleveland, Clements was sadly out of shape and was released. In 1900, he played a few games for the Beaneaters and kicked around briefly in the Connecticut State League.

James William Duncan b. 07/01/71 Saltsburg, PA d. 10/16/01 Foxburg, PA.

One-hundred forty-pound flyweight catcher/first baseman Jim Duncan lasted only one season in the league. He played with Washington and Cleveland. In his 31 game stretch with the Misfits, he participated in exactly one victory, playing first base. In that win, Cleveland broke a 24 game loss string when Duncan's home run in the ninth helped beat the Senators.

Duncan drowned in the Allegheny River October 16, 1901 at age 30.

Ossee Freeman Schreckengost b. 4/11/75 New Bethelem, PA d. 7/09/14 Philadelphia, PA.

Known more for his gregarious eating and drinking behaviors than his ball playing, Ossee Freeman Schreckengost performed on the diamonds for more than 15 years. His goal in life seemed to be to drive his manager's mad. But, Ossee was a competent backstop and decent hitter. "Schreck" had the pleasure of starting his '99 season in St. Louis, then transferring to Cleveland in the Lave Cross deal, and moving back to St. Louis when injuries crippled Perfectos catchers.

Schreck spent 1900 in Buffalo but was in the majors to stay for eight years beginning in 1901. That season Ossee played on a fine AL Boston squad with ex-Misfit mates Tommy Dowd and Charlie Hemphill. Schreck split catching time with Lou Criger, hit .304, and caught Cy Young. In 1902, Schreck backstopped briefly in Cleveland before being traded to the Philadelphia Athletics. For the next six and one-half seasons, Schreck handled some of the greatest pitchers in the game; Eddie Plank, Chief Bender, and free-spirit Rube Waddell. The manager of the team was stern Connie Mack.

Pitcher Waddell, who chased after fire engines for fun, among other things, became instant friends with his battery mate Schreckengost. Stories about their exploits together are legend. To intimidate enemy batters, Schreckengost would soak his mitt before a game so that Waddell's fastballs would sound like they were exploding.

In a restaurant one night, the two ordered steak, but Schreck complained to the waiter that his meat was too tough to be cut with a knife. After the waiter returned with another piece, Schreck again found the same problem. Then, Ossee ordered a hammer and nails. The waiter responded thinking that ballplayers always ask for the strangest things. When the tools came, Schreck marched downstairs to the lobby and hammered the steak into the wall. A near riot ensued (*TSN*, July 11, 1929).

The most famous tale of Waddell and Schreck involves animal crackers and "pizzaza" sandwiches. In days when ballplayers roomed together they slept in the same bed. Schreck and Waddell complained so loudly of each other's bedside eating habits to Mr. Mack, that Connie was forced to write a forbade clause into their contracts. One contract forbade eating animal crackers while the other prohibited pizzaza sandwiches, especially those with limburger cheese and onions. Both men liked to devour the delicacies in bed. The story has been told so often that it is unclear who exactly was the cracker fancier and who gulped the sandwiches.

On another occasion, Mack was so worried about Schreck's drinking habits that he ordered first baseman Harry "Jasper" Davis to try to convince Schreck to stop. Davis was convincing and soon Schreck replaced his alcohol with milk shakes; 15-20 a day! Often, Davis would accompany Schreck to the fountain but once Davis went alone. When Davis asked the soda jerk for a shake the boy said, "Do you want the kind Mr. Schreck gets?" Davis easily agreed and saw the boy reach beneath the counter and fill half the glass with sherry.

In a July 4th doubleheader in 1905, Ossee caught 29 innings. That same year the Athletics made it to the World Series but lost to the Giants in five games. Christy Mathewson tossed three shutouts for the New Yorkers. In the winter of 1905, Schreck paid a visit to an old minor league haunt, Youngstown, Ohio. He went in diamonds and furs, something quite unheard of for a ballplayer.

Schreck also had the unusual distinction of doubling into a triple play. An old newspaper clipping picks up the story: "With the bases loaded and none out in a game against Cleveland, Schreck slammed a long fly over the center fielder's head that looked for a minute that it might be caught. The runner on third played it right by gluing to the bag figuring he could score after the catch, but the runner on second dashed over the third while the runner on first pulled his freight for second. As he neared third, the runner who had been on second saw the runner standing on that bag and turned and hot-footed it back toward second. The runner who had been on first had already turned second base, and the two passed each other running in opposite directions between second and third, the man who had been on first being automatically out under the rules of passing an advance runner. In the meantime, the center fielder had managed to knock down Schreck's hit with one hand but failed to hold it, and Schreck kept on running. The runner on third was so busy shooing the runners off base that he failed to start for the plate until the ball had been returned to the infield, then Lajoie, taking the throw from the center fielder, threw to the plate and nailed the man trying to score as he slid in. That made two out. Schreck had passed second during the fuss, which entitled him to a two-base hit, but seeing two runners already jammed on the line between second and third Schreck turned and dashed back. The catcher, after tagging out the man trying to score and seeing Schreck on his way back, threw to Lajoie who tagged out Schreck, completing a triple play without a run being scored." (Sep 11, 1922, source unkn).

The A's slumped in 1906. Hopelessly out of the pennant race, Mack suspended Schreck for the duration of the season after Ossee was out all night. Schreck played one more productive year but in 1908 he was sold to the Cubs, where he ended his big league career. In 1910-1911, Schreck retired to the minors and hung on with a team in Fort City, Pennsylvania for a while as a first baseman. After hanging up his mitt, Schreck was employed in a cafe in Philadelphia. He died in 1914, just after his old pal Waddell had passed on.

Charles Louis Zimmer b. 11/23/60 Marietta, OH d. 08/22/49 Cleveland, OH.

Chief Zimmer spent 26 years in baseball, gaining a reputation as the first Iron Man catcher. Curiously enough, he began his sandlot career with an Ironton, Ohio team at 21 years of age, giving up as a carpenter apprentice to become a ballplayer. Zimmer spent some time in the minors before playing a few games with the 1884 Detroit National Leaguers. The next season, Zimmer appeared briefly with New York of the American Association. Unfortunately, Zimmer's play was less than spectacular.

It wasn't until 1887 that his long professional association with the city of Cleveland took wing. Zimmer was discovered hitting .409 with Poughkeepsie of the Hudson River League and was signed by Secretary Davis Hawley for $500 (Phillips). He caught a couple of years with Cleveland of the American Association before moving to the 1889 National League franchise.

From the beginning, Zimmer began boasting that he kept himself in such athletic shape that he could catch every game. A teetotaler who also didn't smoke, Zimmer shared duties with Sy Sutcliffe in 1889. By 1890, Zimmer was ready to squat all season...and did. All the more remarkable was that he fashioned a finger glove and worked with no shinguards or chest protectors. The beating he received must have been brutal. *Sporting Life* said in late September that a "game without Zimmer would be a disagreeable novelty." (Sep 26, 1890). But, Zimmer had help. That season also marked the debut of Cy Young. To compensate for Young's fastballs, Zimmer padded his small glove with beefsteak. Until 1893, the pitcher to batter distance was 45 feet.

For the next several years, the Spiders became winners under feisty manager Pat Tebeau. Zimmer and Young were great friends and the Spiders made the Temple Cup championships in 1895-1896. Young became a legend and Zimmer was his battery mate. In 1897, Zimmer caught a no-hitter from Young. But, Zimmer also received notoriety for his hitting. Twice he hit over .300 and once, in Boston, Zimmer socked a home run over the fence that landed in a passing boxcar on the Boston-Albany railroad. By the time the train had stopped at Fall River, Massachusetts, it had traveled fifty miles; almost to Rhode Island! (*TSN*, Aug 23, 1949). By 1898, a thirty-eight year old Zimmer had slowed down considerably. He caught only 20 games with Cleveland that year. In 1899, Zimmer stuck around his hometown Cleveland, rather than complete the move to St. Louis.

With the 1899 Spiders, Zimmer hit .342 before going to Louisville. In the bluegrass, he played 75 games and hit .298.

The next season, Louisville was absorbed by Barney Dreyfuss' Pittsburg franchise. Zimmer went along and not only caught the spitballs of Jack Chesbro but played on two Pirate pennant winners as well. In 1903, Zimmer caught and was manager of the Philadelphia Phillies.

He spent the next few years umpiring and managing. In the National League (1904), the Eastern League (1905), and the Southern Association (1907), Zimmer turned arbiter as he had a "temptation to handle the indicator." (Phillips). In 1906, Zimmer managed Little Rock in the Southern Association. As his baseball career was winding down, Zimmer pleaded, "Young ballplayers, let booze alone and save your money while you are in the business, as it don't last long.." (*TSN*, Dec 5, 1907).

Later in life, Zimmer mastered the art of cigar making (though he abstained himself) and the "intricacies of laundry manipulation." He designed furniture for his home, using his early talents as cabinet-maker. In hometown Cleveland, Zimmer worked as a city building inspector. Zimmer always delighted in proclaiming himself as the oldest living catcher, being a few months senior to Connie Mack. Zimmer also reveled in telling others that he never had a sore arm, a broken finger, or even a bruised fingernail.

MISFITS Gallery

Jim Hughey

Joe Quinn

Charlie Hemphill

Dick Harley

Lave Cross

Tommy Dowd

O. Schreckengost

Chief Zimmer

Tommy Tucker

Louis Sockalexis

Joe Sugden

Due to the team's and player's obscurity, photographs of the Cleveland Spiders remain rare. Note how a few of them have "St. Louis" stitched on their uniforms.

Major League Baseball's Longest Road Trip
July 3-Aug. 23, 1899

(Cleveland victories in bold)

Opponent	Date	Score	W/L
Pittsburg	July 3	7-1	L
Pittsburg	July 4	4-3	L
Pittsburg	July 4	7-6	L
St. Louis	July 6	9-4	L
St. Louis	July 8	5-4	L
St. Louis	July 8	6-2	L
St. Louis	July 9	11-4	L
Philadelphia	July 11	5-1	L
Philadelphia	July 12	4-2	L
Philadelphia	July 13	5-1	L
Baltimore	July 14	14-1	L
Baltimore	July 15	10-0	L
Baltimore	July 15	5-0	L
Baltimore	**July 17**	**7-2**	**W**
Baltimore	July 17	21-6	L
Washington	**July 18**	**5-4**	**W**
Washington	July 18	11-4	L
Washington	July 19	7-4	L
Washington	July 19	6-2	L
Washington	July 20	4-0	L
Washington	**July 21**	**5-3**	**W**
Washington	July 21	5-3	L
Atlantic City	Exh.	**10-3**	**W**
Atlantic City	Exh.	**6-5**	**W**
Atlantic City	Exh.	12-8	L
Baltimore	July 27	8-5	L
Baltimore	July 27	9-4	L
Baltimore	July 28	6-1	L
Baltimore	July 28	8-2	L
Louisville	July 30	9-2	L
Louisville	July 30	16-13	L

Philadelphia	Aug. 1	7-5	L
Philadelphia	**Aug 1**	**6-2**	**W**
Philadelphia	Aug 2	8-5	L
Philadelphia	Aug 3	6-1	L
Philadelphia	Aug 3	4-0	L
Chicago	Aug 5	4-0	L
Chicago	**Aug 6**	**10-9**	**W**
Boston	Aug 8	18-8	L
Boston	Aug 9	7-3	L
New York	Aug 12	13-1	L
New York	Aug 12	6-2	L
New York	Aug 14	7-6	L
Brooklyn	Aug 15	6-2	L
Brooklyn	Aug 16	13-2	L
Brooklyn	Aug 17	20-2	L
Brooklyn	Aug 18	4-2	L
Pittsburg	**Aug 19**	**8-3**	**W**
Chicago	Aug 20	8-7	L
Louisville	Aug 22	15-6	L
Louisville	Aug 23	13-3	L

For a seven week period in July and August, the Cleveland Spiders played 51 consecutive games on the road (including 3 exhibitions) — the longest stretch in major league history. The trip began with 13 straight losses.

In all, Cleveland played 48 League games in 52 days, compiling a 6-42 won-lost record, with all their wins part of doubleheader splits. Their .125 road trip percentage nearly matched their season percentage. The Spiders also ended the season with 36 straight games on the road. The Misfits' whistlestop tour through the National League was no fault of their own.

fielders:

Thomas Joseph Tucker b. 10/28/63 Holyoke, MA   d. 10/22/35 Montagne, MA.

As the 1899 National League campaign ended, Tommy Tucker announced his retirement from "diamond warfare." Wrote *Sporting Life*, "Wait 'till the old war horse hears the bugle blast in the spring." (Oct 21). But, Tucker would never play another league game.

Like many veterans, Tucker stayed in the game because baseball was in his blood. In 1900, as he had done for 16 years earlier, Tommy manned the first sack for Springfield of the Eastern League. He hit .279. In July of 1901, Tucker played briefly with New London of the Connecticut State League (.253) before moving on to Meriden in 1902 (.258). In a game that season, Tucker scrapped with another first baseman from his National League past, Roger Conner. Tough Conner played 18 seasons in the majors mostly with New York teams before retiring in 1897. But, 39-year old Tucker and 45-year old Conner went at it. When their on field brawl wasn't enough, they coincidentally met each other at the train station and came to blows again (Phillips).

During his baseball off-seasons, Tucker was employed in a Holyoke paper mill. Fathering one son and one daughter, Tucker's son entered the newspaper business.

Joseph J. Quinn b. 12/25/64 Sydney, Australia d. 11/12/40 St. Louis, MO.

Second baseman-undertaker-manager Joseph's Quinn's one-year managerial record is easily the worst ever. He won but 12 of 116 contests. It is not, however, the measure of the man. Quinn was put in the undaunting position of tending to a farm team for the St. Louis Perfectos. Perhaps no man suffered more for the syndicate ball idea. Through it all, Quinn was a fine gentleman and the team's most rational spokesman.

Quinn played two more league seasons after 1899. In 1900, Quinn split time in St. Louis and Cincinnati. In 1901, Quinn's 17-year stint ended with the Washington Senators of the newly formed American League. He was released in August of that year after hurting his arm so badly that he couldn't toss the ball to first base (Phillips). Then, for a time, Quinn returned to his Iowa roots. There he played ball with Des Moines of the Western League until 1902. Quinn was named manager of the team the next season until criticism forced him to quit. He remained as the team's second baseman.

After his playing career, the humble Quinn resumed his undertaking profession full time. Two of his sons were ball players. John was a promising third baseman as a St. Louis amateur, even given a trial by John McGraw. But, John died tragically young in the 1920s and was buried by his father. Another son, Joseph Jr., gave up baseball to be his dad's business partner (*TSN*, May 21, 1936).

As a 70-year old, Quinn recalled the watch and diamond he was given in the 1890s by *The Sporting News*. Quinn kept the diamond separate "because it doesn't make sense to wear any frills like that in my business." (*TSN*, May 21, 1936).

Robert Henry Lochhead b. 3/29/76 Stockton, CA d. 8/22/09 Stockton, CA.

Coming from the California League, minuscule Harry Lochhead spent his rookie season as the Misfits regular shortstop. He batted a light .238 with only nine extra base hits. "Shortstop" was a bit of a misnomer for Lochhead. He stopped a few but made 81 errors in 146 games at the position. (Monte Cross of Philadelphia led the league with 90 at a time regulars bobbled about 50 a season). Baseball historians said Lochhead threw right, but often that meant right in the dirt or right over first baseman Tommy Tucker's head.

After his wanderings in 1899, Lochhead went on a baseball barnstorming tour in California. In 1900, he was back on the rutty diamonds of the California League with Stockton. Lochhead showed little batting punch and made his share of errors. Forsaking Stockton, Lochhead jumped to the Montana State League. In 1901, he played 10 games in the fledgling American League with Philadelphia and Detroit. He hit a buck thirty. Beaumont, Texas was Harry's next baseball stop in 1902. Lochhead fizzled, broke a leg, and returned to his home state of California in July of that year (Phillips).

An old photo show Lochhead posing, hands on hips with the word "Gilt Edge" written on his uniform. An early American parlance, "gilt edge" meant top-notch or best. Lochhead certainly couldn't brag of that distinction with the Misfits.

George T. Bristow b. May 1870 Paw Paw, IL d. unkn

Described by *Sporting Life* as "every inch a ball player," outfielder George Bristow had the pleasure of batting against Cy Young in his first league game. He went hitless. Shortly thereafter, George sprained an ankle and never played big league ball again. He was released to minor league Kansas City in mid-May, 1899.

Lafayette Napoleon Cross b. 5/12/66 Milwaukee, WI d. 9/06/27 Toledo, OH.

For the first 38 games of the 1899 season, Lave Cross did his best to manage the Misfits. He won only eight. Lave was probably quite happy to leave Cleveland, but disappointed he couldn't coax a better record from his charges. Considering Quinn's mark amid a season of constant distractions, Cross did just fine. In St. Louis, he batted over .300.

Cross lasted only 16 games with the Cardinals in 1900 and was sent to Brooklyn. In 1901, he began a five-year association with Connie Mack's Philadelphia Athletics. Cross was a standout, contributing bat, glove and athletic savvy to two pennant winners. Lave captained the team and even occasionally subbed as manager when Mack was away scouting or on business. In the 1905 World Series against the Giants, Cross made only two hits but he needn't felt bad. No one else hit either in the pitching dominated classic. Every game was a shutout, including three by Christy Mathewson.

Cross was released as a 38-year-old from Philadelphia in 1906. In April, Cross was honored with a planked shad testimonial dinner by editor Francis Richter of *Sporting Life* for his long baseball service in that city. Present at the 175 guest affair were American League President Ban Johnson, National League President Harry Pulliam, Philadelphia owners Shibe and Billy Shettsline, managers Mack and Hugh Duffy and the Philadelphia American and National League players. Overall, Cross had played 14 years in Philadelphia in the majors. No other baseball player had been so honored (*SL*, Apr 21, 1906).

Lave Cross closed out his 21 year big league career with two poor Washington Senators teams. Afterwards, Cross played and managed in the minor leagues until 1912 with New Orleans, Shamokin, Charlotte, and Haverhills.

A student of the intricacies of baseball, Cross attended a 1914 game at Shibe Park and picked off the visiting player's signs that were "not worth a tinker's darn." (*TSN*, Feb 27, 1915). Cross had always maintained that the best teams did not need signs.

Cross ended his illustrious career having participated in four different leagues; the American Association, Players League, National League and American League. He finished with a .292 career average in over 9000 at bats with 1300 runs batted in. Why Cross in not in the Hall of Fame is a mystery, but many believe that his brief association with the Cleveland Misfits tarnished his outstanding reputation.

Suter G. Sullivan b. 10/14/72 Baltimore, MD d. 04/19/25 Baltimore, MD.

Lave Cross' third base substitute, Suter G. Sullivan also filled in where needed. That included a brief stint as doctor to re-set Joe Sugden's floating cartilage.

In 1899, he hit .245 but fielded quite well at third, making but 23 errors. By contrast, Pittsburg's Jimmy Williams made 66 and Philadelphia's Bill Lauder committed 62. Whether or not Sullivan played ball after 1899 is speculation. Chances are that he hung around in the minor leagues, probably competing for the Cleveland Blues in 1900. From then on, details are sketchy (Phillips). One thing is certain; after his Misfits experience, Sullivan vanished from the league.

Arthur William Krueger b. 9/17/76 Chicago, IL d. 2/20/61 St. Louis, MO.

Arthur William Krueger was another of the many Misfits players cursed by bad breaks. He began his big league life with the 1899 Clevelands. In Krueger's first game in uniform in mid-September, Cleveland blew an 8-1 lead and lost to Washington 15-10. Two days later, the Clevelands broke their long losing streak and defeated the Senators 5-4. But, for the next four weeks, neither Krueger nor his Misfits teammates could win a game.

For the next three seasons, Krueger was shifted around the infield, performing for the St. Louis Cardinals and hitting decently. In 1903, he went to the World Series-bound Pittsburg Pirates. But, late in the year, Krueger was beaned behind the ear by a pitch from slowballer Bill Reidy. Knocked unconscious for two days, Krueger recovered, but his career didn't. His batting average plummeted. The Phils signed Krueger in 1905, but his hitting never did improve. Krueger ended with a .251 career average in the league.

For the next seven seasons, Otto bounced around in the minors in Kansas City, Lawrence, Saginaw, Montgomery, Galveston, and Scranton. He would later reminisce about his athletic days: "Some of the gloves we had were cut out above the knuckles like the kids wear while shooting marbles. And the ball was so soft you could almost wrinkle it when you pinched it. But, it didn't feel soft when you stopped a hot one with your hand or when you were hit by one of them." (*TSN*, Mar 1, 1961).

Richard Joseph Harley b. 9/25/72 Philadelphia, PA d. 4/03/52 Philadelphia, PA.

Despite occasional acclaim, leftfielder Dick Harley turned his position into a circus, leading 1899 National League outfielders in errors with 27. He hit .250. The Misfits were his third consecutive cellar dweller. In 1900, Harley appeared in just five games with the Cincinnatis but in 1901, Dick again patrolled the left garden with Cincinnati's tail-end team. Again, he led the league in errors with 30. So, in a span of five seasons, Harley not only played for three of the worst league teams ever, but he led the league in errors in 1898, 1899, and 1901. In 1902, Harley moved to Detroit of the American League where he met up with his old teammate Sport McAllister. In 1903, Harley found himself with a third place Cubs team. Dick couldn't stand winning and retired.

Harley, always known as a gentleman, exchanged words in a game with Baltimore's John McGraw. When the opportunity arose, Harley slid into McGraw and opened a cut in the third baseman's legs. McGraw seemed to affect people that way.

After his playing days were over, Harley went into the coal business and then coached college ball in his native Pennsylvania at Pitt, Penn State, and Villanova.

Thomas Jefferson Dowd b. 4/20/69 Holyoke, MA d. 7/02/33 Holyoke, MA.

Tommy Dowd's baseball misfortune continued after his season with the Misfits. In 1900, he toiled for minor league outfits in Chicago and Milwaukee. In 1901, the American League's Boston team snatched up a balding Dowd and put him in left field. The Bostons were an excellent squad composed of stars like Cy Young, Ossee Schreckengost, Jimmy Collins, Chick Stahl, and Buck Freemen. The club finished second. Dowd promptly retired.

At the beginning of the 1902 season, Dowd took some cash he had been saving and tried and failed to buy the New London team in the Connecticut State league. He settled for a broken down three-city club in the New York State League. The squad played their "home games" in Amsterdam, Johnstown, and Gloversville. Dowd owned, managed and recruited. Unfortunately, the club started the season with three wins in their first twenty-three games (identical to the Spiders). Recruiting then became impossible and Dowd's efforts were practically laughed out of the league (Phillips). The story sounded all too familiar. Disgusted, Dowd took the field again as a 34 year old in 1903, playing with a group of semi-pro collegians in Baltimore. For the next several years, Dowd coached and managed college ball clubs in New England.

Louis M. Sockalexis b. 10/24/71 Old Town, ME d. 12/24/13 Burlington, ME.

It is next to impossible to separate myth from reality in the baseball career of Louis "Chief" Sockalexis. Hughie Jennings said, "Sockalexis had the most ability of any man who ever played the game." But, Sockalexis' baseball life was cut short by his addiction to alcohol. He might as well have been an athlete dying young. His league totals showed only 94 games in three years.

Born a full-blooded Penobscot Indian in Old Town, Maine, Sockalexis attended Holy Cross University (1895-1896) and Notre Dame (1897). Early on, his athletic accomplishments became legend. He was as strong as an ox and fast as a deer. Once, playing center field at Holy Cross, he chased down a batted ball into the fenceless field's woods, fired it back to the infield and held the batter to a triple. Observers said the throw measured 414 feet. Another time, Sockalexis swam across the Blackstone River to catch a fly for the final out in a ball game. Sockalexis transferred to Notre Dame where he got his first taste of liquor.

Cleveland slugger Jesse Burkett discovered Soc in 1897 for the league and urged manager Patsy Tebeau to sign the swift outfielder. Enormous fanfare accompanied his debut. A March 1897 *Sporting Life* describes Sockalexis as a "massive man with gigantic bones and bulging muscles." In Chief's first game, he faced the great Amos Rusie of the New York Giants in the Polo Grounds. With partisan New Yorkers shouting anti-Indian epithets, left-handed batting Sockalexis whacked a home run in his first at bat. The next time, he smashed another home run. His small Indian fan club in attendance went wild.

In another memorable game in Chicago, Sockalexis came to bat in the ninth inning with his team trailing 3-0 and the bases loaded. Rising to the occasion, Sockalexis bashed out another home run to put his team in front. In the bottom half of the inning, he made a stunning one-handed catch to preserve the Cleveland win. Afterwards, so the story goes, Sockalexis was taken to a local tavern by teammates. The innocent Indian from two Catholic schools was induced to drink to celebrate his heroism. He would never recover. From then on, Soc's 1897 season slipped into decay. His hitting and fielding fell off dramatically. On the 4th of July, Sockalexis celebrated a little too much by jumping out a second story window of a brothel. Though he couldn't play, he could still drink and Sockalexis was often seem hobbling about in search of liquor. But, it wasn't only alcoholism that did in Sockalexis. The United States was just recently removed from the last Indian Wars. Newspapers and fans alike ridiculed Sockalexis' ancestry. One scribe went so far as to call Soc a direct descendant of Sitting Bull. This is quite far fetched since Sitting Bull was a Sioux (James 55).

To try to curb his habit, a frantic manager Tebeau tried to get to Soc's pocketbook. First he fined Sockalexis. It didn't work. Then, Tebeau gave him raises, but that tact didn't work either (Hatch 39). Sockalexis had appeared in 66 games and batted .338.

In 1898, Sockalexis swore off to Tebeau and begged for another chance. In May of that year, Sockalexis was traveling in a train carrying army recruits. Three of the men harassed Soc as being a Spaniard. The comment was especially damaging since the United States was at war against Spain in the Philippines. The remarks hurt the proud Indian and he ended up in a fight with the soldiers (*SL*, May 7, 1898). Tebeau had seen enough of Sockelexis and released him. Sockalexis wandered out of Cleveland and through Hartford and Lowell in the Eastern League. That year, he appeared in only 21 big league contests, fielding and hitting poorly. Sockalexis' drinking had made him a sick man.

In 1899, Frank Robison did not take Sockalexis or his contract to St. Louis. Robison probably assumed that Tebeau did not need a broken down outfielder for the Perfectos. Robison was right. But, Louis did make another try, having convinced manager Lave Cross that he was ready to play again. This time, Sockalexis lasted but seven contests. It was his swan song in the big leagues.

"They like me on the ball field and I like firewater," said Sockalexis in 1900. However, "they" were not league brass. Sockalexis was resigned to show off his athletic skills in his native Maine. He would wow admirers with his batting, throwing, and running exhibitions in Hartford, Lowell, and Bangor. Sockalexis even did some officiating. The enticement for his shows? More liquor. Over the following years, Sockalexis played with the Castine, Maine town team. He still put on shows in temperance, and suffered fits of wild play in between.

In 1912, Sockalexis worked briefly as a ferryman near Old Town. In 1913, Sockalexis had a $30 a month job as a woodcutter in a lumbercamp. On Christmas Day in 1913, Sockalexis was found dead of heart disease. Inside his shirt were newspaper clippings of his heroic 9th inning versus the White Sox in 1897.

Sockalexis was one of baseball great tragedies. He came into the game like a fastburning comet, and alcohol helped him to fame out. But, Louis Sockalexis did leave an important legacy. Frank Merriwell's dime novels, written by Burt Standish, used Sockalexis as an inspiration. Sockalexis prompted others to wax rhapsodic in poetry of his athletic talents. The greatest tribute though came from Cleveland baseball fans. A few years after Soc's death, a contest was conducted by a Cleveland newspaper to re-name their American League team. More fans picked "Indians" and thus the Cleveland Indians were born.

Charles W. Ziegler b. 2/02/75 Canton, OH d. 3/16/04 Canton, OH.
Hailing from the Interstate League, infielder Charles W. Ziegler spent three weeks with the Misfits and appeared in exactly two games. Subbing for Joe Quinn in his debut, the *Cleveland Plain Dealer* said Ziegler "did not burn any grass in the vicinity of second base." (Sep 25). For the season, he secured two hits in eight tries. In 1900, Ziegler spent some time in Philadelphia, enough for three games at third base; batting .272.

Charles Judson Hemphill b. 4/20/76 Greenville, MI d. 7/22/53 Detroit, MI.
Lefthanded hitting Charles Judson Hemphill was a 23-year old rookie outfielder with the St. Louis Perfectos and the Cleveland Spiders in 1899. He joined the Clevelands in early August and suffered through 58 losses in 62 games. On August 6th, Hemphill appeared as a defensive replacement for Sport McAllister who took over at first base when Tommy Tucker got too loud. The Spiders narrowly won that one in Chicago, 10-9. Two weeks later, the Spiders won in Pittsburg 8-3, as Charlie banged out four hits. When the Spiders squeezed by the Giants 4-2 on August 25th in Cleveland, it was the only time Hemphill could doff his cap in front of the home fans. Twenty four straight losses later, the Misfits defeated Washington 5-4. Those were the only victories that Charlie was a part of on the Clevelands.

The first year of the new century saw Charlie in Kansas City. He hit .319 and earned praises for his baserunning, sacrifice bunting, and solid fielding. The new Boston Puritans of the American League signed Charlie in 1901 to play right field. In left field was Charlie's old teammate Tommy Dowd. That year, Charlie hit a modest .261. Hemphill returned to Cleveland's AL squad for a few ball games in 1902 before playing several years with the St. Louis Browns. Charlie didn't hit a whole bunch, but remained in the majors on guile, defense and speedy baserunning maneuvers. Hemphill's bunting abilities were described in a contemporary paper: "He has the faculty of dropping a martyr lick whether the pitcher serves up a fast ball, a slow one, one that is high, or one that kisses the plate." Hemphill was also noted for his batting eye which gave him the nickname "Eagle Eye."

In 1905, his seasons with the Browns were interrupted, but Hemphill led the American Association in batting, cracking .364 for St. Paul. Hemphill became a New York Highlander from 1908-1911. A writer described him as playing "corking ball" for a mediocre New York outfit. At thirty-five, Hemphill's league days were over. In 1912, he managed a poor Atlanta minor league team and was fired for being out of shape. He was later sold to Columbus and St. Paul.

First Baseman Tommy Tucker

Artist: Michael D. Arnold

OTHER PERSONNEL AND NOTES

George Muir

He was the traveling secretary of the Cleveland team. As the season concluded, Mr. Muir was offered a diamond locket by Joe Quinn and members of the team. He deserved better- more like a medal for bravery. Muir was the only man present at all Cleveland games, home and mostly abroad.

Besides his secretarial duties, Muir's task was to give Misfits players their notices of release and make announcements of new players to the press. In that capacity, Muir was a busy man. Thirty-one players wore the Cleveland liveries in 1899.

Henry P. Edwards

It could be said that the loneliest man in Cleveland was Henry P. Edwards. His job: official scorer at Cleveland home games. Needless to say, he didn't have a lot to do. Hired by Frank Robison because other sporting writers were constantly flaying the Cleveland baseball management, Edwards also worked with the daily *Recorder* in Cleveland as managing editor (Spink 330).

After his Misfits odyssey (non odyssey), Edwards wrote about light harness racing for the weekly *American Sportsman* and later became the sporting editor of the *Plain Dealer*.

Elmer E. Bates

A writer for *Sporting Life*, Elmer Bates' loyalty to the Cleveland players and fans was unswerving. After all, the magazine was "the loyal champion of clean sport."

From the beginning of the St. Louis/Cleveland franchise shift, Mr. E. Bates waxed rhapsodic on the baseball team composed of castoffs and tried hard to support them whatever their endeavors.

In July, Cleveland losing woes had prompted Bates to write an eloquent essay on the rationalization of being defeated. It almost sounds like something that cartoonist Charles Schulz would have Charlie Brown say about his sandlot team.

By September though, and into the campaigns waning days, Bates was so disgusted that, like the players, he was merciful for the season's end.

Nicholas Young

For seventeen years, Nicholas Young served as National League President. Before then, he was secretary and treasurer of the league all the back to its origins in 1876. Young was oft-called "Uncle Nick" affectionately.

Young's presidency survived the 1890 Players League and the upheaval of the new rival AL in 1901. But, it was the impossible job of being responsible for his umpire crews that he was most often criticized. In the wild and wooly 1890s, umpires and Young were blasted for showing favoritism, having poor judgement, and poor eyesight. Ironically, Young was stricken blind in 1914.

The Robisons and the St. Louis Cardinals

For the next few years, the trolley kings Frank and M. Stanley Robison owned and operated the St. Louis Cardinals. Frank assumed his traditional role as top dog. Stanley was his second fiddle.

The 1900 version of the Cardinals absorbed several talented players from the four folded 1899 teams. Fireball John McGraw and his chubby sidekick Wilbert Robinson came from Baltimore. So did Bill Keister. Patsy Donovan made the move from Pittsburg. Nobody came from Cleveland. But, manager Tebeau feuded with everyone and quit. McGraw was injured and refused to manage. Cy Young won only half of his decisions. The team went bust. McGraw went to the Giants.

The 1901 edition lost Cy Young to the AL Bostons. However, a fine pitching triumvirate of Jack Harper, Jack Powell, and Willie Sudhoff surfaced. Jesse Burkett led the league in hitting and bantering with fans from his outfield position. The Cardinals flew into the first division. It was to be the Robison's last hurrah. Upset by the St. Louis ownership and wanting a fresh start in a fresh league, many of the Cardinals jumped ship across town to the St. Louis Browns.

By 1902, Rhody Wallace, John Heidrick, Jesse Burkett, Harper, Powell, and Sudhoff were all Brownies. The Cardinals, now a team composed of cast-offs, slid into the second division... and stayed there. Three years later, Frank Robison's ill health gave way to brother Stanley operating the team full time. The franchise continued to derail and fashioned back-to-back 100 loss campaigns in 1907-1908. In September 1908, Frank Robison was stricken while listening to scores of a Cardinal game by phone. In the 9th inning the Cardinals lost the game. Robison fell dead of apoplexy (*TSN*, Oct 1, 1908). He was 56.

M. Stanley Robison's tenure with the Cardinals wasn't much better. In 1905, after Kid Nichols and Jimmy Burke had failed, Stanley tried his hand at managing the team. It wasn't easy. Baseball pitching forgettables like Wish Egan, who wished he could have won more, and Win Kellum, who won the year before in Cincinnati flannels, populated the team. Another pitcher was Buster Brown, probably better suited to another profession- like selling shoes. But, Stanley did have ancient Jake Beckley at first base and promising rookie outfielder Homer Smoot.

After Stanley let himself go as manager, things got even worse. Perhaps, Stanley's practical ways weren't suited to baseball. Incredibly, Robison was in an accident shortly thereafter, falling off his own trolley car. A few years later and recovered from his injuries, Robison noticed his health was failing. He took a trip to Panama to try to bolster his health but instead contracted blood poisoning. In late March, 1911 Stanley Robison died of heart complications as his Cardinals were preparing for spring training.

For a while, it was feared, there was no one to own the team. However, a relative of the Robisons, Helen Schuyler Britton, took over the franchise upon the death of Stanley Robison.

Strangely enough, the Robison legacy shows two distinct baseball ownerships in Cleveland and St. Louis. In Cleveland the Robison's were relatively successful in the 1890s. A Temple Cup championship in 1895 was their crowning achievement. In St. Louis, in the period 1899-1910, the Cardinals franchise was a disaster. It was in the syndicate year of 1899 that the Cleveland franchise hit a nadir while kowtowing to the St. Louis club. That 1899 Perfectos team, whom Frank Robison and many thought was a pennant contender, fizzled. Somehow, it seemed fitting that the Cardinals under the Robison's never really achieved success, perhaps as a penance for the Cleveland debacle of 1899. Despite all this, Alfred H. Spink wrote in his baseball history that the Robison's were "friends and supporters of the National game when love and sentiment were the only inducements and when to back a club meant to dig down in the pockets at the close of each season to meet the deficit which was always in evidence." (*The National Game*, 301). But the question begs, how much digging did the Robisons do for the downtrodden Spiders in 1899?

Player Development

Cleveland Spiders player development, or lack thereof, was a calamity throughout the 1899 campaign. The original manager-to-be, Bill Joyce, demanded too high a salary . The Robison's scoffed and named Lave Cross as captain. Almost all of the starting lineup was rumored to go to St. Louis. Among them were Cross, Joe Quinn, Tommy Dowd, Tommy Tucker, Ossee Schreckengost, and Dick Harley. When Cross finally did go to the No. 1 syndicate team, Quinn was named as manager.

The attempts to secure pitching prospects failed miserably. Tony Mullane and Fred Klobedanz, two men with professional experience and success, washed out in May trials. Two others, amateurs Eggleberth and Smyth, never pitched a game in Cleveland flannels, or anywhere in the big leagues. Instead, the Misfits were left with the likes of Charlie Knepper, Crazy Schmit, Harry Colliflower, and Frank Bates.

With little practice time, the players began the season out of shape. By the time they were physically fit, they lost and lost and lost. There was the usual assortment of injuries and ailments besides dead armed ball tossers. George Bristow sprained an ankle. Joe Sugden was out with malaria. Dick Harley was spiked. Tommy Dowd had a stomach problem and a jammed finger. Charlie Hemphill needed glasses. Sport McAllister had a "bum mit"and an assortment of hand injuries. Louis Sockalexis was sent packing for his alcoholism.

Inexperience also played a part. Several Misfits were just beginning their careers. Harry Lochhead was a rookie shortstop. Otto Krueger and Charlie Ziegler were infant infielders. George Bristow and Charlie Hemphill were first year outfielders. Pitchers Bates, Colliflower, Harper, Knepper, Kolb, and Maupin were just learning National League batters. Other players were washed up veterans like Jack Stivetts, Jim Hughey, Kid Carsey, and Jack Clements.

And, of course, the Misfits almost never heard the cheers or adulation of fans. When they did, the yells seemed not genuine but rather tinged with a mixture of pity. This factor, vital to a ballplayer's psyche and ability to perform, must have decimated the Clevelands.

Curse of Rookies vs. Misfits

Oddly enough, there exists a strange anomaly in the case of rookie pitchers who twirled against the Spiders late in the season. Opposing NL managers, realizing the ease in beating Cleveland, simply gave rookie pitchers a chance. Their reasoning must have been that if those youngsters couldn't defeat Cleveland, whom could they beat?

For a period from August 20 to October 12, five raw hurlers were handed the ball against the Misfits. Dick Cogan of the Cubs was the recipient of the Cubs' 9th inning comeback versus one Mr. Schmit. Cogan won out 8-7 his only appearance of 1899. Harry Wilhelm of Louisville beat Harry Colliflower 13-3 and hit a triple and homer to boot. Wild and fast Emil Frisk didn't stop pitching against the Misfits until he had three victories; 9-7, 10-2, and 6-2. All of Frisk's friskings came at the expense of Colliflower. Pittsburg's Chummy Gray was no friend of the Spiders and beat Jim Hughey 4-1. Finally, Savage Thomas Thomas of St. Louis braved a chill and handed the Misfits a 10-3 setback. Hughey took his customary loss in the affair.

Yet, of those five pitchers, none of them lasted any amount of time in the leagues. They all had a "cup of coffee" and were gone. Frisk appeared in the most games- 20. Gray had a nine game career in his solitary season of 1899. Thomas also lasted but nine games in the majors. Wilhelm hurled five contests in his only season. Cogan performed in all of eight games. So, a sort a curse existed against these unfortunates who pitched opposing Cleveland.

Appendix B
Team Nicknames

OFFICIAL: Cleveland Spiders

PRESS GENERATED: Misfits, Exiles, Discards, What-do-you-call 'ems, Forsakens, Remnants, Outcasts, Orphans, Transfers, Cast Offs, Cast Adrifts, Innocents, Wanderers, Wandering Willies, Tramps, Excursionists, Caudal Appendages, Clevelanders, Homeless Ones, Nomads, Quinn's Queers, Harley-Quinns, Leftovers, Insurgents, Tourists, Tail Enders, and Barnstormers.

Bibliography

Newspapers and Periodicals

The Baltimore Sun 1895, 1899.
Boston Daily Globe 1899.
Brooklyn Daily Eagle 1899.
Chicago Daily Tribune 1899.
Chicago Record 1899.
Chicago Times Herald 1899.
Cincinnati Enquirer 1899.
Cleveland Plain Dealer 1895, 1898, 1899.
Cleveland Press 1899.
Jamestown, NY newspaper date unknown.
Louisville (Ky.) *Courier Journal* 1899.
New York Times 1899.
Philadelphia Bulletin 1899.
Philadelphia Enquirer 1899.
Pittsburg Dispatch 1899.
Pittsburg Leader 1899.
Pittsburg Post 1899.
St. Louis Globe-Democrat 1899.
Sporting Life 1890, 1897, 1898, 1899, 1906, 1911.
The Sporting News 1890, 1899, 1907, 1908, 1915, 1917, 1929, 1935, 1936, 1949, 1959, 1961.
Washington Post 1899.
Washington Star 1899.

Books

Alexander, Charles. *John McGraw*. New York: Viking Penguin, 1988.
Allen, Lee. *The National League Story*. New York: Hill and Wang, 1961.
Beebe, Lucius, and Charles Clegg. *Hear the Train Blow*. New York: Grosset & Dunlap, 1952.
Condon, George E. *Cleveland: The Best Kept Secret*. Garden City, NY: Doubleday, 1967.
Curran, William. *Mitts*. New York: William Morrow, 1985.
Einstein, Charles, ed. *The Fireside Book of Baseball*, 4th edition. New York: Simon and Schuster, 1987.
Flexner, Stuart Berg. *I Hear America Talking*. New York: Van Nostrand Reinhold, 1976.

Gerlach, Larry. "Umpire Honor Rolls." Society for American Baseball Research, Baseball Research Journal, 1979.

Grayson, Harry. They Played the Game. New York: Books for Libraries Press, 1944.

Hatch, Francis. "Maine's All-Time Greatest Baseball Player." Source unknown.

Hurlbert, Gordon. "The Worst Season Ever." Society for American Baseball Research, Baseball Research Journal, 1979.

James, Bill. *Historical Baseball Abstract*. New York: Villard Books, 1986.

Leavitt, Bud. "Louis Francis Sockalexis." Source unknown.

Leitner, Irving. *Baseball: Diamond in the Rough*. New York: Criterion Books, 1972.

Lewis, Whitey. *The Cleveland Indians*. New York: Van Rees Press, 1949.

Lowry, Philip J. *Green Cathedrals*. Manhattan, Kansas: A.G. Press, 1986.

Mathewson, Christy. *Pitching in a Pinch*. New York: Stein and Day, 1977.

Phillips, John. *The Cleveland Spiders Who Was Who*. Cabin John, Md.: Capital Publishing, 1988.

_____. *The 99 Spiders*. Cabin John, Md.: Capital Publishing, 1988.

Porter, David, ed. *Biographical Dictionary of Sports: Baseball*. New York: Greenwood Press, 1987.

Reichler, Joseph, ed. *The Baseball Encyclopedia*, 2d edition. New York: Macmillan, 1973.

_____. *The Baseball Encyclopedia*, 3d edition. New York: Macmillan, 1976.

Reidenbaugh, Lowell. *100 Years of National League Baseball*. St. Louis: The Sporting News, 1976.

_____, and Amadee Wohlschlaeger. *Take Me Out to the Ballpark*. St. Louis: The Sporting News, 1983.

Schlossberg, Dan. *The Baseball Catalog*. Middle Village, NY: Johnathan David Publishers, 1986.

Shannon, Bill, and George Kalinsky. *The Ballparks*. New York: Hawthorne Books, 1975.

Smith, Robert. *Hits, Runs & Errors*. New York: Dell, 1944.

Spink, Alfred H. *The National Game*. St. Louis: National Game Publishing, 1910.

Suehsdorf, A.D. *The Great American Baseball Scrapbook*. New York: Random House, 1978.

Sullivan, Mark. *Our Times*. New York: Chales Scribners' Sons, 1926.

Thorn, John, and John B. Holway. *The Pitcher*. New York: Prentice-Hall, 1987.

Voigt, David Q. *American Baseball*. University Park: Pennsylvania State University, 1980.

Index

(1899 Cleveland Spiders in bold)

inmates 125, 133; misfits advertisement 7, 23

Clingman, Billy 32, 33, 129

Cobb, Ty 184

Cogan, Dick 127, 204

Colgan, Harry 170

Colliflower, Harry 101, 102, 103, 104, 106, 107, 111, 115, 118, 125, 129, 130, 135, 137, 139, 140, 141, 148, 149, 150, 154, 162, 167, 168, 171, 172, 174, 180, 181, 203, 204; debut 101; as entertainer 181; jokes about name 180; rests arm in sling 149-150; as umpire 180-181

Collins, Jimmy 12, 16, 78, 80, 81, 118, 134, 135, 196

Comiskey, Charles 15, 161

Connecticut State League 112, 184, 192, 196

Conner, Jim 114, 145, 147

Conner, Roger 192

Connolly, Thomas 163, 170

Coogan's Bluff 121

Cooley, Duff 90, 91, 108

Corcoran, Martin J. 183

Corcoran, Tommy 43

cranks (see also *fans*) 3, 17, 27, 32, 48, 52, 57, 69, 74, 86, 89, 90, 91, 102, 108, 111, 126, 127, 138, 146, 151, 162, 172

Crawford, Sam 150, 172

Criger, Lou 8, 22, 75, 88, 185

Crisham, Pat 51, 94

Cronin, John 172

Cross, Lave 7, 8, 9. 10, 11, 12, 17, 18, 19, 20, 21, 22, 23, 24, 26, 27, 28, 29, 32, 34, 35, 36, 37, 38, 39, 40, 41, 43, 44, 45, 46, 48, 49, 50, 51, 52, 54, 57, 58, 59, 60, 61, 75, 86, 87, 88, 89, 119, 120, 142, 155, 159, 162, 166, 167, 168, 177, 185, *189*, 193, 194, 197, 203; arguments with Burns 38, 49; dear-life practice 48; grand slam 89; Hall of Fame 194; homing pigeons 166; named manager 9; perfect harmony 46; testimonial dinner 194; transferred to St. Louis 59-60

Cross, Monte 90, 91, 108, 109, 110, 111, 151, 152, 153, 193

Cunningham, Bert 23, 32, 105, 163

Cuppy, Nig 2, 3, 4, 8, 26, 74, 75, 89

Cuyahoga building (Ceveland) 26, 111

Dahlen, Bill 57, 68, 70, 124, 125, 138

Daily, One Arm 15

Daly, Tom 68, 69, 124, 125

Davis, George 75, 76, 121, 122

Davis, Harry 185

Day, John 61, 71, 83, 120

Delahanty, Ed 18, 90, 91, 108, 109, 111, 151, 152, 153, 159, 165, 170

Delilah 178

DeMontreville, Gene 158

Dewey, Admiral 98

Dexter, Charlie 29

Dillon, Pop 169

Dineen, Bill 49

Doheny, Ed 61, 71, 120, 132

Dolan, Joe 152

Donahue, Red 51, 90, 111, 152

Donahue,Tim 115

Donely, Jimmy 9

Donlin, Mike 120, 165, 167, 168

215

McCormick, Barry 35, 38
McCreary, Tom 68
McDonald, Jim 74, 79, 123, 147, 171
McFarland, Dan 99
McFarland, Ed 81, 109, 151
McGann, Dan 101, 102, 155
McGarr, James "Chippy" 4, 86, 88, 122, 134, 135, 136, 143, 160
McGinnity, Joe 93, 103, 158, 160, 161
McGraw, John 17, 50, 51, 92, 93, 94, 95, 100, 103, 104, 105, 120, 143, 150, 153, 158, 159, 160, 161, 165, 171, 179, 180, 192, 195
McGuire, Deacon 2, 125, 138, 184
McJames, Doc 69, 123, 125, 139
Mack, Connie 12, 13, 182, 184, 185, 186, 188, 194
McKean, Ed 4, 8, 41, 74, 75, 86, 87, 88, 89, 116, 119
McManus, Frank 157
McPhee, Bid 43, 142, 1172
McQuaid, Jack 46
Madison, Art 41, 42, 65, 85
Magee, Bill 23, 33, 90, 91, 109, 156, 157
Magoon, Topsy 92, 94, 95, 103, 114, 127, 147, 148
Manassau, Alfred 133
Mathewson, Christy 83, 185, 194
Maupin, Harry 8, 10, 11, 12, 14, 23, 24, 44, 48, 59, 65, 70, 71, 83, 148, 182, 204; credentials 14; to the dogs 44; token appearances 70
Meekin, Jouett 63, 135
Mercer, Win 49, 97, 98, 101
Merriwell, Frank 134, 198

Mertes, Sam 114, 128, 146, 147, 148, 160, 170
Miller, Dusty 28
Miller, Ralph 50
Mohave Desert (California) 135
Montana State League 193
Morehead (Lochhead) 7, 20
Mudville 133
Muir, George 27, 34, 72, 128, 142, 154, 201
Mullane, Tony 42, 43, 203
Murphy (groundskeeper) 21

Nash, Billy 17
National Association 1
National Geographic Society 112
National League 1, 2, 5, 7, 12, 13, 14, 15, 16, 17, 20, 24, 27, 29, 34, 35, 39, 43, 44, 48, 51, 52, 62, 63, 67, 70, 71, 73, 75, 77, 79, 83, 84, 96, 102, 103, 107, 122, 128, 131, 132, 137, 138, 139, 143, 148, 155, 159, 163, 164, 169, 172, 175, 176, 177, 181, 183, 186, 187, 191, 192, 194, 195, 201, 204
National Park (Washington) 96, 100, 153, 155, 157
New Castle, Pennsylvania 77, 78
New Century (dictionary) 90
New York State League 196
New York Times 59, 76, 121, 122, 126
Nichols, Kid 2, 14, 15, 53, 60, 117, 118, 121, 134, 135, 202
Nicol, Hugh 18
Nolan, The Only 1
Nops, Jerry 94, 95, 143, 178
Notre Dame University 196

Oberlin College (Ohio) 1, 73

216

picked off 41; released 142; shoves Casey 57; shoves Wagner 57; stands still 146; versus Griffith 17
Turkish baths 92
Turner, Tuck 18

Union Association 15
Union Depot 130, 137
Union Park (Baltimore) 92, 95, 104, 158, 160

Van Haltren, George 63, 75, 121, 122
Veach, Peek-a-Boo 2
Villanova University 8, 196
Virtue, Jake 2
Von der Ahe, Chris 5, 7, 18
Von der Horst, Harry 4

Waddell, Rube 162, 179, 185, 186
Wadsworth, Jack 2
Wagner, Earl 49, 50
Wagner, Honus 22, 33, 46, 89, 105, 106, 129, 130, 155, 163, 178
Wallace, Bobby (Rhody) 4, 8, 32, 40, 75, 88, 89, 155, 168, 178, 202
Warner, Albert 84
Warner, John 76, 122
Washington Evening Star 48, 95, 97, 156
Washington Park (Brooklyn) 57, 58, 68, 123, 124
Washington Post 47, 99, 100, 50, 153, 154, 156
Watkins, Bill 41, 84
Weehawken Field (New Jersey) 596
West Side Grounds (Chicago) 36, 127, 146

Western Association 175
Western Canada League 183
Western League 7, 9, 10, 58, 63, 156, 161, 162, 164, 192
Weyhing, Gus 47, 101
Wilhelm, Harry 129, 204
Williams, Jimmy 42, 83, 84, 85, 194
Willis, Vic 15, 56, 80, 81, 129, 133, 134
Wilson, Highball 152, 182
Wilson, Parke 61, 72, 75, 76, 123, 131
Wilson, Zeke 26, 40
Wisconsin-Illinois League 179
Wolverton, Harry 35, 36, 38, 60, 113, 114, 115
Woods, Walt 24, 128
World Series 185, 194, 194
Wright, G.B. 8

Yeager, Joe 70
Y.M.C.A. (Washington, D.C.) 104
Young, Cy 2, 3, 4, 8, 9, 20, 39, 87, 163, 169, 182, 185, 187, 193, 196, 202
Young, Nick 29, 35, 39, 50, 79, 100, 103, 107, 143, 148, 150, 164

Ziegler, Charlie 162, 174, 198, 204
Zimmer, Chief 2, 3, 4, 8, 27, 28, 32, 35, 39, 43, 54, 57, 58, 59, 60, 63, 65, 105, 130, 187, 188; bad bounce 43; Cy Young's catcher 2; home run 45; released 63; as umpire 187

About the Author

J. Thomas Hetrick has written two books about 19th century baseball—*MISFITS! Baseball's Worst Ever Team* and *Chris Von der Ahe and the St. Louis Browns.* The latter book was a Finalist for the Seymour Medal, a peer award given for the best book of baseball history or biography in a year.

A member of the Society for American Baseball Research (SABR), Hetrick has indexed *Ball Four* (Jim Bouton), *Minnesotans in Baseball,* and *Baseball in 1889: Players vs. Owners* (Daniel Pearson) for the organization. On occasion, he's presented his research at chapter and SABR National meetings in St. Louis, Boston, and Pittsburgh. In 2001, Hetrick spoke at the Baseball Hall of Fame in Cooperstown, New York.

Hetrick also owns and operates Pocol Press, a small press publisher located in Northern Virginia. He can be reached at info@pocolpress.com.

Appendix C

1899 Cleveland Spiders Roster and Statistics

WON-20 LOST-134
MGRS: Lave Cross 8-30
Joe Quinn 12-104
AWAY: 11-102 HOME: 9-32

VS. FIRST DIVISION: 8-76
VS. SECOND DIVISION: 12-58
ONE RUN GAMES: 8-19
DOUBLEHEADERS: 0-19-12

Pitchers	B	T	HT	WT	YR	W	L	ERA	G	GS	CG	IP	H	BB	SO	AB	H	BA
Frank Bates	L	R	5'7"	168	2	1	18	6.90	20	20	17	153	239	105	13	68	15	.221
Kid Carsey	L	L		168	9	1	8	5.68	19	9	8	77.2	109	24	11	36	10	.278
Harry Colliflower	L	L	5'11"	175	1	1	11	8.17	14	12	11	98	152	41	8	76	23	.303
Jack Harper	R	R	6'0"	178	1	1	4	3.89	5	5	5	37	44	12	14	11	2	.182
Still Bill Hill	L	L	6'1"	201	3	3	6	6.97	11	10	7	72.1	96	39	26	31	4	.129
Jim Hughey	R	R	6"		4	4	30	5.41	36	34	32	283	403	88	54	111	18	.162
Charlie Knepper	R	R	6'4"	190	6	4	22	5.78	27	26	26	219.2	307	77	43	89	12	.135
Eddie Kolb	R	R			1	0	1	10.13	1	1	1	8	18	5	1	4	1	.250
Harry Lochhead	R	R			1	0	1	0.00	1	0	1	3.2	4	2	0	541	129	.238
H. Maupin	R				2	0	3	12.60	5	3	2	25	55	7	3	0	1	.238
Sport McAllister	S	R	5'11"	180	4	0	1	9.56	3	1	1	16	29	10	2	418	99	.237
Crazy Schmit	L	L	5'10"	165	4	2	17	5.86	20	19	16	138.1	197	62	24	70	11	.157
Jack Stivetts	R	R	6'2"	185	11	0	4	5.68	7	4	3	38	48	28	5	39	8	.205
Willie Sudhoff	R	R		165	3	3	8	6.98	11	10	8	86.1	131	25	10	31	2	.065
Highball Wilson	R	R	5'7"	165	1	0	1	9.00	1	1	1	8	12	5	1	3	1	.333

Catchers	B	T	HT	WT	YR	G	AB	H	2B	3B	HR	R	RBI	BB	SB	BA	S.A.
Jack Clements	L	L	5'8"	204	16	4	12	3	0	0	1	0	0	0	0	.250	.250
Jim Duncan	R	R	5'8"	140	1	31	105	24	2	3	2	9	9	4	0	.229	.257
O. Schreckengost	R	R	5'10"	180	3	43	150	47	8	3	0	15	10	6	4	.313	.407
Joe Sugden	S	R	5'10"	180	7	76	250	69	5	1	0	19	14	11	2	.276	.304
Chief Zimmer	R	R	6'0"	190	15	20	73	25	2	1	2	9	14	5	1	.342	.479
Infielders																	
Lave Cross	R	R	5'8"	155	13	38	154	44	5	0	1	15	20	8	2	.286	.338
Otto Krueger	R	R	5'7"	165	1	13	44	10	1	0	0	4	2	1	1	.227	.250
Harry Lochhead		R			1	148	541	129	7	1	1	52	43	21	23	.238	.261
Joe Quinn	R	R	5'7"	158	15	147	615	176	24	6	0	73	72	21	22	.286	.345
Suter Sullivan	R	R			2	127	473	116	16	3	0	37	55	25	16	.245	.292
Tommy Tucker	S	R	5'11"	165	13	127	456	110	19	3	0	40	40	24	3	.241	.296
Charlie Ziegler					1	2	8	2	0	0	0	2	0	0	0	.250	.250
Outfielders																	
George Bristow		R			3	8	8	1	1	0	0	0	0	0	0	.125	.250
Tommy Dowd	R	R	5'8"	173	9	147	605	168	17	6	2	81	35	48	28	.278	.336
Dick Harley	L	R	5'10"	165	3	142	567	142	15	7	1	70	50	40	15	.250	.307
Charlie Hemphill	L	L	5'9"	160	1	55	202	56	3	5	2	23	23	6	3	.277	.371
Sport McAllister	S	R	5'11"	180	4	113	418	99	6	8	5	23	31	19	6	.237	.297
Louis Sockalexis	L	R	5'11"	208	2	7	22	6	1	0	0	29	3	1	0	.273	.318
Jack Stivetts	R	R	6'2"	185	11	18	39	8	1	1	0	8	2	1	6	.205	.282

Sources: *Macmillan Baseball Encyclopedia, National Baseball Hall of Fame, Richard Topp.*
Strikeout data not available for batters.

226

www.ingramcontent.com/pod-product-compliance
Lightning Source LLC
Chambersburg PA
CBHW052036090426
42739CB00010B/1929